In the Neighborhood of Zero

Frontispiece: Photo taken in the backyard of the Spanos house on Sunapee Street. *From left to right*: Costas (younger brother Charles, age 14); Vaios (father, age 56); me (age 18); Aristides (younger brother Harry, age 16). Courtesy of the author.

In the Neighborhood of Zero

A World War II Memoir

WILLIAM V. SPANOS

University of Nebraska Press .. Lincoln & London

Publication of this volume was assisted by
The Virginia Faulkner Fund, established in
memory of Virginia Faulkner, editor in chief
of the University of Nebraska Press.

Library of Congress Cataloging-in-
Publication Data

Spanos, William V.
In the neighborhood of zero :
a World War II memoir / William V. Spanos.
    p. cm.
ISBN 978-0-8032-2681-4 (cloth : alk. paper)
1. World War, 1939–1945—Personal narratives,
American. 2. World War, 1939–1945—Prisoners
and prisons, German. 3. Prisoners of war—
Germany—Biography. 4. Prisoners of war—
United States—Biography. 5. Ardennes, Battle
of the, 1944–1945. 6. Dresden (Germany)—
History—Bombardment, 1945. 7. Spanos,
William V. I. Title.
D805.G3S716 2010
940.54'7243092—dc22
[B]
2009033454

Set in Minion by Kim Essman.

To the memory of those who died in the firebombing
of Dresden, February 13–14, 1945, my neighbors

Hovering over
their microcosmic map,
no periplum,
They,
in shining brass,
push their prosthetic armada
to its destination,
unleash its murderous load, and,
when the unexpecting city below
goes up in turbulent flame,
cry, "good show, old chaps."

Caught in that rain of terror,
we, down here,
under Their abstract gaze,
the living and the dead,
in the midst
of fire and brimstone,
all the boundaries razed,
become
A neighborhood of zero.

"Did you ever return to Dresden, Professor Spanos?"

"I never left there."

Conversation with a student,
after a lecture on Kurt Vonnegut's
Slaughterhouse-Five

Contents

Preface

In the wake of September 11, 2001, the George W. Bush administration, appealing to the deeply backgrounded American exceptionalist ethos, took advantage of the nationalist fervor precipitated by Al Qaeda's attack on U.S. soil to launch its global "war on terror," the invasion of Afghanistan and then Iraq in the name of (American) civilization. In a ruthless reduction of the cultural and political complexities of the planet, complexities in large part produced by the imperial arrogance and depredations of Western Europe and its contemporary heir, the United States, President Bush declared to the world, "You're with us or against us." Since then, and despite alienating the United States's traditional allies and the vast majority of the people of the so-called Third World in the process of imposing American-style democracies on alien cultures, this president and his neoconservative intellectual deputies systematically exaggerated the threat to "American homeland security" to produce the sense of national emergency—the state of exception that has increasingly enabled the executive branch to ignore civil and human rights—and thus to facilitate the imposition of its paradoxical global agenda: the American Peace.

Although the catastrophic possibilities of this extremist cultural and political strategy are immense, the strategy itself is not new. Indeed, it is one whose origin appears to be simultaneous with the origin of the American national identity itself. I am referring to the "American jeremiad," which, since the New England Puritans, has had as its fundamental purpose the instigation of collective anxiety and an enabling sense of renewal by focusing on a frontier beyond which is a wilderness inhabited by an evil enemy who threatens its security, unity, and civilizational energy. This strategy played a decisive role in the formation of the American national identity and its chauvinistic attitude toward "foreigners" ever since the Puritans adapted this appeal to the notion of a national "awakening"— reminding "backsliders" of their "chosen calling"—as a means of securing and renewing its disintegrating collective consensus, the "Covenant." In a highly orchestrated speech to the American people on September 11, 2006, President Bush, commemorating the attacks on the World Trade Center and the Pentagon, appealed to this Puritan/American tradition in the face of growing skepticism about the war in Iraq. It is not accidental that he concluded his speech by asserting that the "American calling" in the wake of the attacks on the American homeland was to win the global war on terror and, echoing the Jeremiahs of the American past, from Jonathan Edwards through Daniel Webster to Samuel P. Huntington, called for "a third Great Awakening."

The following memoir about my experience in World War II, written a long half-century later, particularly the "legendary" Battle of the Bulge in December 1944 and the nearly forgotten firebombing of Dresden, is not, therefore, intended to be "objective," simply another of the numerous narratives of that "good war" written by the official custodians of the American national memory or by ventriloquized American veterans who have contributed to the longevity of the exceptionalist mythology of the American national identity. I mean the mythology that "America," different and superior to the decadent "Old World," had been "elected" by God or History to fulfill His or Its benign purpose in the world's wilderness. On the contrary, my memoir is frankly intended as a counter-memoir, a dissident remembrance of, a witness to, this "just war," whose cumulative glorification has been recently reiterated in *The Greatest Generation* (1998), the encomium to the America of World War II and the American soldiers who fought it written by the popular former anchorman of NBC Tom Brokaw, and in *The War* (2007) produced by the prestigious documentary filmmaker Ken Burns.

In thus offering this counter-memory, my purpose is not by any means to disparage the multitude of young men who fought, were wounded and maimed, taken prisoner, or died violent deaths during that terrible global war. It is, rather, to *remember* the singularity of the war and to call into question the insidious ideological uses to which the dominant culture in the United States has insistently put its "sacrificial" victory over the barbarian enemies in its aftermath: during the Cold War, the Korean War, the Vietnam War, and, not least, in the wake of Al Qaeda's attacks on the American homeland, when the Bush administration, aided and abetted by the culture industry, even more than the preceding ones, systematically invoked the memory of America's call to its young men in the 1940s in behalf of its historically ordained global mission. I mean its exceptionalist war on terror and the imposition of American-style—that is, capitalist—democracies on alien (barbaric) cultures to make the world "safe for" civilization. Against a cultural memory that has attributed sophisticated consciousness to them, it should be remembered that these American young men, like me, were mostly uneducated and inexperienced boys. The vast majority had only a minimal sense of the history that precipitated the war. And once we were plunged into the waking nightmare of combat, it was not grand narratives of our nation's eventual victory that motivated us; it was primarily *survival* in a larger totality that was beyond our experience to think. However we recounted our experiences after the war or however it was recounted for us by historians and the media, it was, as the telling margins of their stories invariably suggest, not so much our will to contribute to a clear-cut higher cause—freedom, democracy, civilization, America—that was our primary motive in combat as it was this sheer will to survive a global momentum of violence beyond our ken.

In keeping with this haunting and dislocating reality about the American soldier in World War II, I want to say at the outset that the young boy I write about in the following pages now, fifty years after the event, is in some fundamental way foreign to me. This is not only because the minute particulars of his thoughts, feelings, and actions in the seemingly unending midst of that infernal moment has been obscured by the great lapse of time. It is also and primarily because the interim between that time and this, not least the long and arduous process of "education" out of the darkness of ignorance—which is to say, the illusions of "disinterested" truth—has rendered my identity radically different from his. In the painful process of writing about him, I was often taken aback by a sense of alienation not only from his physical appearance but from his mind and soul. What, I thought, had that young bewildered boy, who, as the saying goes, "didn't know his ass from his elbow," and the turbulent history into which he was flung to do with me? What right do I have to speak for him, to narrate his story? Am I imposing my late, postmodern identity and sense of the world under the aegis of America on the singularity of his experience? Am I mimicking in reverse the prevailing, triumphalist, story about the young men who fought World War II?

And yet I do somehow recognize this boy, especially certain apparently isolated particular gestures of body and soul that keep leaping out at me, as if to assure me that he is my kin, as I strain, often with shameful tears in my eyes, to remember him and what he went through. And these intimations have to do with precisely his vague but insistent intuitions, precipitated by the circumstances of his captivity and, above all, the horrific firebombing of Dresden to which he bore witness—his experience in an infernal zero zone, as it were—into the unbridgeable disparity between the way his youth was represented for him by the American "world" after his return and the acutely existential way he was himself experiencing it. To put these intuitions another way, they have to do with his sense of being a minute and expendable, but necessary, pawn in a larger scheme that was way beyond the range of his comprehension.

In a way I began writing this book about my experience as a prisoner of war in Dresden, Germany, on August 16, 1945, the day the government of the United States announced the end of World War II—immediately after it had dropped atomic bombs on Hiroshima and Nagasaki, Japan. I knew then that, despite my will to forget what I had undergone in that brief, traumatic five-month period of my life, I had to write the book. I also knew what I wanted it to say. And that was because I felt I had borne witness to a massive crime against humanity that no appeal to reason, not even to the saving of countless other lives, could justify. But that knowledge was essentially visceral. I had neither the worldly experience nor, therefore, the breadth and depth of mind and, above all, the language that would make the haunting sense of it that was buried in my being, right down to my capillaries, overt and intelligible to the others to whom I felt responsible. It has taken me a lifetime to achieve that breadth and depth of mind and that language. Only now, in the twilight of my life, after many years of obsessively teaching and writing around this singular and unspeakable event—I am convinced that it has all been preparatory—have I been able to do away with the scaffolding that has cluttered everything I have written. To put this divestment as William Butler Yeats does in one of his greatest but still to be understood poems, I have been able to come down "to where the ladders start / In the foul rag-and-bone shop of the heart."

For this liberation from the prison house of abstraction, I am paradoxically grateful to all those materialist intellectuals and scholars—the existentialists, the phenomenologists, the feminists, the neo-Marxists, the poststructuralists, the postcolonialists—whose works I read voraciously after the war. Reading modern Western civilization itself against the grain, they refused, in one way or another, the victors' interpretation—an interpretation from above—of the richly various complex world, the shattered world below.

On another, more personal, register I want to express my deep-felt gratitude to all those who accidentally crossed my path during the infernal journey I was bound upon—Doris, Tom Yukie, Bob Wagner, Jerry, Claire, my unknown fellow soldiers in the garbage pit, the British soldier in Stalag iv-b, the unnamed foreman in the factory at Rabenau, Brigitte and Frieda, even Persephone, and not least Aris. These nobodies in the world below, as I reiterate in a woefully inadequate language of mourning, "came and went." Nevertheless, in reminding me, each in his or her or its own way, that there was care in the abysmal world into which we had been thrown, they left their indelible mark on the sensitive skin of my being, an inventory to be read and deciphered—and brought back to life—at a later time.

More immediately, I wish to thanks my former student and beloved friend Assimina Karavanta. For a very long time after my return to the world, I, like many others who had suffered the lunatic violence of the war, found it virtually impossible to speak directly of my traumatic experience to my family, my friends, my colleagues. When I was asked about it, I responded, of course, but invariably in a way that suggested that what had happened to me was no more important than all the other war stories they had heard. My silence was the consequence not simply of the unspeakable horror of what I had experienced but also, as I have said, of my feeling that I was not in command of a language commensurate to the task of adequately representing the meaning it had for me. Over the years I was often goaded by my memory of that dreadful time into beginning the process of writing, but the spark it ignited always died out in the face of the enormity of the project. This was especially the case during the benighted years of the Vietnam War, when, adopting the strategy of "attrition" against an invisible enemy, the United States was destroying Vietnam "in order the save it for the free world." It was, in fact, not until the spring of 1999 that, thanks to Mina, I made the decision to begin writing the book.

We were sitting one evening on the front porch of my house in Castle Creek, New York, drinking wine and talking about the role that the myth of American exceptionalism had played in the first Gulf War. Somewhere along the way, the subject of the massive B-52 bombings of North Vietnam came up. And to underscore the undiscriminating brutality of America's conduct of that war—its indifference to the distinction between combatants and civilians—I mentioned that I had been in Dresden during the Allied firebombing that reduced that venerable German city to rubble and killed an untold number of people, possibly over a hundred thousand, in one night and day air raid. This parenthetical personal reference to an epochal event that the official histories of the war—the legacy of the complicity between the state and the culture industry—has more or less erased from history had a powerful impact on my European interlocutor, and it shifted the focus of our conversation. She asked me to tell her what happened, and during the next hour or so, loosened by the wine and her intense interest, I did. Deeply disturbed by my personal "story"—

and its unexpected implications about the United States—she wondered why I had not written about it, especially, she reminded me, given that I was always telling my students that the responsibility of the intellectual is, above all, to bear witness. In response, I told her that the singularity of my experience demanded a kind of writing of which I, steeped in the academic jargon of literary criticism and theory, was incapable. "But, Bill," she replied, "you've just done what you're saying you can't do. Please believe me." This combination of Mina's ironic reference to *la trahison des clercs* and the enthusiasm with which she received my story instigated my decision to begin writing after many years of procrastination.

Since then, roughly ten years ago, when I began tentatively to translate that buried time in my life into writing, my book has benefited greatly and in multiple ways by the care and generosity of several academic and personal friends: my *boundary 2* colleagues, who have encouraged my intellectual heresies through the many years of our association—Paul Bové, Dan O'Hara, Don Pease, Michael Hayes, Jonathan Arac, Cornel West, R. Radhakrishnan, Ronald Judy, Lindsay Waters, Kathryn Lindburg, and Jim Merod; the memory of my parents, Vaios and Marigoula, whose abiding love enabled me to survive the horror; my sister, Olga, whose beautiful face was a talisman in that time; my brothers Stephanos, Aristides, and especially Costas (Charlie) and his grace-filled wife, Joy, whose care has encouraged me to resist the ravages of time; my beautiful niece, Theo Spanos Dunfey, who became my unofficial agent after reading the manuscript in one sitting; my sons, Aristides and Adam, and my daughters, Maria and Stephania, who have let me be, even at this late date. Last but not least, I thank from the bottom of my heart my former wife and dear friend, Susan Strehle, Adam's mother, who has listened to me read as I have written—and has been moved to tears more than once by what she has heard.

Finally, I want once again to single out and express my gratitude to my friend and *boundary 2* colleague Donald Pease. At a *boundary 2* conference on the "Future of Literary Studies in the Academy" at Pittsburgh University in October 2007, I read a brief section of the chapter from my memoir on the firebombing of Dresden, which I had introduced by saying that, though what I was about to offer had nothing to do with literary studies, it might suggest, to those who knew something about the early years of the journal and/or had followed my errant scholarship over the years, "where I had come from." Because I had to catch a flight back to Binghamton an hour or so later, I wasn't able to stay to hear how my reading was received. Two days later, however, I had an e-mail note from Don, who was now in Berlin, telling me how much he was moved by "my passing on what was beyond the telling." Responding to my repeated use of the phrase *zero zone* to characterize the "place" that was Dresden after the apocalyptic firebombing, he went on to say that, as he heard it, that zero zone, which was the unspeakable consequence of the firebombing, was also, and because of that, a zone in which the social bond as I had been taught to feel it by "America," had been broken. It was this "revelation," he suggested, that enabled me to respond the way I did to the dead of Dresden, the "figures in the rubble who had been reduced to nonexistence," and turned that burned-out nonplace into "the neighborhood of zero."

I cannot, of course, be certain that the story that follows will be received by my readers as the testimony to the horror of the Allies' firebombing of Dresden I intend it to be, not to say to the redemptive "neighborhood of zero" it revealed like an epiphany. Indeed, I am profoundly aware of the abyssal gap remaining between my feeble words and the unspeakable singular event itself. But I am satisfied at least that what I have written about this event has retrieved something of that boy's life—some semblance of his awakened being—from the oblivion to which he and so many millions like him have, for all the encomiums to the "sacrifices of our greatest generation," been relegated by the banalizing Word of the custodians of the American cultural memory.

It is with great pleasure that I express my gratitude to Heather Lundine, editor-in-chief of the University of Nebraska Press, for her warm response to and generous support of this work, and to the staff of the press, who guided it through publication, particularly Elizabeth Gratch, whose copyediting was full of care.

In the Neighborhood of Zero

1. Departure and Border Crossings

Reflection is disinterested. Consciousness [life] is relationship, and it brings
with it interest or concern; a duality which is perfectly expressed with the
pregnant double meaning by the word "interest" (Latin *inter esse*, meaning (i) "to be between," (ii) "to be a matter of concern").

SØREN KIERKEGAARD, *Johannes, Climacus
or De Omnibus Dubitandum Est*

I am a Greek American, the second son of five children born to parents
who, in an effort to escape the wretched poverty of the "Old World,"
emigrated to the United States—first to Manchester, New Hampshire, the home of the Amosgeag Mills, the largest cotton factory in the
world at that time—in the first decade of the twentieth century. In the
first years, before they were married, my proud father, Vaios, unwilling
to work in a factory where "higher-ups" reduced the immigrant laborers to groveling nonentities, found employment with a railroad gang laying tracks west of Kansas City. My mother, Marigoula, whose father had
emigrated to the United States a few years earlier and had accumulated
enough money managing a *kafenio* (coffee shop) to send for her and her
sister, Katerini, began her adult life at the age of eleven in a shoe factory,
where, in order to gain employment, she had to hide cast-iron weights in
the pockets of her billowing ankle-length skirt to bring her weight up to
the factory's "rigorous" requirements. After they were married, my par-

ents moved briefly to Worcester, Massachusetts, where my father learned the barber's trade, and then, enticed by several young friends who had moved earlier from Manchester, to Newport, New Hampshire, a small mill town in the Lake Sunapee region, where they decided to settle down to raise a family.

Despite the Greek community's effort to preserve its old-world culture—the first generation of Greek American children, for example, attended Greek school after each day of public school—I became "assimilated" to the American way of life in my adolescence. After graduating from high school in 1941, I was conscripted into the U.S. Army, fought in World War II, and after the war, went to college under the GI Bill of Rights, taking my Bachelor of Arts degree at the prestigious liberal arts college Wesleyan University, my Master of Arts at Columbia University, and in 1964, after teaching two years at Mount Hermon Prep School in Massachusetts, my doctorate in English literature at the University of Wisconsin in Madison. On completing my academic work, I taught at the University of Kentucky for a couple of years, then at Knox College for several more, and finally at the State University of New York at Binghamton. During my career there, from 1972 to 1989, I founded and edited *boundary 2: a journal of postmodern literature*, which over the years became one of the most prestigious literary journals in North America, if not the world. In the process my numerous publications earned me a national reputation as a leading American critic and scholar.

Looked at superficially, in a way predetermined by the benign myth of "the American melting pot"—and all too easily celebrated by most Greek Americans and other ethnic minorities of that era—my life would appear to embody the fulfillment of "the American dream." Seen from the perspective I painfully acquired in the process of growing up, however, not least during my service in the U.S. Army between 1943, when I was drafted at the age of eighteen, to my discharge in September 1945, shortly after the German surrender in May and the horrific atomic bombing of Hiroshima and Nagasaki brought the war in the Pacific to its shocking end, this narrative of my "immigrant success" undergoes a radical change of terrain. It not only discloses the underbelly of the benign American exceptionalist narrative—the deeply backgrounded idea that the United States, chosen by God or History, is different from and superior to the decadent Old World—and the nation's unilateral missionary commitment to "ameliorate" the conditions of the poor and oppressed, the benighted and the downtrodden. It also foregrounds the silent hyphen between my Greek and American selves which, in a more recent language, has rendered me a hybrid. It is not my intention in this inaugural chapter to provide a narrative of my life as a Greek American. It will suffice for my purpose to focus on a certain aspect of my adolescence which affected my conflicted experience as an American soldier and combatant in World War II.

I never felt at ease in the New England I was growing up in, a provincial world that was constituted, on the one hand, by an Anglo-Protestant elite I initially felt was patronizing to the ethnic minorities who worked in the mills and the shoe shops they managed and, on the other, by a relatively impoverished and uneducated "Yankee" working class that, in large part, maintained its dignity and superiority by identifying the ethnic minorities in the village as unwelcome intruders. But at that time I did not consciously see the two constituencies that lorded over us in these respective terms. On the contrary, despite my unease—and in large part because what my schooling was massively inscribing into my being was the benignity of the American way of life—I attributed this persistent disorientation and my sense of dislocation to the limitations of my ethnic culture. I was, indeed, a barbarian. What I remember most vividly— to my present shame—about those early years was, therefore, my willful effort to suppress my lowly "Greekness" and to assimilate myself into the higher ways of the dominant Anglo-Protestant culture. I was becoming a ventriloquized dummy.

Nor were my parents, particularly my father, helpful in pointing me toward an alternative way of comporting myself in the Yankee world I precariously inhabited. Unlike many of his immigrant friends, who were committed wholeheartedly to assimilation, my father was deeply torn by his pride in his Greek heritage and his admiration for the idea of "America" as the land of freedom and opportunity. He had enlisted in the U.S.

Army in 1918, and though the war ended before he was called to overseas duty, he took great pride in his service and was disappointed about not being able to serve his adopted country in combat. On being discharged a year later, he, like many ethnic Americans who had served in World War I, joined the American Legion and participated actively in its meetings and ceremonies. I remember from my childhood how proud he was to wear the navy blue American Legion uniform, always dry-cleaned and neatly pressed, on the Fourth of July and other celebrations sponsored by the Newport chapter, how upright he bore his six-foot, well-built body as he marched in the parades, his dark handsome Mediterranean face intent on the proceedings, how reverently he saluted the American flag. My guess is that my father always bore himself in that manly manner, but I am certain that it was enforced by his pride in having been a soldier in the American army. When, for example, on the rare occasions he would grant me the opportunity of walking with him to his barbershop early in the morning, he would invariably turn, look down, and chastise me as I struggled heroically to keep up with him. "Vasili," he would say in Greek, "stand up straight [*orthos*] and walk like a soldier [*san stratiotis*]. When you grow up, do you want to be like those 'unwashed' [*apliti*] who think they're God's elect and hate us only because we're Greek?"

The dignity of my father's comportment in public, which I then attributed to his having been a soldier, was compelling, despite the ambivalences I harbored about my identity. My older brother, Steve (Stephanos), six feet, six inches tall and conscious, like my father, of his handsome and striking presence, joined the Junior American Legion Drum and Bugle Corps, eventually becoming its drum major, and a couple of years later, when I was thirteen or fourteen years old, I followed suit. This is not to say that I, like my brother, was drawn to the military. I don't remember precisely why I joined the corps. In retrospect, I think it was symptomatic of my desire to gain relief from the gnawing anxiety precipitated by my sense of alienation and the unrelenting discrimination I experienced growing up in that provincial Yankee environment. At any rate, by the time I graduated from high school in June 1941, as the war in Europe and the Pacific was raging, I had pretty thoroughly repressed my Greek identity, to the dismay of both my mother and father, and had become, or so I thought, "Americanized." (My father called me an "American hamburger" [*Amerikanikos keftedhas*].) As a result, I accepted at face value the now prevailing notion that the victory of the United States in World War II depended on the absolute patriotism of the ethnic minorities—Italian Americans, Jewish Americans, Irish Americans, Polish Americans, Greek Americans, Spanish Americans, French Americans, Finnish Americans, even German Americans—who were fighting it, a notion, however, that the repetition of these images of multicultural camaraderie in the numerous war films we watched as civilians eventually rendered vaguely duplicitous. It was with this sense of ambivalence—or, rather, this compensation for the anxiety of a future dislocation—that, after donning the American uniform on being drafted into the U.S. Army, I left Newport in the spring of 1943.

My thoughts on the Boston and Main train transporting me and twelve or so other inductees from Newport to Fort Devens in Massachusetts were wildly confused. I was in many ways glad that the separation from my family would enable me to think and act independently of the Greek cultural context in which I had grown up (our family was traditionally authoritarian and hierarchical). But I also felt that the separation from my father and mother, my younger brothers, Harry (Aristides) and Charlie (Constantinos)—my oldest brother, Steve, had been drafted several months before—my sister, Olga, and my high school girlfriend, Kathryn (Kitty) Carey, was a violent sundering that left me desolate, alone in a bewildering, huge, and ominous world that I was not equipped to deal with. The other inductees in the compartment seemed to be excited by the prospect that lay before them. They joked knowingly about "our town fathers," who, surrounded by American flags, had sent them off at the railroad station with canned patriotic speeches recalling the "unforgotten heroes" from all the Newports of the United States who had nobly sacrificed their lives defending America—and civilization—against the barbarian Huns in World War I and were answering its sacred call once again. But the peculiar kind of animation they manifested seemed to suggest that they had also been inspired by the very patriotic sentiments they were mocking. As I brooded over the difference between my conflicted emotions and what seemed to me their equanimity, if not enthusiasm, it occurred to me, as a barely audible whisper, that most of these inductees, several of whom I knew in some degree or other, were, like me, members of working-class ethnic families. I didn't perceive—indeed, I was at that stage of my life incapable of inferring—the complex social implications of this situation. My fellow inductees on the train were, as I was, simply Americans called to duty on behalf of their country. Nevertheless, this subversive thought had occurred and would increasingly haunt me throughout the time of my military service.

A few hours later we arrived at Fort Devens, a huge staging area about thirty miles west of Boston, the purpose of which was to commence the process of transforming a diverse and amorphous swarm of young, undisciplined civilians into American combat soldiers. During those first days we were assigned to our temporary units, divested of our civilian clothing in exchange for fatigues, khakis, and, most ominous, a set of "dog tags," shorn of our long hair, and given dental and medical examinations. These fast-moving events remain a blur in my memory. The rapid and dislocating pace of the metamorphosis made it impossible to process them. What I remember about this transforming time, primarily because it contradicted my inscribe expectations, was that most of the commissioned and noncommissioned officers who presided over the process treated us as if we were the scum of the earth, a comportment that was no doubt strategic, but seemed to me like a continuation of the contemptuous discrimination, epitomized by the epithet "Greaseball" I had suffered growing up in Newport. I remember in particular hearing a sergeant who, a few days after our arrival, was marching several of us in lock step to the dental clinic say in disgust, "Didn't your parents teach you jerk-offs what a toothbrush is? Well, you ignorant shit-faces, the U.S. Army will, you'd better believe it."

But in that deeply depressing blur there was Frank Sinatra, who had captured the hearts of virtually every teenage girl in the United States. His soothing liquid voice echoed the nostalgia and shamelessly sentimental dreams of lonely young Americans stationed and fighting in other remote places in the world:

I'll be seeing you
In all the old familiar places,
That my heart embraces
All night through.

His voice to me, at that time of disruption, was in part a stay against my confusion, because his songs reminded me of a part of my life at home I enjoyed a lot—listening to the Lucky Strike radio program Sinatra hosted in the evenings after dinner or mimicking his uncannily moving improvisational phrasing for Kathryn as we stumbled and stuttered through the uncertainties of adolescent sexual attraction. But it was also no doubt because he was an Italian American from Hoboken, New Jersey, who had somehow managed to transcend his working-class ethnic roots without at the same time denying them. All through my stay at Fort Devens I sang in my mind all the songs I had learned by heart listening to the recordings he made with the Tommy Dorsey Orchestra and after he had gone solo. In retrospect it was not a substantial stay against chaos, but it was, for all I knew at that innocent time of my life, a sustaining solace. And I confess, despite the resistance to sentimentality I developed over the years—and the volatility of Sinatra's politics—his voice remains to this day a comfort in difficult times.

Less than a month after arriving at Fort Devens, my uncertainty about where I would be sent for basic training came to an end when, to my dismay, I was informed at reveille roll call that I had been assigned to Camp Wheeler in Macon, Georgia. According to rumors circulating at Devens, the camp was in the heart of the "redneck" South and had the ominous reputation of being a "hellhole" for new soldiers, especially for those from the decadent northeastern states. A couple of days later I and about fifteen or so inductees I didn't know, uniformed but, in my case at least, psychologically ragged, were herded into an army truck that drove us to Springfield, Massachusetts, where we boarded a huge black funereal train bound for our dreaded destination. As the train shuddered its way out of the station, I, who had never traveled past Boston, perceived this coerced trip into the deep South as a symbolic journey.

In excruciating slow motion, the train, like a black mechanical serpent, ground through Massachusetts and Pennsylvania and into the South, through a various but familiar landscape dotted with seemingly thriving towns, into an alien landscape burned to a crisp by the heat of an unrelenting sun, the towns, far more distant from each other than those in the North, unreal in their languid, amorphous, and dull sprawl. My sense of dislocation, of the abyssal hole that had opened up at the railroad station in Newport a month earlier, began to deepen. I suddenly realized how ill prepared I was to encounter a looming future far from "home" and haunted by the specters of loneliness, violence, and death. Curling myself up, fetus-like, in the corner of my window seat, my abstracted gaze willfully directed outside the suffocating space of the compartment filled by my uniformed "comrades," I conjured an image of myself standing melancholically beside Kathryn under a lamplight at the doorstep of her apartment on Ash Street and called on Frank Sinatra, my principal of last resort:

When purple shadows start to welcome the dark,
I'll take the same old stroll through the park,
And I'll cling to you, dear,
Just as though you were here.

We arrived at Macon late in the evening of the second day, and an army truck transported us to a sprawling, ugly army camp a few miles beyond the city limits in the middle of a uniformly flat plain of red earth as vast as the eye could see. A huge fiery sun was setting on the distant horizon, transforming the dull expanse into what seemed a lurid red wasteland. It was terrifically hot, the air was heavy with humidity, and our clothes were soaked in sweat. This, I thought with fear and trembling, was to be my home for the next thirteen weeks.

The rumors about Macon, the camp and the city, we had heard at Fort Devens were not far from the truth. The sergeant who was in charge of my platoon was a young Southerner, reddish blond cropped hair, blue-eyed, severe: a fanatic disciplinarian, always dressed in starched fatigues that seemed to crackle as he walked, determined to reduce our minds and bodies into deadly weapons. A gold crucifix hung around his neck. "The Nazis or the Japs you're going to be facing soon are cunning killer machines," he would say in inaugurating a punishing exercise in the heat of the day, adding contemptuously, "You won't survive long, you can bet your sorry asses, if you go into combat with them filled with the civilian ideas you learned up there in the North." I knew that he was right about discipline. It was indeed a kind of invisible armor. But I couldn't help feeling that he and most of the noncoms who ruled our waking and sleeping lives with iron fists were themselves machinelike killers, not simply indifferent to but in some sense contemptuous of the errant life that is being human. Throughout the grueling thirteen weeks of basic training, conscious of my desire to survive, I willed myself to be "trained," despite feeling that some of the exercises—the hand-to-hand combat; the day-long, painful, full-pack marches; the extended rifle drills in the heat of the unbearable afternoon Southern sun—were acts of revenge for some kind of unspecified crime we Northern trainees had collectively committed before coming to their beloved army.

Most of the members of my platoon became acclimated to these soldierly imperatives. But however much I tried, I simply could not become a "good soldier." I was often reprimanded by our platoon sergeant for not making my bed properly, for the wrinkles in my dress uniform and the stains in my fatigues, for the missteps I made in marching drills, for not seeming attentive to commands, for the speck of dust that remained in the barrel of my M1 rifle after cleaning it. Eventually the sergeant concluded that I was a "goldbrick"—the equivalent of a pariah—or so I surmised, after realizing about halfway through basic training that I had been increasingly assigned to kitchen police duties after the workday was over.

I was in fact not a goldbrick. During basic training I became an excellent marksman on the rifle range. I even won a coveted "Expert Riflemen's Badge" in the process. And I excelled in simulated combat conditions, for example, crawling on my elbows, rifle cradled in my arms, through barbed wire under machine gun fire. But I must admit I was "a loner," reluctant to belong. There was something in me that resisted being disciplined, a hard-to-fathom recalcitrance, which in some vague way, and despite my effort to suppress it, I felt had to do with the hyphen between my Greek and American selves: the contradiction between the unhappy actualities of my life in the small mill town in New England and the American promise.

I remember vividly, as if it had happened yesterday, one morning sometime near the end of basic training that epitomized this disturbing impulse. The reveille bugle had raucously announced the dawn of another day, the sergeant, dressed as usual in crisp fresh fatigues barking at the foot of the long barracks room, "Rise and shine, you mother fuckers; time to drop your cocks and don your socks." That was the usual routine, but somehow that morning the sneering voice penetrated my being like a dagger thrust into my stomach, right there where that recalcitrance silently abided. I woke up, staggered through a shower, made my bed, dressed in fatigues, grabbed my rifle, which I had carefully cleaned and polished the night before, and ran out the door to take my place in the third row of the platoon to await rifle inspection by our unit's lieutenant. When after a few minutes he finally arrived, the sergeant shouted, "Teeeeenhut!" We came to rigid attention, our combat boots echoing with a decisive thud as they collectively hit the asphalt pavement. Then the lieutenant called out, "At ease!" and, putting on a clean pair of white gloves, began the tense process of rifle inspection.

This daily disciplinary exercise consisted of the following phases: as the inspecting officer stepped up to face the trainee, the neophyte in one fluid motion would sharply raise his rifle diagonally across his body and grab it below the barrel with his left hand, disengage his right from the stock, whip it up to the bolt, pull the spring open, and release the rifle— at the very moment that the lieutenant shot his hand up to take the rifle, peered into the empty chamber and then the barrel, and thrust it back at the trainee, who would then release the bolt (which sprang back with great force to close the chamber) and bring the rifle back to the ground.

As the lieutenant moved from one trainee to another, repeating the motions over and over again, interminably I thought, it suddenly struck me that the labored solemnity of this scene was a colossal farce, and the impish itch inside me began to awaken as I tried desperately to coax it back to sleep. And then, as if conjured, the lieutenant was standing before me. I brought my rifle up in front of me and went flawlessly, indeed with unusual grace, through the ritual motions until the lieutenant grabbed the rifle out of my hand, looked into the chamber, and thrust it back at me. I received it with my left hand, but when I brought my right up to release the bolt, my left thumb somehow got in the way and the bolt, like a hammer, smashed back into my thumbnail. I screamed in pain and dropped the rifle on the lieutenant's foot. A moment of awful silence, amplified by my scream of pain and the clatter of the fallen rifle on the pavement. Then the platoon, my comrades-in-arms, burst out laughing. Was this disruption an accident, the result of my overanxious desire to perform well? Or was it that irrepressible impish recalcitrance that abided furtively inside me? Whatever the actual cause, I now, in retrospect, understand this ludicrous symbolic moment as a symptomatic effort to deconstruct a received ritual that promised some kind of liberation as in fact a ritual in which the brainwashed washed the brains of the innocent young . . . for what? That was the question that, despite my awareness of the civilized barbarism of the Nazis, came increasingly to haunt me throughout the three years of my service in the U.S. Army.

Another aspect of my experience at Camp Wheeler that struck me as disturbingly odd had to do with race. We had been told, without registering the irony of that benign commitment, that the U.S. Army did not discriminate. But I found at Macon that this was decidedly not true. Of the thousands of young men taking basic training there, there were no blacks among us. It was emphatically a white—and crudely masculine—world. For a while I attributed this absence of blacks to the camp's location in the segregated South, where to my dismay blacks rode standing in the rear of buses; were not allowed to eat in white restaurants, drink from white water fountains, or use white toilet facilities; and were consigned to the "buzzards' loft" in movie theaters. The military, I assumed, sent black inductees to camps in the North to protect them from this kind of degrading discrimination. But the realities of life in the camp quickly disabused me of that assumption. I soon found out that there were, in fact, black soldiers in the camp, but they were segregated from the space occupied by the white inductees by being consigned to the motor pool—and heavy-duty labor—and, if I recall correctly, their own pxs and barracks. When, disturbed by this revelation, I asked ncos who were familiar with the camp to explain this humiliating divide, they invariably replied that blacks—all too often they referred to them as "niggers"—were belligerent, always prone to provoke violence. "If these blacks were allowed to mix with white soldiers, the camp would become a war zone."

One evening, while I was on kp duty peeling potatoes in the mess hall kitchen and talking with one of the permanent cooks, an amiable Southerner I had gotten to know, he told me about an incident that had occurred that morning in the camp stockade, which, as I recall, was not segregated.

"A white and a black prisoner in the stockade, a couple uv giants," he said, "were ordered by the mps in charge ta dig a latrine. They'd dug a big hole in that there hard red earth, waist high, all the time, as ya'll might expect, cursin the fuckin fates and each other for what was happenin to them. There's no debatin that. But what happened next between those motherfuckers—that's somethin else. In a fit of exasperation the white guy told the nigger that he, the white, was doin more diggin than him, one shovel-full ta his four. Without sayin a word, the nigger jumped out of the hole, lifted his shovel high over his head, and brought it down, pow! full force, on the white guy's skull, splittin it in two."

There was a pause, while I caught my breath. And then he went on. "I'm not a nigger-hater, ya'all, like a lot uv my buddies. I'm for livin and lettin live," he said, "but ya'll have to admit that they're just not like us, even the white guy he brained. Ya just cain't rely on them people; they're too unpredictable, mean-spirited, like jungle animals that can't be civil. That's why they don't make good soljers."

I listened to this horror story and its moral in silence, appalled by the contradictions. But knowing that nothing I could say in response would destabilize the deep certainty of his convictions, I said nothing.

For a while I entertained the possibility that this ugly racism was restricted to the U.S. Army camp at Macon. But I soon found out that it was, in fact, the official, if unannounced policy of the American military com mand, indeed, of the American government. I experienced this shameful and disturbing paradox everywhere I was assigned after basic training: at the Army Specialized Training Program at the University of Alabama, at Camp Atterbury in Indiana, at the staging area in Cheltenham, England, and most dramatically for me, in the European combat zone. For the huge convoy of army trucks—"the Red-Ball Express," it was called—that drove the 106th Division, of which I eventually became a member, across France from Le Havre to the Ardennes Forest in Belgium, where we took up combat positions, were manned entirely by black soldiers. The shock of this contradictory witness—not simply the segregation but the menial nature of the tasks assigned to black Americans as opposed to the decisively important tasks assigned to white Americans—crystallized my earlier intuition that, despite the grandeur of the American cause in which I was about to become bodily engaged, there was something "rotten in the state of Denmark."

What I remember most acutely about my time at Camp Wheeler was the "party" the noncommissioned officers of our platoon arranged for us after we completed basic training to celebrate our having become "shit-kicking GIs." By that time most of my fellow members had indeed become a "manly" collective, precise in their bearing, careful in their dress, masculine about their sexual prowess, confident in their soldierly calling. Or so it seemed to me. I too was relieved that basic training was over and that the degradations to which we had been subjected in the process of being "hardened" by military protocol—the NCOs invariably identified this term with erection—had come to an end. But unlike my comrades, I didn't feel that I had "arrived." Despite the yearning of one side of me to be, I was not one of them. In fact, my sense of dislocation had been intensified. I belonged and didn't belong to the collective. It was with this unbalancing sense of being an outside-insider that I went to our "last supper," as the noncoms called it.

At about four-thirty in the afternoon of the Saturday of the last week of basic training, we all piled into an army bus, procured by our noncoms, which was to take us out to the countryside between the army camp and the city to a roadhouse restaurant specializing in Southern barbecued chicken. The short ride was tumultuously merry. Under the spell of release we sang popular songs—the Andrew Sisters's "Don't Sit under the Apple Tree" and Bing Crosby's "White Christmas" (both of which I detested)—mimicked the drawling commands of our sergeants, playfully criticized each other's failures as good soldiers. On finally arriving at our destination about an hour later, we were led by a couple of waiters in long grease-stained white aprons through a large bar and lounge, relatively empty but already flickering garishly with multicolored lights, country music coming from a large juke box blasting away at an almost intolerable volume, into a private dining room decorated with large photographs of female nudes and furnished with a long wooden table laid with paper plates and plastic cups extending across the length of the rectangular room. The three noncoms took their privileged places in the middle of the table on the far side of the room, and the rest of us seated ourselves wherever space was available. When the company had settled down in their chairs, the first sergeant, a career soldier who had supervised our basic training by delegating his orders of the day to his lower-echelon aides, stood up and, striking the table with his fist, called us to attention: "Tiiiiieeen . . . hut!" We all rose simultaneously, en masse, like jack-in-the boxes. And he, with a grin of satisfaction, said in his Southern drawl, "Now ya'll acting like American soldiers. Thirteen weeks ago you suckers would be falling all over yourselves processing that God 'amighty command in your Northern pussy-like pea-brains." He paused, looking benignly around the table, and then barked, "At ease!" We took our seats again, many of us with visible pride.

Then, pounding the table for our attention again, he launched into a speech praising the American flag and the country it gloriously represented, vilifying the brutal Nazis and especially the "yellow Japs," reminding us of America's historical mission, ordained by "the Big Man Above," "to save the world for democracy." That, he emphasized, not without betraying a certain remnant of doubt, depended entirely on the collective goodwill of an ethnically diverse multitude—"you Pollocks, Dagos, Kikes, Greaseballs, Frogs, who owe our country." And looking at us, seemingly one by one, with a penetrating gaze, he concluded, "Wherever you guys are assigned on this here planet, you're all gonna get the job done for old Uncle Sam! . . . Now let's party!" signaling to a waiter who was standing at the door to the kitchen. The sergeant's speech was greeted by most of my fellow soldiers with enthusiasm. "Here! Here!" "Right on, Sergeant!" "Let us at those fuckin Krauts and Japs!" I, too, like Ishmael, went through the motions. But our Ahab's speech—the difference between the doubtless idealism of his sentiments and the crude and clichéd language he used to express it—turned my stomach inside out. Once again, I couldn't repress the nauseating feeling that I didn't belong in this company, even though I was a part of it. "A-part," I kept saying to myself, "a-part."

As the double kitchen door leading into our dining room parted, the sergeant shouted through the din, "You can look but don't touch!" and a number of beautiful young waitresses, dressed in short black satin skirts and see-through silk or linen white blouses opened at the neck to reveal most of the cleavage between their breasts, came through one by one carrying large trays laden with garnished golden-brown chicken, corn-bread, French fries, and cold slaw. The whistles and catcalls were tumultuous. To the knowing delight of the noncoms, the waitresses flirted with us while they served the succulent-looking chicken, bending low beside each man in such a way as to induce ripples down their ample breasts. Despite my embarrassment—I had never encountered this sort of thing before—and my realization that the whole scene had been programmed, the bare flesh of young women intermingled with the thick, spicy aroma of the roasted chickens took on a sensuality that filled the room with a far more primal aura than that produced by the sergeant's nationalistic speech. After the waitresses had served us, they left but soon returned, one after the other, to more whistles and catcalls, with large pitchers of beer. Once again the first sergeant banged the table with his fist, bringing the company to another silence and, raising a plastic cup of beer in front of him, said, "A toast to America, to our beloved South, to our beloved U.S. Army, and—" he paused with a comradely grin, "to our Southern women you Northern shit-faces will be fighting for to make amends. Let the festivities begin!"

After the cheers subsided—I'd like to think they were the expression of relief rather than approval, but I was not certain—we began our last supper, and the beer began to flow. I had drunk beer before on occasion but never in excess, simply because I didn't like the taste of it. That night, however, in a mighty effort to silence my demonic recalcitrance, I drank with a vengeance, cup after cup after cup . . . until the lights went out.

The next thing I remember I was lying face down in a puddle of vomit in front of the roadhouse—a pandemonium of loud echoing country music, raucous voices coming from every direction, and phantasmic blue, red, yellow, and white lights blinking randomly—my arms spread out and my fingers, raw and bloody, desperately clutching the earth, which, I realized with terror, was intent on throwing me off her red back. "No, don't! Please, don't!" I remember repeating. And then the faces of the first sergeant and several of my "buddies" bathed in the lurid surreal light and raucous sound, hovering above me, laughing good-naturedly: "This Spanos kid . . . he's getting there!"

A week after this last supper the assignments we had been waiting for in fear and trembling were announced in our barracks room. To my astonishment—and admittedly, great relief—I, unlike all my comrades, who were called to service in military units all across the country, was assigned to a unit of the new Army Specialized Training Program (ASTP) at the University of Alabama in Tuscaloosa. Apparently, the military command in Washington has been informed by the field commanders in Europe of a shortage of combat engineers and, no doubt in anticipation of a not-too-distant Allied invasion of the European continent, had established this program at a number of universities in the South (I think) to fill this lack. I'm not sure how or why I was assigned to ASTP. I was not particularly talented in mathematics and the sciences. I did, however, vaguely remember taking something like an aptitude test at Fort Devens, but as I recall, there was no specific consequence attributed to it. At any rate, in late September or early October 1943, under the aegis of a mysterious abstract authority, I boarded a train at Macon that took me to Tuscaloosa. On arriving at the beautiful University of Alabama campus, we were bused to the ASTP quarters, a student dormitory, in which, to my delight, we were assigned not to barracks but to rooms for two.

My stay at the University of Alabama was a welcome respite from the heavy-duty rigor—indeed, the hard labor—of basic training and, not least, from the agonizing crude simplifications of the complexities of the world we actually lived in. Despite my awareness that the university was segregated, the comparative easiness of life in the program was comforting. Above all, I found the normal level of conversation far more elevated, various, and engaging than the ventriloquized talk at Camp Wheeler in Macon. And this general pleasure was enhanced by the friendship I soon developed with two of my fellow ASTP students, Tomas Yukie, my roommate, a Yugoslavian American from upstate New York, and Bob Wagner from Buffalo, New York, both of whom had been drafted out of college, the one from Cortland Teachers, the other from Niagara University. Tom, my elder by a couple of years, tall and gaunt, whose face reminded me of a Modigliani portrait, was a serious, straight-laced young man who, convinced of my confusion, assumed responsibility for guiding me though the perilous entanglements of the unpredictable nomadic world into which we had been thrown. He was, in retrospect, my Virgil during those months at the University of Alabama before we parted company, not at the gates of Purgatory but of Hell.

There was nothing I said, no matter what the topic, that he didn't find errant, a false turn toward disaster. "Bill, old boy," he would say in his precise and somewhat stilted way, "you have to take control of your destiny. You cannot wallow in ambiguities as you always do. Simplify, as Thoreau said. How in the world, in its increasingly mystifying way, are you going to survive youth, love, loneliness, war?" Bob Wagner, on the other hand, short, burly, and barrel-chested, was a saturnine fellow given to playfully undermining the idealizations of our friend Tom, a kind of Sancho Panza to Don Quixote. "Ambiguities," he would say in response to the stiff purity of Tom's vision, "are what the world's all about. You listen to him, Bill, and you'll wind up in the mouth of a cannon. You've got to keep your eyes on the ground, my friend, not in the sky." "The ground," he would say, with a certain pride in his wise and learned paradoxes, "the

tangled and bloody ground's our friend, not the sky. Remember Thales?"
And the delightful war of words would commence.

To me this kind of semi-serious but always challenging banter was not
simply a reprieve from the boring crudeness of the usual talk at Camp
Wheeler. It also was revelatory. The play of its unexpected movements
enabled me to see that the United States consisted of two incommensurable worlds, not so much of class or culture but of quality of mind, one
inhabited by people who valued thinking, the other by those who were
indifferent or hostile to its impracticality and always spoke in banali-
ties. What I delighted in was not a growing sense of knowingness that allowed me to feel superior to my former comrades at Camp Wheeler. It
was, rather, a newly discovered sense of the complex richness of the life
of the mind, the sense that the resonant potentialities that thinking discloses were indissolubly related to the radical uncertainties of my being
in the world—to my dislocation, my being in-between. In the company
of these two new and unlikely friends it suddenly occurred to me that
I was growing up, that I, in all my programmed minuteness and irrele-
vance, was an integral part of an immeasurably large and unfathomable
world, frightening but also somehow enabling.

During my stay at the University of Alabama I took courses in advanced algebra, trigonometry, and calculus, all preparatory to my projected
courses in civil engineering. I had no natural aptitude for the mathemat-
ical sciences, but assuming that my successful completion of the project would earn me a commission and a kind of combat duty that was, I
thought, more peripheral and safer than being an infantryman, I willed
myself to master them. Against my natural inclinations I worked at learning formulas, equations, and paradigms long after Tom—a mathemati-
cal genius, I thought—had gone to bed. Eventually the rigorous logic informing these mysterious signs began to become clear. In fact, I began to
envision myself as an engineer building or rebuilding roads and bridges
in terrain that had been retaken by our Sherman tanks and infantry soldiers, far above the body-shattering violence below.

But that future, too, like all the previous ones since departing from
Newport, was not to be. In the spring, after spending four or five months

at the University of Alabama, our ASTP unit was suddenly, without advance notice, dissolved and transferred en masse to Camp Atterbury outside Indianapolis, Indiana, to take up assignments in the newly formed (or re-formed) 106th Division. This turn—which, if I remember correctly, involved the entire Army Specialized Training Program—was shocking. But its cause was not difficult for us to imagine, even though it was not officially announced. The war in both the Pacific and in Europe was intensifying. The American army had invaded Italy from North Africa and had defeated the Italian army on the mainland. Anticipating victory in the West at long last but inhibited by the far-flung areas of its operations, the American military command was beginning to feel the need for more manpower. And as it turned out—it was in the winter of 1943, and the Soviet armies were counterattacking the Germans in the East—the American and British forces under General Dwight Eisenhower were planning the decisive act of the war in Western Europe: the invasion of France.

At this point the war began to impinge menacingly on my consciousness. I had always been aware of the war but not, for some reason, perhaps because I had concentrated on the transformations it produced in me or because I had considered myself to be a nonentity in this epochal event, in a way that affected by sense of safety from harm. I had felt somehow immune or beyond the scope of its violence. Now as the war reached its tentacles into this remote campus in the deep American South, I became acutely aware of the imminence of a disruptive process that, like a whirlwind, would hurl me across an ocean into the killing fields. But even more important, this utterly unexpected turn activated in my mind an awareness of a massive indefinable but transcendent omniscient entity, not god but a national abstraction—the U.S. military command, the American government, the American public, or some dominant constituency of it—that was determining my every gesture from a remote distance. It was this abstraction personified in the ubiquitous figure of "Uncle Sam," his omniscient and inescapable gaze reaching into all the nooks and crannies of America, his bony long finger pointing at all the "me's" who had thought ourselves to be irrelevant nonentities. The figure gave us an identity and at the same time accusingly called to us, "I want you!"

Under the relentless gaze of this indifferent but commanding eye, I and my friends, Tom and Bob, were assigned to the new 106th Division at Camp Atterbury, I, for no reason I could fathom, to the communications platoon of an infantry company of the 423rd Regiment, and they, as I recall, to infantry platoons of the 422nd and 424th. This separation of our triumvirate was for me a serious blow. I had taken great comfort and had achieved a kind of equanimity in their company. But I resigned myself to the arbitrary and often cruel dictates of Uncles Sam's seemingly fickle finger. After arriving and settling into our respective units at Atterbury, we made it a point to get together on weekends, when we had leaves of absence. But as we oriented our priorities to our new particular contexts, these meetings became less frequent. Eventually they ceased altogether. In fact, to my acute and abiding regret, I never saw Tom and Bob again. Nor did I ever find out, except in imagination, what happened to them during the disaster that befell our division in Belgium. It was the case in that turbulent time of modern history. They simply came and went.

As a member of the communications platoon of my company, I spent most of my time training to become proficient as a telegraph and radio operator. I was, of course, grateful for not having to undergo the rigorous and backbreaking training to which the infantry soldiers were being subjected and that in anticipating the horrors of combat—erroneously—I would be a secondary figure to the infantryman. But I also felt guilty for feeling this way. In spite of the ambiguities that haunted me, I believed in America's cause and felt obligated to do my share, however little it might be, to achieve it.

The Western Allies invaded Normandy in June 1944 and were fighting major battles all along the northern coastline of France. My brother Steve, I was informed in a letter from my father, was in the 84th Division fighting at Saint Malo. The war in Europe, in general and in particular, had taken a decisive turn. But I was not one of those perennially Athenian young men to whom Thucydides refers in *The Peloponnesian Wars* who enthusiastically go to war for the sake of glory. Aware of the impending moment that would take me across the boundary that protected me from the violence of war, I was frightened.

But my stay at Camp Atterbury was not entirely marked by this disconcerting subjective tension. There were frequent times of respite, thanks to the weekend passes that enabled us to visit Indianapolis, a city in the heartland of the United States that was far more tolerant of GIs than Macon and even Tuscaloosa. What I remember most vividly about the city was the circle at its center and, more specifically, the dance hall, whose entrance was located between bars, shops, and boutiques along its circumference, where several of us from our platoon would go on Fridays or Saturday nights to drink beer, meet girls, dance, and—hopefully— "make out." At eighteen I had not as yet had sex and was therefore the object of considerable derision by my now mostly older companions. And for that reason, and despite my puritanical moralism—and not least my love for my high school girlfriend, Kathryn—I was eager to consummate what they called alternatively "becoming a man" and, bizarrely, "breaking my cherry."

Like "The Indianapolis Circle," the huge dance hall was circular, covered by a high dark blue dome punctuated by lights that looked like distant stars and, when the band was playing, strobe lights projected red, white, and blue colors that flickered on and off in slow motion around the ballroom. At the entrance side of the dance hall, as I recall it, was a long curved bar and at the far side the bandstand. The orchestras that played there usually were local groups, though on occasion a nationally known orchestra on tour would stop by for a one-night gig. The ballroom on Saturday nights was always crowded, couples near the bandstand, many unescorted girls at one side of the circumference (always a reminder of the depletion of the local population of young men during the war) and, on the other, mostly soldiers, hungry for female companionship, from the camp. Though I loved the music of that era, particularly the swing bands of Artie Shaw, Glenn Miller, Tommy Dorsey, Duke Ellington, and Woody Herman, preferring the standard ballads they played, I was not a good dancer. And despite having been often told that I was "good-looking" or "handsome" or "cute," I was then—and for a long time afterward— extremely shy. As a consequence, though I would try coaxing myself into asking one of the girls at the periphery to dance, I spent those first few

Saturday nights nursing a Coke (sometimes a beer), listening to the music on the sidelines and, I must confess, wallowing in one kind of imagined, self-pitying scenario or another.

One night, however, as I was standing near the bar with a couple of friends, I noticed, not too far down the right side of the ballroom, a pretty young girl looking directly at me. She was wearing a black knee-length skirt and a tight-fitting black sweater, adorned by a gold necklace that emphasized her full breasts. She was swaying slightly to the slow rhythm of a ballad. Her hair was straight and coal black and hung slightly below her ears, the front cut in a curved bang across the middle of her forehead. Though clearly Caucasian, her face, especially the slight almond shape of her eyes, had the look of an Oriental. I looked back, vaguely excited, but was too shy to sustain the eye contact. She then turned her attention away, and, I thought that, to my chagrin, that was that. Shortly afterward, I saw her dancing with another soldier, and at the end of the night she departed with a couple of girlfriends, with whom she apparently had come to the ballroom.

A week later, on my next leave, I returned with a friend to the Circle Ballroom, hoping she would be there and determined, if she was, to ask her to dance with me. For some reason or other we arrived late in the evening. Upon entering the place, I surveyed the crowd and spotted her talking with her friend pretty much in the same place as the week before. She was wearing a dark blue, form-fitting dress cut low at the neck. I had had a beer before I arrived to fortify myself, but my will began disintegrating. I turned to my buddy in the hope of recuperating my composure, but he had vanished. As I was looking for him, I suddenly felt a soft tap on my shoulder, and when I turned, there she was.

"Hi, soldier," she said in a soft voice, "would you like to dance?"

I felt flushed but elated. "Yeah, I'd like that," I said, embarrassed.

We walked onto the dance floor and began dancing to a slow ballad. What an exquisite thrill it was to feel the soft flesh beneath this young woman's dress and her arm gently but firmly wrapped around my back! I had forgotten that feeling—a glowing sexual excitement tempered by a soothing sense of comfort and connectedness—in the throes of my agonized readjustment.

As we danced under the flickering dome, we exchanged brief histories of ourselves. I told her, in so many words, that I was from a small town in New Hampshire, the son of Greek parents, that I had three brothers, two younger than me and one older, who was fighting in Europe, and a much younger sister, that I had graduated from high school and was drafted into the army the year before, and that I had spent my basic training in Georgia and the next several months studying to become an engineer at the University of Alabama in the ASTP, before being assigned to an infantry division at Camp Atterbury. She told me in far more words that her name was Doris Knight, that she had grown up on a farm near Bloomington, Indiana, had graduated from high school a couple of years earlier, and was now working as a secretary for a law firm in Indianapolis, a job that she didn't like because her bosses never let her forget that she was a female. Then there was a long silence, interrupted by sudden enthusiastic bursts of mellifluous speech flowing out of the sweet mouth of my lovely and mysterious partner. Time has shredded the words she spoke to me that night, but the memory of Doris's embrace around which they circulated like butterflies around a red flower remains indelibly inscribed in my mind. The feeling of her soft breasts pressing against my chest, the occasional squeeze of her right hand, the faint touch of her face on my neck—all of it said, "I like you, Bill."

When the set was over, I reluctantly walked Doris back to the circumference from which she had emerged—like Botticelli's Venus, I would now say—and, still holding her hand, thanked her for asking me to dance with her. Struggling for words, I blurted out that I hoped I'd see her again. She smiled but didn't answer. I stood there for an awkward moment wanting to say something memorable, but all I could muster was a flat "Good night." Then, as the band leader was announcing the last set of the evening, I turned toward the bar to seek out my buddy. After finding him, under the influence, I led him into a bus that brought us back to Camp Atterbury.

As I lay anxiously elated in my bunk that night, Doris's lithe body circulating in the firmament of my mind like the flickering lights of the ball-room, I tried to infer a narrative from the various conflicting fragments or impressions that had been inaugurated by the touch of her finger on my shoulder. One was the result of a combination of loyalty to Kathryn and my puritanical moral sense. Why would a young girl, not even twenty-one, go unescorted to a dance hall? Did she go to such dubious social places to be "picked up"? Was the tap of her finger on my shoulder such an invitation? Were the gestures of affection I felt her body making meant to be provocative? From this narrative perspective I painted Doris in an image that my soldier friends would call "a fast girl on the make," to which I responded ambiguously. I disapproved of her apparent promiscuity, which I compared to Kathryn's austere integrity, but I was also sexually aroused by it. After all, my purpose in going to the Circle Ball-room in the first place was in some vague way to find a girl to have sex with. (At that stage of my life I abhorred using the current GI language: "to get fucked," "to find a piece of ass," "to get some pussy.") So, despite my disapproval and my loyalty to Kathryn, I had entertained the possi-bility of a sexual consummation. The other narrative I conjured was the antithesis of the first one. Like so many girls at that time, I thought, when most of the young men from the towns and neighborhoods all over the country were elsewhere in the world, Doris—and, I imagined, Kathryn too—was simply yearning for the pleasurable comfort of male compan-ionship in a world that seemed to sever connections maliciously. And the dance hall was the most convenient place to find it. This impulse, not promiscuity, explained her unexpected invitation and the warm in-timacy of her bodily gestures as we danced. These two contradictory nar-ratives jostled for primary position in my confused head for hours, un-til I finally fell asleep.

As I had hoped, but also each time feared, I met Doris at the Circle Ballroom several times after the first night, and eventually we became closer. As we danced, her bodily movements seemed to become increas-ingly intimate, almost provocative. She would run her fingers through my hair, press her thighs against mine, look deeply into my eyes with what seemed to me enticing desire. Still, I couldn't fathom her motive nor mine. I desperately wanted her. Her sexual vibrancy had become irresistible to my youthful innocence. And this desire, despite my will to remain loyal to Kathryn, was intensified by my awareness that our time together was limited. "Take the gift she's offering you before time takes it into its careless mouth." But on the other hand, I also thought I was falling in love with her and thus felt a moral responsibility to hold back in the name—yes—of a less bestial ending. As I look back to this wonderful but cruel ephemeral moment—another in-between—in my life, I regret not having consummated what Doris seemed to be offering me without conditions. My high seriousness—my sense of an ending, in which things would turn out better than they would had they been confronted by a rash act—what a waste! And I remember the lines of the poet Wallace Stevens, whom I came to love many years later:

Death is the mother of beauty; hence from her,
Alone, shall come fulfillment to our dreams
And our desires.

Whatever that first night might have been, it was not consummated one way or another. Following the invasion of Europe and the considerable losses that epochal moment in the war entailed, the Allies intensified their assault against the German army in the West. The British and American armies were spread thin from southern Normandy to the Netherlands, thus compelling the U.S. military command to call up virtually all of its reserves, prepared or not, in the United States. In early October 1944—I think it was the ninth—the 106th Division, far from having coalesced into an efficient fighting machine, was suddenly ordered by "Uncle Sam" to entrain to Camp Myles Standish in Taunton, Massachusetts, a staging area preparatory to being shipped across the Atlantic to our unknown destination in Europe. I was, again for reasons only comprehensible to a transcendental determination, transferred from the communications platoon to an antitank unit of the 423rd Regiment, where I was assigned as an ammunition bearer. I never saw Doris again . . . She came, and she went.

I remember nothing pertaining to my soldierly existence about the five or six days I floated wraithlike through Camp Myles Standish. What I do remember is my gnawing anticipation of departure, of a decisive severance from everything—places, histories, people—that had hitherto given me some minimal sense of home, stability, and identity, the anxious feeling of being a pawn in the indifferent hands of an incomprehensible force. In particular, and above all, I remember a guilt-fraught but desperately pleading call to Kathryn I made from a telephone booth in Taunton on the second day after our arrival to tell her that I was shipping out to Europe in a few days and to ask her to take the train from Newport to Boston, where I would meet her for an afternoon together before my departure.

"Please, Kitty, come!" I begged (melodramatically). "I have to see you before I go overseas. Europe's so far away!" Despite my knowledge of her mother's prejudice against my ethnic origins, I literally believed at this critical turning point in my life that she would allow her eighteen-year-old daughter to travel by herself to Boston to alleviate my anguish.

There was a moment of silence, as if she had taken a blow in the stomach. Then she replied, "I want so much to come and see you, Bill. Please believe me, but I'm pretty sure Mom won't let me. Hang on, and let me ask her."

A silence of about two minutes ensued, one, it seemed, in which an entire lifetime played itself out. When she returned to the phone, she said in a voice that sounded as if she were holding back tears, "Mom said no, Bill. The idea of taking a train to Boston is out of the question. I'm so sorry!"

I was silent for a moment. The hole I had anticipated had opened up under me. Then I said with resignation, "Yeah, I knew your mother wouldn't let you come, but I had to ask. You know that, don't you? . . . Don't cry . . . I'll be seeing you—" And I hung up.

On October 16, 1944, after undergoing an interminable number of gear checks and information sessions by a Camp Myles Standish cadre of sergeants who seemed to specialize in preparing neophytes for the vagaries of war—I wondered if any of them had been in combat—the 106th was entrained to New York, where we were, to our astonishment, herded not into the dreaded small troop ships we had expected but the mighty *Queen Elizabeth*, which was to ferry us to an unnamed destination across the Atlantic. On the morning of the seventeenth we boarded the huge celebrated vessel, heavy with gear, each man's rifle, steel helmet, knapsack with shovel and pickax, canteen, and duffel bag containing all his worldly belongings—a heavy overcoat, a wool blanket, a dress uniform, an extra pair of fatigues, toiletries, a poncho. It was a slow and resonantly silent process. A steady rain added to the gloom we all seemed to be feeling.

Several hours later, after I and the others in my squad had finally settled into our oppressively small "stateroom," we felt the ship's motors start rumbling and its propellers churning then a shudder and motion. Huddled in an upper bunk in the damp claustrophobic cabin, I thought, "We're finally off . . . But where is the ship taking us?" It was a question that was more than geographical and, thus, devoid of the expectation of arrival. I felt once again untethered, floating anxiously in an insubstantial, worldless world, without reference points, desperately hanging onto the debris of my shattered past.

The voyage across the Atlantic Ocean took about six days. It drizzled almost the whole time, and the sea was constantly high. But because the cabins below were suffocatingly crowded, many of us preferred climbing up to the expansive open decks for the fresh air they offered, even though the wind was chilling, and the rise and plunge of the huge ship and the acrid salt spray made many of us seasick. It was a miserable crossing in excruciatingly slow motion, however fast the *Queen Elizabeth* traveled. And our nervous impatience was exacerbated by frightening images of German submarine attacks of the kind we had all seen in the movies. After the fourth or fifth day on the high seas, however, the weather broke. The rain ceased, the sky cleared, and the sun emerged like a released prisoner or a conqueror. We all swarmed to the bathing decks as though we were on a tropical beach and soaked up the bright, if not terribly warm, glorious North Atlantic sun. At about the same time we were, to our utter relief, informed that our destination was England. On the seventeenth the *Queen Elizabeth* entered the Firth of Clyde, near Glasgow, Scotland, a diversionary route intended to ward off German U-boats. At night we boarded a train that brought us to our much anticipated but hitherto unknown temporary destination, an American military base outside the town of Cheltenham in Gloucestershire, west of London.

Located on a huge picturesque estate whose origins might have dated back at least to the seventeenth century, the camp, consisting of a series of Quonset huts (semicircular prefabricated tin structures), was laid out at the site of a steeplechase course near the main buildings. It did not look anything like a military installation. A huge mansion built in the Renaissance Gothic style presided over a vast, neatly groomed landscape ornamented by flower gardens in the vicinity of the mansion and, farther out, clumps of venerable old trees. This building, it turned out, was the headquarters of the 106th Division military command. The troops, as I remember, were billeted in the Quonset huts and in tents between the steeplechase course and a wooded area some distance from headquarters. I figured that this arrangement was camouflage to render troop concentration invisible to aerial detection. But what struck me was the jarring contrast: an image of what in those days I took to be the height of civilized life informed by the lethal instruments—soldiers and weapons—of barbarous violence. We all had a lot to learn about civilization, Western style.

The time we spent at this unique camp was more or less uneventful. We were subjected to full field pack marches, more predictable orientation sessions, and drill inspections. The war in France seemed to have come to a lull after the American and British armies had driven the German army out of the coastal area of the North Atlantic from Normandy to Holland. But we all knew that this hiatus wasn't going to last long. We had, after all, been called to Europe abruptly and prematurely. We were simply waiting in dread for the inevitable crossing of the English Channel.

To release the tensions of this new in-between, our officers gave us overnight passes on weekends to visit the town of Cheltenham or the small city of Gloucester nearby. This was an opportunity I and my new friend Jerry Feingold, a garrulous, good-natured, and worldly-wise Jew from a New York suburb, whom I had met on the *Queen Elizabeth* during the crossing, always took advantage of. Because we were not beer drinkers, unlike most of our fellow Americans, our usual destination was the USO in the town, where we could drink punch, eat snacks, play pool and games, and, not least, meet girls and dance.

Unlike most American civilians, at least the ones I had encountered in Macon, Tuscaloosa, and Indianapolis, who were all too often indifferent or even hostile to our presence in their communities, these English men and women of the provinces, to my surprise, treated us with kindness and solicitude. I'm not sure why this was so. I had heard that the British were cold-blooded chauvinists who, from their deeply inscribed imperialist perspective—which in the case of the United States involved a long-standing disdain for their former "Yankee" colony—had little but contempt for all manner of foreigners. My guess was that it had to do with the immediacy of the war. Whereas Americans had escaped the disruptive violence of attacks on their homeland soil, the British had been subjected mercilessly to its horror, especially during the Battle of Britain between November 1940 and December 1942, and, not least, to the cruel decimation of their young men over five long years of relentless war. They thus empathized with the young Americans who were passing through their battered homeland into a devouring conflagration. Or so it seemed to me—perhaps because I wanted to minimize my sense of alienation and loneliness in this unfamiliar space. Be that as it may, the USO in Cheltenham became a retreat from the chaos of my thoughts and feelings during the all too brief month of our fated division's stay in England.

Very early on, it could have been the second weekend after our arrival, I met a young English girl, Claire—I can't remember her last name—at a USO dance welcoming the newly arrived "Yanks." She was about my age, maybe a year or two older, blonde and blue-eyed, fair, full-bodied, an astonishing beauty who was also full of the joy of life—and endowed with a lively sense of humor. By that time I had gotten past my inhibitions, at least to the point where I could will myself, despite my incorrigible shyness, to address the opposite sex. When I first saw her in profile standing near the bandstand swaying rhythmically to a slow Glenn

Miller tune, I pointed her out to Jerry and told him that my goal was to win her heart. To that end—with Jerry's guffaw as a challenge—I walked across the floor, introduced myself, and asked her to dance. "Pleased to meet you, Yank!" she answered, accepting my offer and taking me by the hand onto the floor.

As we danced, Claire spoke without inhibitions, for which I was grateful. She told me she had seen me at the USO a week before, indeed, had taken an immediate interest in me because I looked so forlorn, a little boy in a soldier's uniform, and that she had hoped I'd come over and ask her to dance. I was elated by her attraction to me—and the natural ease of her conversation. She was so different from Kathryn—and, for that matter, from Doris; she made it so easy for me to talk. The Glenn Miller piece, "Moonlight Sonata," came to its end, and immediately following it, a fast jazzy instrumental erupted. Taking my left hand and using my body as a pivot, she started jitterbugging, spinning in and away while circling around me, her body swaying rhythmically, her feet moving rapidly and gracefully to the beat of the music, in the process, to my dismay, drawing the attention of many of the soldiers and civilians in the room. When the music had come to its end, she was breathing hard but smiling happily. Her hand still holding mine, she walked me over to the table and bench on the other side of the floor, where we sat down to rest. After regaining her breath, she said with a mock note of remorse, "Did I embarrass you?" Her wild antics had indeed made me feel uneasy, but I assured her that she hadn't. We talked throughout the rest of the evening until closing time. Having seen that I was "making out," Jerry had left. We walked out of the USO into the street; she kissed me briefly on the lips—a peck more than a kiss—and said softly, "Come next weekend, Yank. I'll be waiting for you." She then hurried away down the street and into the night. I stood there dumbstruck but happier than I had been ever since entering the army. I then found a bus that brought me back to the camp.

After this first redemptive encounter, I met Claire at the USO on a number of other Fridays or Saturdays. Our intimacy, to my astonishment, grew on each successive occasion. But strangely each time, after kissing me warmly good night at the entrance of what I came to think of as our sanctuary, she departed alone or sometimes with a friend into the night. I was confused by her mysterious behavior. She took such delight in talking to me, but invariably what she would say in that high-spirited way of hers was restricted to her daily routine—the out-of-the ordinary occurrences at the primary school where she was teaching or, rather, supervising children whose parents lived in London or some other city, the dress she was making and eager to wear for me, or things we had spoken about during a previous meeting. She did not want to know about my past, nor would she say anything about hers. And the future—above all, the future—was off-limits. Although I wanted more, I instinctively understood her reticence. Our worlds, however different, were, after all was said and done, the same: fully of the present, a present that, like a besieged fortress, was trying futilely to keep turbulent history at bay.

One night, however, as we were dancing closely to a romantic ballad with which I was not familiar, Claire suddenly began whispering the words:

I may be wrong, I may be right,
But I'm perfectly willing to swear
That when you turned and smiled at me,
A nightingale sang in Berkeley Square.

Holding me close in her arms, she began quietly to sob.

"What's wrong, Claire?" I asked.

"Nothing, Yank, just a memory that keeps coming back to haunt me."

"Tell me about it."

She pulled herself together, laughed nervously, and said, "It's nothing, really, not anymore."

"Tell me!"

"No point in it."

"Tell me, please!"

There was a pause. Then, in a voice that was half-apology and half-relief, she said, "A chap I knew . . . ages ago . . . was shot down over London." And then she resumed her song:

The moon that lingered over London town,
Poor puzzled moon, he had a frown.
How could he know we two were so in love,
The whole darned world seemed upside down.

"Upside down," I repeated to myself and let it go at that.

A couple of weeks later we met again at the USO. It was now the middle of November, and we could tell from the multiple signs of movement in and around the headquarters of the American military command that "that time" was drawing near. As usual, we danced and talked, telling each other what we had done during the week and how much we missed being together. But Claire's manner was different that night. The tone of her voice seemed more buoyant and carefree than usual and her bodily gestures of affection more intimate. And when the dance was over and the time had come to say good night, she asked me, to my great surprise, to go out with her for a pint of ale. I was, needless to say, thrilled by the invitation and eager to oblige her.

Following the street she usually took after we had parted, we found ourselves five or ten minutes later in a crowded and noisy public house, which, she said, she occasionally frequented with friends. Everyone in the place—old men and women, young British and American soldiers, WAFS (Women's Auxiliary Forces), civilian girls—was extraordinarily animated. It was as if they were celebrating the end of the war—or savoring the last day of a world about to become extinct. Huddled in the corner of the pub, Claire and I tacitly joined the cacophonous rout, which soon came to sound like a polyphonic choir.

As we drank our ale and shouted our intimacies silently across a great distance, Claire took my left hand and began gently to draw hearts with her index finger into my upturned palm. The sensation triggered by this unexpected gesture of intimacy sent an exquisite sensuous shiver through my body into the crotch. As she repeated this, she looked into my eyes in a way I had not experienced before or, if I had, only in a subliminal way. I was elated but also anxious. Was this a deliberate invitation to make love, a gesture released by the alcohol she had drunk? Or was it an unpremeditated act of sensuous affection intensified by the beating wings of the time that was running out on us? Or both? Whatever it was, I was committed to living this night through.

After we had drunk two pints of ale, Claire announced that it was time to leave and invited me to accompany her the rest of the way to her apartment, which, she said, was within walking distance from the pub. I assented, of course, and we left, closing the door on this pleasant noise and opening one that turned out to be our first and last walk together. The late autumn moon—which, to me at that pregnant moment, was a she, not a he as in the song Claire had sung—was high and bright, bathing the blacked-out street with its silvery light. She was not frowning, nor did she seem puzzled. To me she seemed, in fact, relieved to find two young people from different sides of the Atlantic together and quite upright, in an upside-down world. Claire's spirits, no doubt animated by the alcohol, were high. Instead of walking beside me, she announced that she was the moon and I, the earth, then started to dance in a circle around me, repeating the pattern as we walked, all the while whispering, "I love you, Yank. I love you, Yank." Entranced by her exquisite beauty and grace, I violated nature, turning around and around always to meet her bright eyes.

In that communal, innocent frame of mind, we finally arrived at our destination: the small apartment house, on the second floor of which Claire lived. It was facing us from across the street we were walking on, its bright facade lighted by the moon and beckoning ambiguously. To the left was a large brown wet lawn in the middle of which a huge and very old tree—it looked like a maple—rose majestically, despite its bare branches, out of the earth, like a resonantly ambivalent ghost. We crossed the street. Claire walked to the tree, turned, and leaning her back against it, threw her arms wide open and said, almost in a whisper, "Come to me, my steady and good earth." Laughing, I folded her in my arms and kissed her hard, my tongue ever so tentatively parting her receptive lips and touching hers. She broke away, feigning indignation. "Earth," she said, "don't be so Greek!"

As we were playing this childlike game—a game that by this time, despite my moral inhibitions, I was sure was going to end with my making love to my moon—I suddenly felt, to my horror, the urge to urinate. The warm pints of ale I had drunk had begun their subversive work. I was terrifically embarrassed, and thinking that motion would relieve the urge, I started circling the tree, telling Claire that it was my turn to be the moon. But this didn't work. I couldn't control the urge. What to do? In desperation I ran across the street and down a block or so and relieved myself in the dark. For a brief moment I considered the possibility of returning to Claire, but my shame was too acute. There was no alternative but to return to the camp. And so I walked back to the uso, devastated by the dreadful turn of events and wondering what she was thinking as I ran off and then failed to return.

The next morning after a miserable night rehearsing the ludicrous nightmare, I told Jerry my story. Laughing, he said, "You dumb asshole, Spanos, the Brits aren't as squeamish as Americans are about shitting and pissing. Warm ale makes you piss. In such a situation as the one you got yourself into last night, you idiot, you just say, 'Excuse me, my dear, I've got to spend a penny,' and when that penny is spent you return to the state of affairs before the interruption."

That night was the last time I saw Claire. I returned to the uso the following Saturday, but she wasn't there. A few days later our officers announced that we were shortly to be shipped across the English Channel to a combat zone on the Continent . . . She had come, and she had gone.

Early in the week of our departure from Cheltenham, I received a message—I don't remember how I got it—from my brother Harry, who was a first-year student at Harvard, saying that our older brother, Steve, a master sergeant in the 84th Division, had been wounded in action in France, near Saint Malo, and had been transferred to a hospital in Malvern, England, not too far from Cheltenham. The message said nothing about the nature of the wound—it turned out to be a shrapnel wound in the neck from which he recovered—but I took it to be serious because he had been flown to England to be treated. I informed my company commander about this turn in the hope of getting a leave of absence to visit Steve. That, he told me, was absolutely out of the question. It was too late, he said, and besides, "That's war, soldier! We can't put it on hold while you go visiting a wounded brother in a hospital." I was distraught, but there was nothing I could do about it.

The officer was no doubt right, though I thought the way he put it to me was unnecessarily cruel. I was trying desperately to be clear-headed and resolute, but there were no markers, no reference points, no directives around which to concentrate the scatter in my confused head. It was as if I didn't count. (Many years later, in 1998, Steven Spielberg's *Saving Private Ryan* came out, a popular and award-winning film highly praised by the media for its courageous realism. It depicted the entire American military command in Europe organizing its war effort to ensure the survival of the last of several members of the Ryan family. When I saw it, I couldn't help recalling with great bitterness the difference between my company commander's indifferent response on the occasion of my request and Spielberg's mythical gesture showing that in American democracy everyone, high and low, WASP or ethnic, are at center stage.)

A week or so later, on a stormy late November day after a train ride from Cheltenham, the 106th Division boarded troop carriers waiting at the port of Southampton that ferried us across a ferociously volatile English Channel to Le Havre, France. I had crossed what I thought then—mistakenly, it turned out—the last boundary.

2. Captivity

I must die, I must suffer, I must struggle, I am subject to chance, I involve myself inexorably in guilt. We call these fundamental situations of our existence ultimate situations [*Grenzsituationen*, literally, boundary situations]. That is to say, they are situations which we cannot evade or change … In our day-to-day lives we often evade them, by closing our eyes and living as if they did not exist. We forget that we must die, forget our guilt, and forget that we are at the mercy of chance. We face only concrete situations and master them in the world, under the impulsion of our practical interests. But to ultimate situations we react either by obfuscation or, if we really apprehend them, by despair and rebirth: we become ourselves by a change in our consciousness of being.

KARL JASPERS, *Way to Wisdom*

After a rough crossing of the English Channel, the 106th Division arrived at the battered seaport of Le Havre, a city that had been virtually leveled during the Normandy invasion, where a convoy of U.S. Army trucks, "The Red Ball Express," was waiting to transport us to our destination. During the crossing our officers had informed us that we were being assigned to an area in the Ardennes Forest, specifically a mountain area called the Schnee Eiffel, west of the village of St. Vith in Belgium near the Luxembourg border. We were, they said, going to replace the 2nd ("American") Division, a renowned unit, desperately in need of respite, having been in combat since the invasion of Italy in September 1943. Although the ground we were to take over from the 2nd was on the front lines separating the Allies from the German forces, it was, we were relieved to hear, an inactive zone, providing the perfect conditions for easing a raw and inexperienced division into combat action.

On disembarking at Le Havre, my mind was preoccupied by the wintry cold and, not least, the question of what was to come when we had reached our destination. I was nevertheless struck by the discovery that the United States Army convoy that constituted this Red Ball Express was manned entirely by a unit of African American soldiers, who, saying nothing, went through the mechanics of organizing the expedition into the interior as if they were phantoms, not flesh-and-blood bodies. This impression, especially underscored by our conveyors' spectral silence, exacerbated that uneasiness about the United States I had come to feel in Georgia, when I realized that the army I belonged to was segregated. Sometime during that long night it even occurred to me that our guides—black Virgils, I would now call them—were leading us not toward our salvation but to our doom.

The journey through northern France in light snow and bitter cold was surreal. The convoy drove with lights dimmed on winding local roads that took us through small and large villages, where French families huddled in the cold at the entrances of their homes silently waved to us as we passed through, occasionally handing containers of coffee to the men on the trucks when the convoy was stalled because of traffic congestion. In the truck bearing my antitank gun crew we sat together in gloomy silence, our anxiety minimizing the warmth of our huddled bodies. No jokes, no banter, no small talk. We were diminished. The size many of us had achieved in the process of training had withered away. To the French outsiders we may have looked like fearless warriors. On the inside, or so it seemed to me, we were young boys again who had been torn from our homes and transported like sheep across a void into a nameless and threatening space—a real nightmare—by a force whose power I had felt brush against the edge of my consciousness on several occasions since my departure from New York.

We arrived at St. Vith, on the edge of the Ardennes Forest in Belgium, a village that, given the several roads leading into and out of it, must have been the prosperous seat of rich farmland in another age. Now it was a noisy scene of technological chaos exacerbated by deep slush and mud. The 2nd Division—troop carriers, artillery, tanks, armored cars, jeeps— were pulling out as our division was pulling in and debarking. As we were desperately trying to organize ourselves for the trek into the Ardennes, south of St. Vith, to take up our battle positions, the veterans of the 2nd Division—some in trucks, some directing traffic, some securing artillery pieces mounted on trailers, some walking in the mud alongside the departing vehicles—seemed like another species. Gritty, unshaven, with scarves wrapped around their faces, their clothes clotted with mud, they were clearly much older thus us, more "weathered." But it was their youthful high spirits, in contrast to our dour somberness, that struck me. They threw snowballs at us as we were dismounting, mocked our insignia ("the hungry lion's gonna eat shit!"), joked about our youth ("How are you guys gonna kill Nazis with you mouths still sucking you mammas' nipples?") It was that "in-betweenness"—that bewildering and foreboding estrangement of the familiar, ghostly apparition and solid reality—that had once more infiltrated my being, this time in the chaos of the space we were moving into, with a sense of no exit. (Throughout that time and the horrific days that were to follow, I and most all of the foot soldiers of the 106th hadn't the slightest idea about where precisely we were in relation to a "front," which, for us, was simply a word. And no examination of maps of the area in later years ever clarified that uncertainty.) The only relief from this alien world was the comforting thought that we had been assigned to a quiet sector and were not likely to become engaged in action soon.

The snow in the Ardennes was more than a foot deep. The sky, or what we could see of it beyond the towering fir trees, was heavy and threatening with more snow. My squad spent the entire afternoon of that first miserable day putting our fifty-seven-millimeter antitank gun in place at the edge of the forest, facing a clearing—a pasture, no doubt—of high ground that descended gently into a wooded valley, then setting up tripwires strung with tin cans around the area of the gun emplacement. When that Herculean labor was accomplished, we began to dig foxholes big enough to accommodate two of us. As we hacked at the semifrozen ground, we heard artillery explosions in the far distance and were thankful that the war was elsewhere for the time being. Little did we know that it was *there*, precisely, and with a vengeance, waiting to spring.

We hadn't finished digging our foxholes by nightfall, so we cleared spaces near the gun site and set up pup tents in the hope of resting in some degree of comfort during the cold night. My tent-mate, the other ammunition bearer, was Rudi, a tall, gangling Finnish American from somewhere in New England. To ease our way into the thought of sleeping on the ground in freezing weather, he reminded me of his (imagined) indestructible Lapland forebears, who lived their entire lives in such inhuman conditions—and in the dark to boot. But it didn't work. However adamantly idealists claim the power of mind over matter, imagination over reality, matter and reality invariably win where the struggle really counts. Laying huddled with my fellow soldier in that small tent in the forest, cold, wet, exhausted, and forlorn, listening to the occasional, far-off reverberation of artillery fire, the shadows of the giant fir trees hovering over us made the sky seem infinitely distant. And I felt ourselves—Rudi and me, the young soldiers of the antitank squad, the company, and even the regiment and the division—infinitely small, marginal, and vulnerable to the far more formidable, central, and inscrutable forces informing the direction the universe, unbeknownst to us, was taking. The sergeants, the platoon leaders, and the company, regimental, and divisional commanders on whom we relied for order and resolution—the imagination at least of guidance, if not protection—all seemed to me utterly ineffectual in the face of, if not powerless to resist, this invisible puppeteer's commanding hand.

After a very long night the dawn came, leaden, sullen, threatening more snow. Despite not having slept much, I was grateful for the light of day, however feeble it was. As Rudi was cursing his fate, I got up, lighted a can of Sterno, filled my steel helmet with snow, and, taking it by the chin strap, held it over the purple flame until the snow had melted. I washed my face with the pleasant warm water. Then, contemplating the long walk to the field kitchen for breakfast, I got up to relieve myself.

I had not taken more than ten steps when suddenly a sharp crack close by shattered the stillness. With several others who had been startled out of their sleep, I slogged through the deep snow toward the collapsing tent and found a dead body, rifle between its legs, its skull shattered. The soldier had blown his brains out. I recognized him immediately. He was a young Spanish American, a member of one of the companies of my regiment whom I had come to know at a distance at Camp Atterbury. He was a good-looking young man, high-cheeked and olive-skinned, athletic in body, with a great sense of humor. He was an amateur magician who was also an amazing knife thrower. I remember a couple of performances he gave in which he would outline a human body on a wooden panel in chalk and then, from a distance of ten feet or so, would throw his knives, rapidly, one after the other with the intent of coming as close to the outline figure without penetrating it. His aim was uncanny. And I admired his nerves, which were as steel-like as his shining daggers. What had compelled him to commit this appalling act? What nightmare could have been so real to him that this seemingly strong young man would take this means of escaping it? I was bewildered. Someone called a team of medics in. They put the body in a green canvas body bag and hauled it away to wherever the dead in war were taken. For me the mutilated corpse and the blood and brains–spattered snow remained, a can of lumpy red paint spilled randomly on a white canvas.

The next eight or ten days were uneventful. We finished digging our foxholes, added more trip wire around the gun emplacement, and blazed trails back to the field kitchen. Although our horizon was limited to that small space we occupied, I assumed that the larger units to which we belonged were also consolidating their positions the better to attack or withstand attack. The skies were overcast, so there was little air traffic— no bombing runs, no reconnaissance flights or fighter raids in German-occupied territory. Being inside, minute members of an increasingly larger historical context, we saw little beyond the narrow horizon of our installation and knew no more about the immediate situation than these limits allowed. We were grateful for the lull, but the silence was deafening. We didn't know that our inexperienced division was thinly spread out, having been assigned to a front normally occupied by two divisions. We were in limbo . . . waiting.

On the tenth or eleventh day after taking our positions in the Schnee Eiffel area of the Ardennes Forest—it was December 16—the German army, appearing as if out of nowhere, attacked all across the extended front held by the 106th Division. Because our antitank gun was located a mile or so southeast of the village of St. Vith, our unit was not assaulted immediately. But from the variety, density, and persistence of the firing, we knew that the attack was massive and total and guessed that the Germans were intent on splitting the British army in the north from the American army in the south. (This offensive, we learned much later, was intended to recapture Lièges, a supply center in Belgium, and the port of Antwerp in Holland.) Eighty-eight barrages, mortar explosions, machine-gun and rifle fire, and the dull roar of moving tanks, filled the hitherto silent and expectant forest. We carried boxes of ammunition down to our antitank gun while the gunners were preparing it to fire. We hunkered down and waited in this raucous din, our hearts in our taut throats, for our "baptism of fire."

Suddenly the young lieutenant in command of our unit came running toward us through the deep snow, waving his pistol and shouting wildly that the Germans had broken through our lines. He ordered us to abandon our antitank gun and follow him. His purpose apparently was to lead us to an infantry unit, but he was not sure where we would find one. His panic was demoralizing. This sort of thing didn't happen in any of the war movies we had seen in our previous lives. Yet we had no more idea than he did about what to do in this situation. We had lost our bearings. We didn't know then that the entire command of the 422nd and 423rd regiments of the 106th Division would collapse almost immediately after the German army launched its unexpected massive Panzer offensive. And without leadership the uninitiated boys who composed it—after the war I learned that the average age of the troops in our division was twenty-one, considerably less than that of the great majority of American military units—could offer little resistance to the overwhelming concentration of the advancing German juggernaut's firepower.

I was preoccupied by the chaos of our situation. But it did occur to me to wonder how the German army could have massed that close to the American lines without betraying its movements to Allied intelligence. The wintry weather, as the official history generally asserts, had no doubt prevented reconnaissance planes from flying over the area, but was that a sufficient explanation? (Several days later, after being taken prisoner, I bore witness to the vast concentration of men, tanks, armored vehicles, and supply trucks that were pouring into the gap opened up by the breakthrough with astonishing impunity.) Despite my conscious effort to repress it, I saw flickering there in the corner of the eye of my mind the cliché "cannon fodder," now, however, de-sedimented into an image of mangled young corpses piled on top of each other in a lurid, blood red landscape.

The rest of that first mind-shattering day and the next few that followed remain an incoherent blur in my memory, or rather, a series of incandescent but discontinuous images in lurid colors that cannot be incorporated into a comforting narrative structure. There was no beginning, middle, and end to induce a sense of resolution, of finality, then as now. The violence would decrease, then cease, then erupt again, decrease, cease, and erupt, on and on and on and on. This, it occurred to me for the first time, was not a "war story." It was the singular, irreducible, unnameable, and dreadful experience of war. You were a part of a unit but lived it alone. No one could live it for you. Like death.

In the confusion of abject defeat, I had become separated from the other members of my antitank gun crew and had joined a stray group of equally disoriented members of the 423rd Regiment, about twenty or twenty-five of them, seeking to reestablish contact with a larger unit in the hope of . . . who knew what? Resistance? Comfort in the solidarity of death or shameful capture? We climbed through the high snow of a slightly forested incline and, on reaching the summit, found more stragglers, probably seventy-five to a hundred, cut off from their shattered units, in utter disarray, and seeking some way out of the chaos. They turned out to be members not only of my regiment, the 423rd, but also of the 422nd. From this information I surmised in despair (rightly, I learned much later) that the German Panzer divisions had broken through the American lines at the point southeast of St. Vith in the Schnee Eiffel, between the ground held by the 422nd and 423rd regiments and the 424th, had surrounded the first group, and were carrying out a massive mopping up operation after the blitz.

Suddenly, as we were exchanging "information," we heard the shrieking whistle of incoming eighty-eight-millimeter shells and then the explosions on the back side of the hill short of our "position." We began frantically digging foxholes for protection, but that was futile. The eighty-eights had zeroed in on us. The next round of shells a few minutes later was on target. Some exploded as they hit the ground, some above in the trees, raining jagged red-hot shrapnel on us. As I lay curled up at the base of a fir tree, like a fetus reluctant to emerge from its mother's womb— that position would become a constant in my wandering in the zero zone thereafter—I heard in one instant the shrill whirr of a piece of shrapnel and a heavy thud as the sharp, hot steel buried itself deep in the ground a yard or so from my trembling body. Then, amid the yells and screams of the wounded and the dying, I saw, about twenty-five yards in front of me, an American soldier—he looked even younger than me—rise up out of the snow, shouting to rally his comrades against an unidentifiable target, and begin to run in the direction from which the eighty-eights were firing, his rifle in one hand and a hand grenade in the other, raised high above his head, as if that small weapon in his fist contained the power to destroy the entire German army. A shell explodes nearby. The young soldier flies in a flash of fire. *Click*! And comes apart. *Click*! I begin running back down the snowed-covered hill we had ascended followed by several soldiers I don't know.

A couple of days later, after wandering in the forest, in the midst of the unceasing din of large-scale bombardment on what seemed all sides of us, though in the near distance, we encountered another contingency of about fifty Americans. They, like us, had been separated from their units and were headed in a westerly direction along a wide corridor in the forest in search of a stable Allied command of any sort. The group was led by a lieutenant colonel, around thirty-five, his face curiously red, dressed in white. He was straining to appear calm and in command in an effort to assure the ragged group of dislocated stragglers that he would lead them out of this maze with no seeming exit. But I could see that he was no savior. It was easy to tell that he was following the protocols of his military training at a war school, not what he was seeing with his eyes and feeling with his heart. And these abstractions, I felt instinctively, were hardly adequate to the task of deliverance.

He was, regrettably, no more certain of our location in the woods and thus of a plan of action than all the rest of the soldiers he was leading. Nevertheless, he was in command, and they followed. He had formed them into a loose marching column, weapons at the ready, no doubt in order to bolster their uncertain sense of solidarity and purpose and, in case of attack, to concentrate their firepower. Despite our misgivings, my small contingency joined this large motley group, taking our places at the tail end of the column.

For an hour or so we struggled through the stinging cold and the heavy snow, hoping against hope that by some miracle our leader would find a way out of this labyrinth. Whatever this forest path we were taking under his guidance was for the lieutenant colonel—he seemed like a Theseus who, after slaying the Minotaur, had lost the thread Ariadne had given him to find his way out of the maze—for me it was like the earlier ones I had traversed after my squad had been ordered to abandon its antitank gun, leading us into the mouth of the Minotaur, not out of its bestial lair. Not long after joining the group, the distant guns fell silent. We walked quietly, slowly, cautiously, favoring the possibility that it meant safety rather that imminent danger.

Then we heard the rumbling of tanks coming from the very westerly direction in which we were headed. Maybe they were American, I thought for an instant. Instead, we saw, looming out of the forest on both sides, about a thousand yards ahead, four German tanks crawling like primordial beasts toward us, their turrets swiveling into firing position. We started to run toward the more densely wooded terrain on both sides. The tanks' artillery opened up, firing point-blank at us. As I labored through the heavy snow, I saw bodies up ahead flying akimbo, including the lieutenant colonel's—Theseus's. *Click!* Dismembered. *Click!* Torn open by shrapnel. *Click!* Rivers of blood in the white snow. *Click!* The abyssal reality of violent death.

Miraculously, I and another one of my comrades—I didn't even know his name nor he mine—made it into the dense forest, temporarily escaping the Minotaur's bloody jaws. But it was no reprieve. Reprieve, I now realized with a sinking finality, was impossible. We were surrounded. It was now, rather, a matter of one kind of suicide or another—violent death, like the magician's on that first day, which seemed a lifetime ago, or that of the young boy who would defeat the German army with a hand grenade—or the abject ignominy of capture, which, in that innocent, pitiless, and decisive confusion, I considered a simply bloodless form of death.

Having run away from the firing to the point of utter exhaustion, we sat under a tree to recuperate our expended strength, despite the possibility of being overtaken by the German foot soldiers who must have been accompanying the four tanks. What to do? That deeply human and finally unanswerable question for which Americans always had an answer. We decided simply to "go on."

Several hours later—it was around four or five in the afternoon, the forest was getting dark and the weather freezing cold—we stumbled across two more GIs, one to my astonishment who was in the communications platoon of my company in the 423rd Regiment at Camp Atterbury. He was a gentle, easygoing Southerner, a little older than I, whose first name I don't remember but whose last name was Daniels. His story was like ours, except that he had participated in the futile brief effort of the 423rd and 422nd to withstand the German onslaught in the vicinity of St. Vith. Adding to the crushing psychological burden we were carrying, he also told us that the regimental commanders—or was it the commanding general of the 106th Division?—had surrendered to the German army a few days earlier.

The four of us banded together, once more in the futile hope of squeezing through the German cordon and finding a solid American base or line to join. We began walking westward until it became dark and then decided to rest, hoping to get some sleep during the night before resuming our search for an exit out of the maze. My buddy and I had not eaten anything but snow in several days. To our joy, however, Daniels and his friend had some pieces of bread and a couple of small cans of gi rations—cheese and jam—which they shared with us. I remember that for the first time in my life, but not the last, I did not take for granted the food I was given to eat. I chewed the bread over and over until it became a liquid that, combined with the morsel of cheese, I could swallow slowly to savor the unearthly taste. After this welcomed break, we dug a pit in the snow under a tree, and, huddling our bodies together, we spent the night in silence, each enclosed in his deep private world.

The next morning we recommenced our westward trek through the dark and ominous Ardennes Forest. Around one or two in the afternoon we came to a clearing, a steep hill on our right, which seemed to have once been a huge pasture, maybe a third of a mile wide, open from a long way below to the summit. Skirting the edge of the wood, we climbed toward the crest and saw in the middle of the opening a large hole in the ground, which might have been a bomb crater. I volunteered to run across the field to examine it more closely. When I got there, I saw that it was a huge garbage pit of a field kitchen recently abandoned by a German unit. The bottom was full of rotting sauerkraut, potatoes, turnips, wet breadcrumbs, and other waste, including human excrement. The stink of decay was overpowering. Returning to the forest edge, I informed my comrades of what I had found and suggested that, however awful the conditions, we would do well to hide and rest in the pit during the remainder of the day. Seeing that it had been recently abandoned by a contingency of German soldiers, it would most likely be a safe haven, at least temporarily. They agreed, and one by one we ran in a crouch across the field and plunged knee-deep into the slime to wait the night out before resuming our search at daybreak.

I can't remember what I thought during the next couple of hours while waiting for the sun to set. We said virtually nothing to each other. What was there to say? It seemed to me that language itself, in the process of entering the labyrinth into which we had been led, had deteriorated, like the food in the garbage pit, into a kind of an offensive slime. As before, I struggled to remain steady and afloat by grasping at the shards of my boyhood past—my beloved, caring mother and my stern but reliable father, my loving brothers and baby sister, my inseparable wild Irish friend, Bill Kennedy, my girlfriend, Kitty, the two teachers I had fallen in love with, Miss Calloway, who taught me the rudiments of art in the sixth grade, and Catherine Condon, who taught me Latin in high school, both kind, indifferent to my ethnic status, unlike most of the others, conscious of my intelligence and wanting to nourish its potential—and even Frank Sinatra's songs, Doris, and Claire, my caring carefree moon. But they all remained ungraspable phantoms of what seemed in the symbolic stench of the garbage pit a world that had burned itself out. Holding my carbine—the small repeater weapon I carried as an ammunitions bearer—between my legs, I slouched into the nauseous slime once more in the fetal position, closed my eyes, and silently wept.

Wallowing in this morass, each in our own way, we were suddenly awakened to full consciousness by the now familiar shrill whistle of an incoming eighty-eight-millimeter shell. It exploded on the edge of woods to the right. Then another exploded at the same height on the left. Then another exploded ahead of us, just behind the tree line. The firing ceased for a few minutes and then commenced again, repeating the same pattern. The ubiquitous gaze of Germans, like a malicious god's eyes, had sighted us making a run for the garbage pit and was zeroing in on our haven. We instinctively crouched down more deeply in the slime, waiting … this time, however, for the end. But the eight-eights ceased firing again … We waited, paralyzed … five, ten, fifteen minutes in utter silence, but … expectantly. The wind was picking up and made the branches of the trees in the forest moan a kind of dirge.

Suddenly the ghostly form of a German soldier in a white snowsuit stepped out from behind a tree on the right edge of the forest, firing a short, rapid burst from a Schmeiser over our heads—brrrrrrrrrrrrrrrrit—

and shouting, "Hands up, *Amerikaner!*" then returning to cover. A second man, also in white, came out from behind a tree on the left side, firing another deadly burst from his Schmeiser over our heads, shouting, "Hands up, *Amerikaner!*" And a third came from the edge of the forest above us. Then there was a pause and silence. The hiatus in the artillery bombardment, we realized, had been intended to enable German foot soldiers to climb the hill on both sides of the garbage pit to surround us. I was on the side of the pit nearest to that of the tree line from which the first burst had come. Strangely, I no longer felt terrified. Rather, for the first time since my exposure to combat violence, I felt calm and something like in control of my mind, a sense of fatality in this zero zone. We had heard many rumors during the various contacts we had made that the Germans were shooting the prisoners they were taking. One of our group said something about a massacre of American soldiers near a village named Malmedy at the very beginning of the German attack.

As I clean the sludge off my carbine meticulously in the silence, making sure that the cartridge clip is secure in its chamber and the gun capable of firing, I turn to my comrades and say quietly—I am not being heroic—"This is it, friends . . . We've got to decide to fight or be taken prisoners. If we put up a fight, we're dead. If we give up, we'll probably be shot anyway—" But before I have finished, the American at the far side of the pit, whom I don't know, throws his rifle down into the garbage, rises to his feet, and shouts, "I don't want to die!" leaps head first out of the pit. *Click!* The decision has been made. We all drop our weapons, climb out, dripping with rotting sauerkraut, raise our hands above our heads at the complete mercy of the snow angels with Schmeisers, who are now coming triumphantly out of hiding toward us from all around the semicircular tree line. *Click!* I am the last to climb out of the pit. I close my eyes, waiting for the bullet to blow my skull or face away . . . but it doesn't strike. *Click!*

In that eternal instant between life and death something baffling, indeed inexplicable, happened to me. I was barely aware of it at the time, even though it silently affected my experience in captivity. Only after the war, during my first year in college, did this singular "event"—this in-between time, which has haunted me ever since—assume a special significance for me. Reading a biography of the great existentialist Russian writer Fyodor Dostoyevsky one evening in the hope of deepening my understanding of his disconcertingly mysterious novel, *Notes from Underground*, I came to the episode in his turbulent life when, standing in front of a firing squad, a black handkerchief tied tightly around his eyes, he waited for the bullet that would end his life but which, thanks to a last-minute order, was never fired. In that instant he experienced an inexplicable epiphany that utterly transformed his life. Mine—I underscore the comparison, despite the enormous difference of our circumstances and status—at that acutely unique moment in the Ardennes was something like that.

But even now, after meditating upon it for many years—indeed, having made that epiphany the supreme theme of all my teaching, scholarship, and criticism—I cannot, nor will I try to, explain "it" rationally. I will only say that before this terrible revelatory instant with my eyes shut and self-blinded to the unspeakable reality of what loomed before me, I had lived my life simply as life—bare life. But after it—after my dead body's incandescent image flared into my mind—I suddenly came to value life. Hitherto I had felt my life to be irrelevant, or rather, that it had been relegated to the margins by unnamed forces I had assumed were far more important than I was. Facing the stark image of its instant termination, my life suddenly took on infinite possibilities of body and mind, possibilities of which I was never or had only intuitively been aware, the *potential* of empowerment, of real freedom, I would say now, if this word had not been corrupted as it has by modern democracies. And that this empowerment was not only a potential in me but in every human being on the face of the earth. Everyone, high and low, has a history. I vowed, without understanding the vow, and despite knowing my extinction was imminent, that if I ever returned to the world, I would dedicate myself in the name of *this* life to resisting those various inhuman forces, no matter their provenance, that marginalized groups of human beings—denied them histories—in order to feed their own, central, will to power.

I open my eyes to the reality before me. I see for a brief second the German soldiers in white standing in front of us, tense, their rifles pointed at our heads. They are surprisingly young, like us, some of them even younger. Then they burst out laughing at the spectacle of the mythic American soldier dripping from head to foot with the slime of decaying food and stinking of human excrement. *Click!*

Ringed by a dozen or so of these white-clad German soldiers—they seemed like angels of death—our hands over our heads, we were led down the pasture into the forest below, where we were handed over to what seemed to me a military police unit. We were searched and, except for our dog tags, relieved of our valuables then informed that we were prisoners of war (*Kriegsgefangene*) and would eventually be sent to a stalag (prisoner of war camp) in the interior of Germany. When these formalities were over, the military police unit marched us along a path in the forest that led, after an hour or so, into a road entering St. Vith, now in the hands of the victorious German army.

The spectacle we witnessed as we walked into and out of the village was a surreal nightmare. Coming in, the road was strewn with gutted American supply vehicles, armored cars, troop carriers, jeeps, an occasional tank, and dead bodies in various postures of rigor mortis. I remember one in particular. Lying on a mound of muddy snow by the side of the road beneath a thick damp sky; the corpse's eyes were wide open, and its right arm was pointed skyward, as if bearing witness to a miracle. Going out of the village, the middle of the road was clogged with German vehicles moving triumphantly westward accompanied on the right shoulder by a seemingly disciplined column of Germans soldiers extending as far as the eye could see and, on the left shoulder, a ragged column of American prisoners of war, in various states of shock, gauntness, and fatigue, also extending as far as the eye could see, each looking at the other intently but from such seemingly different perspectives—jubilant victory and abject defeat.

As I walk out of the village, overwhelmed by this disheartening spectacle, I catch the eye of a German soldier across the way. He is about my age and height, though fair, his rifle slung over a heavy dark green overcoat laden with an ammunition belt and hand grenades. At first I think his gaze, shadowed by the rim of his steel helmet, is victoriously malignant. "We've defeated you decadent Americans in the name of our Führer's new world order!" And I, in utter despair, accept the judgment. But then, as he passes by my line of vision, I think I see something else in his eyes, something infinitely gentle—and questioning. And I respond. *Click*!

> I shot him dead because—
> Because he was my foe,
> Just so: my foe of course he was;
> That's clear enough; although.

But it was too late. He glided back into the unknown world ahead of him. And the redemptive vision blacked out. That young man, too, had come and had gone.

On the basis of what I had seen behind me and was seeing ahead of me, I could not help but feel that the German army had defeated ours and that the last ray of hope—for me? for Europe? for America? for civilization?—was extinguished. The dark night of the world had descended. That, at least, however melodramatic it sounds today, is what I felt then, as I contemplated that coming and that going, that new and even more vacant inbetween. We did not know at that abyssal time, as we were being herded into the German interior, that the breakthrough at St. Vith and the Schnee Eiffel would culminate in what came to be called by the media the "Battle of the Bulge," that, in fact, the victorious army we prisoners of war were observing in horror was moving into a decisive catastrophe. We did not know that the German army's decimation of the too widely deployed 106th Division and its push, under General von Rundstedt, toward Liège and Antwerp, was then being interrupted by the 101rst Airborne Division and remnants of other defeated American units at Bastogne, a few kilometers from St. Vith, and that it would eventually find itself in a pocket around which the Allied armies—the American and British forces in the north and General Patton's tank corps in the south—would converge at its mouth and close it off. We did not know that this convergence and the ensuing battle in the depths of the Ardennes would end in the virtual destruction of the mighty German war machine in Western Europe. We did not know that, in some fundamental way, the Battle of the Bulge, simultaneous with the Soviet army's defeat of the German armies in Belarus in the East, was the beginning of the end of World War II.

Since the end of the war, the official and popular histories (including Hollywood's versions) of the now mythic Battle of the Bulge have represented the action of the 106th Division positively. Acknowledging that it was ill prepared to resist a formidable attack and that it had been deployed far too thinly along a much wider than normal salient, these received histories also claim that the German assault on the 106th beginning on December 16 was unexpected. Because of the poor weather conditions, which precluded reconnaissance flights, it has been said, the Allied military intelligence was entirely unaware of the massive buildup of German forces prior to its offensive. Following the directives of this scenario, these retrospective histories of the battle have minimized, if not entirely overlooked, the importance of the immediate and bizarre "failure" of Allied intelligence in favor of representing the very young and uninitiated soldiers of the 106th Division as embattled heroes in an impossible situation (a representation that was welcomed by most of the veterans of the division who had surrendered and were taken prisoners). Despite the horrendous odds, they—especially the troops positioned in the Schnee Eiffel defending St. Vith—fought heroically, however brief their stand, in a valiant effort to slow down the overwhelming German assault. And according to these histories, which invariably invoke the memory of the heroic defenders of the Alamo in the telling, it was the delay of the enemy's advance achieved by these beleaguered, courageous, and noble young American innocents that provided the far more seasoned Allied units to the north and the south of St. Vith (the British and Americans under General Montgomery and the American tank corps under General Patton) time to move in to close the bulge.

Remembering again and again that shattering time of my youth, I have often been compelled by its ambivalence to wonder, despite my desire to resist the impulse, how accurate I had assessed my circumstances at the moment of my capture. Was what happened to me and my comrades in the 424th and 422nd regiments of the 106th Division indeed the consequence of unforeseen circumstances—bad weather, a failure of intelligence, fate—as this received history of the Battle of the Bulge concluded? The contingent realities I experienced throughout those tumultuous and chaotic days in December 1944 would seem to support this affirmative answer. From inside, however—from the extremely limited perspective of an anonymous player; a minor, insignificant, and not very knowledgeable, participant—in this epochal world event that affected millions of human beings not only in the West but in every part of the world, any other alternative explanation was barely conceivable. But from the larger perspective I have gained from living and thinking about American history since World War II—from the period of Indian removal through the period of Manifest Destiny to the Cold War, particularly the nation's devastation of Vietnam in order to "save it for the free world" and its present bloodless "realist" geopolitics in the Middle East—the question will not be laid to rest. It continues to haunt me. To rephrase it, we were untried adolescent American soldiers, thrust into these vulnerable circumstances—replacing a veteran combat unit, deployed to defend an abnormally wide sector—to spring a decisive trap for the German high command under Field Marshal Gerd von Rundstedt? Were we simply pawns in a preconceived scenario, planned at the highest level of Allied authority, that was intended to allow a break through the lines at St. Vith and thus enable the Allied armies in the north and south to converge and close the bulge, surrounding and destroying the German army?

The next few days after joining the huge column of American prisoners of war leaving St. Vith were unrelentingly bleak, certainly no "walking through a winter wonderland." Under the supervision of a small detachment of guards strategically placed at intervals along the side of the road, we were forced to march toward an unknown destination in the interior of Germany as the German troops were making their way into the village and beyond. It was bitter cold, our sweaters and combat jackets hardly adequate against the freezing temperature; we were hungry, having eaten almost nothing in several days; we were physically and emotionally exhausted; we were filthy, not having washed or changed clothes in over a week. And we were utterly demoralized. Our guards' job was to keep the erratic column moving. To them, it seemed, we were nothing more than a massive obstacle in the way of the triumphant advance of the German army coming from the opposite direction. Routinely one of them would prod the barrel of his rifle into the back of a straggler, shouting obscenities, sometimes in German, sometimes in English. On occasion one would strike a prisoner in the legs or on the shoulder with his rifle butt to compel him to move faster. As we marched eastward, like the cadaverous bodies of the damned, into hell, we saw more abandoned American vehicles, some overturned and riddled with jagged machine gun holes. And on occasion an American body, pale faced, its limbs in rigor mortis. Most disturbing of all, I saw a number of prisoners of war who had fallen by the wayside, no longer capable of continuing the grueling pace set by our guards, and, in anguish, foresaw their inevitable fate in that cruel and hopeless situation.

I can't remember how long that forced march lasted. Even though clock time had become a blur to most of us, I think we walked for several days and nights, with intermittent and occasionally extended halts along the way to rest after we had advanced beyond the combat zone. During those precious halts we were each given a small piece of bread and some watery soup to eat. All through this time, which, like everything that had happened to me since the beginning of the German assault, seemed interminable, I remember the appalling silence interrupted only by the monotonously uneven rhythm of the thuds of our multitudinous boots crushing the heavy snow and wondering when and how this journey would end. I guessed we were being marched to a stalag, a destination that I began to look forward to. These facilities, I had learned in one briefing or another in England, had at least to conform to the Geneva Conventions, which to me, in my innocence, meant rest, food, and shelter.

Under the aegis of our guards we crossed the fabled Rhine River, like the dead in the Greek myth who crossed the River Styx under the unforgiving eye of Charon, not into the Elysian Fields but into a hostile Germany (near the city of Koblenz), where the civilians, vengeful over the unrelenting Allied bombings, cursed and spat at us as we made our sepulchral way through their bombed-out streets. Eventually, after the third or fourth day, we arrived at around noon at our immediate destination, the huge railroad yards at Limburg an der Lahn, an important freight hub a few kilometers southeast of Koblenz, where a huge train of battered boxcars was waiting to take us deeper into Germany. By the time we arrived, the number of prisoners of war in the column, all Americans, and mostly of the 106th Division, had swollen to two or three times its original size, as smaller groups coming from tributary roads joined the main mass. There must have been at least a thousand, perhaps as many as two thousand, of us, a number that underscored my sense of the magnitude, decisiveness—and ignominiousness—of our defeat.

Immediately on our arrival, the guards lined us up along the side of the freight train, divided us into groups of about sixty to each boxcar, and, when this was accomplished, herded us into them in preparation for departure. This process lasted throughout the rest of the day until nightfall. When we were all inside, the guards bolted all the doors of the train. Words, no matter how precise and supple, are inadequate to describe the horrific conditions in these boxcars, which at an earlier time carried cattle to slaughterhouses. Once the doors were closed, the minimal space of our existence was so dark that we could barely see each other (though many of these boxcars had been previously strafed by Allied fighters, leaving several jagged gaping holes in the sides that allowed a minimum of light to penetrate the darkness and fresh air to moderate the stench).

The number of prisoners in each car far exceeded its spatial capacity. Our weary and by now stinking bodies were jammed so close together that it was impossible to rest in any sense of the word. Despite our exhaustion, we nevertheless squirmed in acute discomfort, like flailing fish caught in a trawler net. In one corner of the car there was a large open tub with a board across the top that was intended as a toilet facility. It was virtually impossible to stand up and move under such circumstances. When someone felt the need to shit or piss, he had to climb on and over other bodies—and bear the sting of their curses—before arriving at his destination and then to suffer the indignity of performing the act in public. As a result, many of us relieved ourselves in our helmets in the hope—often unfulfilled—that they and their contents would be passed from one prisoner of war to another until it could be discharged out of one of the holes in the broken wall of the boxcar. There was also, and not least, the intolerable smell, growing increasingly strong as the hours passed, of excrement pervading our suffocating space. What, I wondered, was it about human beings that enticed them to become so inhuman as to want to reduce their fellows' lives to the status of nonhuman life? What was this dehumanizing journey going to be like once it had commenced? How would one survive in this living and soon to be moving tomb?

It was under these unbearable conditions that we spent Christmas Eve in the Limburg railroad yards. We were all aware of it. As we waited for the train, which sat idly, its locomotive firing up in the far distance ahead, to begin its infernal journey into the German interior, several of the inmates of our boxcar remarked bitterly on the irony of our predicament. One, on the other end of the car from where I sat, even began singing the Christmas song Bing Crosby had made popular in the United States the year before, "I'm dreaming of a white Christmas / Just like the ones I used to know." But despite his tentative effort to bring us together as Americans, the rest would not—or could not—pick up on his lead. It seemed to me as if the distance between the song's "children playing in the snow" and us, who were mired helplessly in the present hell of our own excrement, was too far to travel. A loud oppressive silence, amplified by the distant huffing of the locomotive engine, reigned over the dark and silent gloom of the boxcar, each of the sixty of us confined not only in that odorous internal space but also in the solitude of our damaged internal selves.

And so in that silent but unholy night I curled up once more in a fetal ball, closed my eyes, and tried to conjure those Christmas Eves in Newport that I had spent with my family in what seemed another lifetime: the turkey dinner at nine o'clock at night my mother had been preparing all afternoon, not least the delicious stuffing of hamburger, diced potato, raisins, apple slices, walnuts, and herbs blended in the juices of the turkey; the gathering of the family at about ten-thirty, after the lights had been turned off, around the brightly lighted and flickering Christmas tree; the singing of Christmas carols, invariably supplemented by my mother's singing a Greek folk song about *Hristougena* (Christ's Nativity) or about the daring exploits of the Klefts—the Greek guerilla warriors who fought the Ottoman occupiers of Greece—in the wintry nights; and finally the opening of the presents stacked haphazardly at the base of the tree, most of them intended to replace items of clothing that were worn-out, but one or two, like the World War I fighter airplane kit for our older brother, Steve, to satisfy each of the children's particular inclination.

But when I called these images up, the irrepressible present—the infernal world of the boxcar, expanding outward to encompass the whole world—would interrupt, melting them into oblivion like the images of burning celluloid projected on a screen. If the Nativity of Christ—the night the Savior was born—could not prevent the inhumanity of our captors and the terrible physical and spiritual pain we inmates were suffering, why, I asked myself, should we celebrate it? His coming promised peace on earth and goodwill toward men, a "new year." But the world of shit we were forced to inhabit belied those glad tidings. Yet . . . the matter was too complicated for my inexperienced and uneducated mind to process. And then I began to cry inside, repeating, "Mama! Mama! Mama!" like a child calling his mother to come and console him.

Many years later, while on a sabbatical in France, in 1974, I, my wife, and our children visited the twelfth-century cathedral St. Lazare, at Autun, in Burgundy to look at the masterpieces of the great sculptor Gislebertus. This visit, as I recall, was undertaken not too long after visiting the memorial of the Battle of the Ardennes Forest at St. Vith in Belgium, where I had found, not without registering the resonant irony, that the official designers of this monument to that epochal world event had eternally mismatched the insignia (the lion's head) and the number of my division (the 106th).

On entering the precincts of the west entrance of the cathedral, I was stunned by the brilliantly executed facade overlooking the portal. It was the iconographical scene of the Last Judgment, with a highly stylized, that is, immutable, Christ seated centrally on a throne, arms outspread pointing to the Apostles with his right hand and to the scale of judgment in which St. Michael weighs the souls of the terrified and cowering humanity with his left. Below a bar separating these symbolic scenes, one sees the saved heads uplifted, led by bishops on the right, and the damned, in multiple postures and expressions of terror and sorrow, being herded into hell by an angel with spread wings. What captured my eyes immediately was a small but powerfully resonant detail: in the middle of the left side of the bar under which the damned are depicted, two huge hands, which have broken through the bar, hold one of the damned around the neck, as the latter, eyes and mouth wide open, expresses terror, grief, and hopelessness. Having recently retrieved the burning memory of my capture, I was compelled to recall the hellish conditions in the boxcars that were carrying us into the interior of Germany. I not only identified this younger tortured self with the damned, particularly the one whose head is enclosed in the gigantic hands, depicted in Gislebertus's frieze, but also felt that those disembodied noose-like hands around the victim's neck expressed, far more precisely than I could at the time, that insistent and profoundly troubling sense I had felt from the time of my capture to the time I was consigned to the miasmic world of the boxcar of a "higher cause" that used us, made us accountable—we innocent children or "lower" members of the human species—for its sublime purpose without revealing its "end."

Around eight or nine o'clock at night after another day's excruciating delay, we heard the locomotive start to cough in the distance ahead and the guards calling each other up and down the tracks to board the freight train. About a half-hour later, as I sat squeezed in a corner of the boxcar anxiously anticipating the next stage of our journey, the air-raid sirens suddenly started to scream their raucous warning. The guards still remaining in the yard shouted to those on the train to get off, and, without any apparent concern for the thousands of prisoners in the boxcars, they ran off to the air-raid shelters underneath the Limburg terminal for safety. Through the holes in the wall I could see intermittently the beams of searchlights moving across the wailing night sky. Then in the distance I heard the drone of bombers. It was, we learned later, one of the legendary night bombing units of the British raf, whose target that night was the railroad yards of Limburg. Sealed in the boxcars, with no means of getting out before they arrived, we realized with horror that we were at the mercy of our own bombers.

Then something extraordinary—and terribly ironic—happened. As we sat cowering in our boxcar expecting the inevitable once again, we heard the grating of the door bolt sliding open. One of the prisoners (it turned out), in a gesture of heroic lunacy—how else could one put it?— had squeezed through an opening in one of the boxcar walls and had begun unbolting as many of the doors of the train as he could, releasing a multitude of prisoners from their confinement into, as it immediately turned out, worse circumstances. Along with many other prisoners ahead and behind us, we evacuated the boxcar and began running in every direction in search of shelter from the imminent attack. As we ran, scattered yet in a strange unison, like a stampede of cattle or the turbulence of fractals, the bombs began to fall out of the angry sky. Multiple explosions lighted up the railroad yard. In that hallucinatory light and sound I saw from the corners of my eyes a number of bodies to my right and left arching upward and then down along with debris accompanied by screams of pain.

In that maelstrom my impulse was to lie down and wait for the explosion that would end my life, but for some reason—hope in the face of hopelessness, I think—I continued to run. Eventually, after crossing what seemed an infinite number of railroad tracks—in reality it took no more than a couple of minutes—I saw an incline ahead of me at the edge of the railroad yard. It was broken in the middle by a high retaining wall that on the right jutted up against a squat concrete windowless building, maybe a pillbox. Gathering my remaining strength, I made for this possible haven and, on arriving, found an indent in the wall where it joined the building. I curled up in the corner, my arms folded around my head, and waited. A bomb exploded on the hill above me not more than thirty yards from the wall. A blast of fiery light and thick hot air hit my head like a baseball bat. And then I blacked out. When I recovered consciousness—it must have been a mere instant after the explosion—my head was throbbing and my right ear ringing mercilessly, but I realized that the retaining wall had saved my life.

After completing their mission, the bombers turned and left, leaving a number of fires burning, some American dead and wounded strewn all over the railroad yard. But the prisoner of war train remained, strangely, entirely intact. Like so much of the war to which I had borne and would bear witness, the heroism of that young American who had unbolted the boxcar doors to save his comrades had turned out to be complicit with the Allied instruments of their death and maiming.

In the aftermath of that terrifically ironic British bombing of the Limburg railroad yard—which, in the name of decisive victory, had to be indiscriminate about what it destroyed to achieve its end—I had an intuition that would become one of the supreme philosophical and ethical themes of my adult life: that war is not an anomaly but the extreme form of Western humanity's rage for order—its (finally futile) will to reduce to nothing everything in time and space that resists it narrative logic, which is to say, its inability to let being be. This intuition, as I will suggest later in my story, was deepened not too long afterward, during the firebombing of Dresden. But it was not until several years after the war, when I read Herman Melville's great un-American American novel, *Moby-Dick*, that these early intimations took on conscious articulation. I am referring to his decisive ironic disclosure of the destructive—and self-destructive—consequence of America's paranoid will to power over being (the white whale). The nothing that Ahab would annihilate annihilates him:

The prophecy was that I should be dismembered; and—Aye! I lost this leg. I now prophesy that I will dismember my dismemberer. Now, then, be the prophet and the fulfiller one . . . Come, Ahab's compliments to ye; come and see if ye can swerve me. Swerve me? Ye cannot swerve me, else ye serve yourselves! man has ye there. Serve me? The path to my fixed purpose is laid with iron rails, whereon my soul is grooved to run. Over unsounded gorges, through the rifled hearts of mountains, under torrents' beds, unerringly I rush! Naught's an obstacle, naught's an angle to the iron way!

When the sirens had blasted the all-clear signal, the German guards came out of their shelters to round up the scattered prisoners. I was now outside the area of the railroad yard, and for an instant it occurred to me that I might try to escape. Shaken to my marrow by the nearby explosion and remembering that I was at least a hundred kilometers inside Germany, however, I abandoned that thought no later than it came to me. So I returned to the train, where the guards were assigning some of the prisoners who had been medics the task of collecting the fallen bodies, separating the dead from the wounded—there must have been between forty and sixty of them—and treating the wounded soldiers as best as they could. By the time this gruesome task was completed, several trucks had arrived to bear both piles of mutilated bodies away to their unknown destination.

Instead of herding us back into the train, as we were expecting, our guards, for some reason I could not fathom—it may have had to do with rebuilding tracks ahead that had been destroyed by the Allied bombers— lined us up in pairs in a column and marched us in the dead of night out of the railroad yard. About a half-hour later we arrived at a prisoner of war camp (Stalag xii-a), where we spent the night in an enclosed canvas tent adjacent to the main wooden buildings of the prison compound. In the morning we were fed something that tasted remotely like coffee and bread then rounded up and led out of the camp toward the Limburg railroad yard. In the daylight we saw what the darkness of the night before had obscured. It was a huge tent camp close by but distinctly separate from the one in which we had spent the night. Its four sides were enclosed by a barbed wire fence fifteen to twenty feet high. And it contained what seemed a vast number of Russians captured on the Eastern front in various stages of bodily—and probably mental—decay. Many of them were lying on the frozen ground, too weak to move, their curiously striped gray and black clothes in tatters. Others, more like cadavers than human beings, were standing against the fence, clutching the barbed wire with their emaciated fingers and peering at us mysteriously as we walked by. One, at the far end of the barbed wire fence, the yellow, leatherlike skin of his face stretched tight against the bones of his skull, reaches through the wire, his skeletal palm and fingers upturned. He says nothing, but his sunken eyes blaze behind their bony sockets. *Click!*

I had heard that the Nazis discriminated between their enemy in the West and their enemy in the East, that they conceived of the Bolshevik Slavs to be an inferior race, like the Jews, that they treated Russian prisoners, when they deigned to take them, with unspeakable cruelty, as if they were not of the human species, that they were guilty of "crimes against humanity." This horrific experience seemed to confirm with a vengeance what I had heard, and I was appalled by the German command's inhumanity.

Somehow, however, I felt I was bearing witness to something else, something deeper, in the blazing eyes of that Russian prisoner of war. I couldn't explain to myself what I saw there at the time, except that it had something to do with everything that had happened to me since becoming a soldier, especially with the German breakthrough. Even today, as I try to recall that distant time from the perspective of what I have learned about living in a volatile world dominated by the United States since the end of World War II, I cannot finally give that experience a name. Suffice it to say that in the wake of the RAF bombing, particularly the killing and maiming of my fellow prisoners of war, I came, by way of a vague but irresistible leap, to associate this resonating disturbance with my realization that the Germans who perpetrated and condoned this inhuman violence against the humanity of the Russian prisoner of war were of the same culture as the creators of the *Mass in B Minor*, of *Don Giovanni*, of *Faust*, of *The Magic Mountain*, that they, like the British, French, and Americans they were fighting, were members of Western culture. Those spectral eyes, in other words, seemed to reveal an ironically terrible limitation endemic to Western civilization at large. What I saw, I reiterate, was at that moment only a vague intuition. After the firebombing of Dresden, however, this shadow became a spectrally present question: was what I bore witness to in that seemingly accusing gaze of the emaciated Russian prisoner of war—a human life utterly stripped of its dignity—a symptom of a certain inhumanity inhering in a civilization that distinguished itself from, claimed superiority over, other cultures by appealing in a fundamental way to its benign humanity?

Having been marched back to the Limburg railroad yard, we were herded once again into the dreaded forty-and-eights to resume our journey. I cannot remember the exact itinerary of this train laden with broken young men, except that it was to bear us eastward across Germany to an unknown destination, an unknown that increased my sense of its symbolic nature. But this was secondary to our immediate situation. What I remember most vividly about this journey into the unknown was its devastating effect on my soul. In the wake of the accumulative shattering of all the stabilities I had known as a child, I came to see it as a rite of passage into hell: an infernal journey. The space of our confinement, as I said earlier, was agonizingly small, which made movement, especially getting to the crude toilet facility in the corner of the boxcar, virtually impossible. The foul smell of human excrement—some of the prisoners had diarrhea ("the shits," we called it)—was overwhelming. It was difficult breathing through the nose, but because of the close quarters, it was also difficult breathing through the mouth. And the seemingly unending duration of the journey made this abominable situation even worse. We suffered these degrading conditions through seven or eight days as the train made its slow way toward its destination. On the first or second day en route, the train was strafed briefly by Allied fighters, probably seeking another target. After that it traveled only at night. During the daylight hours, when the train was at rest, we remained confined in the suffocating boxcars. The only respite occurred sometime in the morning hours when our guards let us out to relieve ourselves along the rail tracks and to feed us a watery potato soup and bread from a portable field kitchen. It was a small mercy for which we were all grateful, but it could not redeem the estranged and uncanny world we inhabited.

In the process of writing about this moment in my rite of passage, I found, in an old leather box of valuables my mother had left to me after she died, a dust-covered file containing a typewritten letter and a telegram to my parents signed by Adjutant General J. A. Ulio of the U.S. Army after I was taken prisoner. The letter, dated January 13, 1945, notifies them that "your son, Private First Class William V. Spanos, 31,269,818 [the number on my dog tags], has been reported missing in action in Germany since

21 December 1944," expresses the government's regrets, assures them that "the case" is not "closed," and ends by informing them that "the personal effects of an individual missing overseas are held by his unit for a period of time and are then sent to the Effects Quartermaster, Kansas City, Missouri, for disposition as designated by the soldier." The telegram, dated May 3, 1945, a few days before the end of the war, when I was wandering in the bombed-out streets of Brux, in northern Czechoslovakia, reads: "The Secretary of War desires me to inform you that your son PFC Spanos William V [I was, as I recall, a corporal at the time of my capture] is prisoner of war of German Government based on information received through Provost Marshal General. Further information received will be furnished by Provost Marshal General."

In rereading these official notifications after so many years, I was, needless to say, appreciative of the American government's effort to provide my distraught mother and father with information about my status overseas. But I must confess I was repelled by the bureaucratic language through which this information was conveyed to them. In these communications I, like the thousands of young men in the letters sent by the American government to inform their parents that they were killed, wounded, missing in action, or taken prisoner of war, was little more than an object of statistics, my dreadful experience reduced to a bloodless abstraction: KIA, WIA, MIA, POW. A body stripped of everything but life. What, I wondered, as I reread these, must my mother and father have felt, when on the days of their arrival they encountered the irreconcilable disparity between the abstract words they read and their helpless flesh-and-blood son who had disappeared from the face of the earth or into a distant war-torn world? No appeal to the difficulty of the state's problem of communicating this kind of information can mitigate the degrading insult inflicted by such letters and telegrams on the humanity of the parents of the soldiers who were killed or wounded or taken prisoners.

Similarly, in recalling my recurring wartime intuition that I, like all my fellow "GIs," was a disposable pawn manipulated by a larger and far more important and powerful but unknown force, it occurred to me that the official histories and the media that represented the war in its aftermath had passed over the actual experience of the prisoner of war and that the huge number of veterans of the stalags accepted this silence. This was no doubt because the historians, the journalists, and even the filmmakers, who purported to focus their lenses on the ordinary soldier, perceived the war in large, indeed totalizing, conceptual terms: the Allies and the Nazis, democracy and totalitarianism, the strategies of commanding officers, the movements of armies, victories and defeats, and so on. They minimized, if they did not entirely reduce to counters, the singular individual soldiers who were being killed or wounded or, especially, taken into captivity. But this silence was, I think, also because the historians, the journalists, and the Hollywood filmmakers wanted, at all costs, to avoid the risk of evoking the suspicion that American prisoners had been taken captive because they had lacked the courage or will to die pro patria.

Having experienced the unspeakable horrors of captivity as an American soldier in World War II, I have found most of these histories, like the communications from the war office to my parents, woefully inadequate, indeed misleading. In glorifying that war, as in the recent case of Tom Brokaw's book *The Greatest Generation*, or the common soldier, as in the case of Ken Burns's documentary *The War*, they marginalized American prisoners of war and, like the U.S. high command, tacitly reduced their singular experience of captivity to an indifferent statistic. Put more bluntly, they silenced their potentially heretical—that is, antinationalist—voice by speaking abstractly for them.

The freight train carrying its cargo of war prisoners finally arrived at its destination on the seventh or eighth day of its easterly progress. It turned out to be Stalag IV-B, a camp near Mühlberg, east of Leipzig, and not too distant from Dresden in Saxony, close to the Russian front. It was a huge camp, housing several thousand prisoners of war in large, austere wooden barracks and circus-style tents surrounded by a high barbed wire fence and observation towers manned by machine gunners. The inmates were mostly British, but, if I remember correctly, there were also many prisoners who came from the Western allied world—Canada, France, Holland, Belgium, Norway, the United States (though there were none from the Soviet Union)—as well as from several of the colonies of Britain and France, above all, India and Africa. Many of the prisoners at Stalag IV-B had been inmates since early in the war. But to put this mass of deprived humanity in terms of nationalities and cultures, as it has been done almost universally by the official histories and the media, would be to distort the reality. After several days in the camp I began to realize that many of my fellow inmates had lost, or were in various stages of losing, their national and cultural identities, that the deprivation not simply of human rights but also of the basic amenities of civilized life—sanitation, clothing, and bodily nourishment, above all, food—had reduced all too many of them to instinctual life, to the elemental condition of biological survivors. Tobacco was capital, and the knife was the arbiter of conflict.

That world of the stalag, I soon came to believe against my will, was not a world; it seemed to me more like a jungle, in which everyone was a prey—the heart of darkness, I would say, if that phrase had not been deprived of its meaning by the imperial imagination. It was nothing like the world represented after the war in movies such as *Stalag 17*, starring William Holden, and *Von Ryan's Express*, starring Frank Sinatra, or the long-running television comedy *Hogan's Heroes*, in which the camp becomes the setting for the play of the self-reliant, practical, and humane genius of ordinary Americans. The real camp was, rather, an infernal space, where the brutal and degrading reality of the cage prevailed. Having felt my sustaining past and my sense of community slipping away as I journeyed into the unknown interior of Germany, I was frightened by all I was seeing in the camp.

Shortly after arriving at Stalag IV-B, for example, I was accosted by a couple of British prisoners, both, I noted with some surprise, considerably older than me, smartly dressed in their immaculate jumpsuits and polished boots, conveying in their demeanor a sense of well-being and cunning in a space exuding lack—ill health, destitution, hopelessness. They wasted no time in coming to their point. Knowing I had only recently been captured, they assumed I was likely to have a pack or two of cigarettes and wanted to know if I'd be willing to trade them for bread. I told them I had no cigarettes but got the distinct impression that they didn't believe me. One of them took the liberty of reaching across to feel one of the pockets of my field jacket. I was startled. To these British prisoners I wasn't a comrade, an unfortunate ally who, like them, had been captured and was suffering the hell of dislocation and the hostility of the enemy. I was, it seemed from their crude manner and actions, simply an object to be exploited. They eventually withdrew but not without leaving me with the distinct impression that their visit was fraught with threat and that they would return.

As I was trying to process this disturbing encounter, another prisoner, a Canadian it turned out, around thirty I guessed, approached me. Introducing himself, he told me he had been taken prisoner in the disastrous British and Canadian raid on Dieppe on the northern coast of France in August 1942 and had been in Stalag IV-B ever since. He wanted to know how the war was going, whether the Allies were advancing, as rumor had it, or were in retreat, as the German guards were constantly announcing, and where and how I was taken prisoner. I told him the bad news about the German breakthrough at St. Vith (not knowing that it was the beginning of a decisive Allied victory) and the particular and general circumstances of my capture, indicating my doubts about the official rationale for the conditions that led to the collapse and surrender of my division. In the process of telling him my "story" his severe demeanor began to soften. And when I had ended, he seemed, to my surprise—and, given my earlier encounter with inmates of the camp, my relief—to manifest concern for my fate, probably, I surmised, because of my vulnerable youth. He told me he had witnessed what had recently transpired between the two Brits and me and that unfortunately the camp was filled with inmates like them who went to extremes to ensure their survival, indeed, that he was one of them.

I can't remember exactly how he put all this, but the gist of it was something like this: "Early on after being captured at Dieppe—it seems an eternity ago that I was dragged into this utterly other world—I figured out that the Germans who ran Stalag IV-B weren't going to adhere to the laws of the Geneva Convention, especially those having to do with feeding POWs. That's primarily because they don't have enough of it to feed their own people but also because they're simply indifferent to our needs. We're their barbaric enemies, after all. I learned all too soon that to survive in Stalag IV-B I had to abandon all the values I had learned in the so-called civilized world, break all its laws. Or rather, I had to act out overtly what they concealed. To care for someone else is to put yourself at risk, like throwing your weapon away in a battle. To survive you have to be a cutthroat, as you've already seen." At this point he reached into the front pocket of his worn heavy jumpsuit and pulled out a Red Cross jackknife, and, opening out the long menacing steel blade, he slashed the air in front of him, saying, "This steel, old chap—and your will to use it— is your armor in this hell."

Then he told me that because the inmates, like those two Brits who had accosted me, were older and seasoned survivors, this bloody camp was no place for a "young chap" and advised me to take the risk of signing up for an *Arbeitskommando*. These, he explained, were small supervised groups of prisoners of war who were sent out to farms to work in the fields or to villages to do odd jobs such as cleaning the streets, removing the garbage, repairing roads that had been bombed out, or to small factories to work the machines that were always being left idle by the conscription of the labor force by the German army. As members of such working commandos, he said, prisoners of war had easier access to food, to more comfortable shelter, and to better sanitary conditions. "Not least," he said, "you'll escape the inhuman laws of the stalag. It's too late for me," contradicting himself, "I'm a denizen of this brutal world. But you, old chap . . . you don't belong in this zoo. I could tell by the way you told your story. If you stay in this godforsaken place, I don't think you'll last a month. You're too innocent to survive."

I was frightened by what this hardened veteran of stalag life had said about its codes of existence, but I was also touched by his kindness, not unaware that his solicitude countered everything he had said about himself. I thanked him for his good advice and told him I'd follow it. We shook hands. He wished me good luck then turned, crossed the floor— I noticed a slight but distinct limp—and melted into the crowd on the far side of the huge room. I never saw him again. He too, I now thought consciously, had come and had gone.

That night—or was it the one after?—was December 31, New Year's Eve, the night, precisely between eleven and midnight, I turned twenty years old. With the events of the last ten days or so colliding helter-skelter in my mind like the parts of a machine that has gone haywire, I laid down on the cold ground of the circus tent to recuperate some semblance of order, some sense of my former identity, out of the fractured morass I had become. It was a painful and futile attempt. In many ways New Year's Day for Greek families—and I think this was especially true of mine—was a far more important holiday than Christmas, indeed, than any other in the year with the exception of Easter. We called it Agios Vasilios's (Saint Basil's) Day, after the great Byzantine theologian and bishop of Caeserea (329–79), who was eventually elevated to sainthood by the Byzantine church. Because of his lifelong efforts to ease the wretched life of the poor and oppressed, no doubt, he eventually became something like a primal and always present awakening natural force in the eyes of the Greek peasantry, a force somewhat akin to the fertility gods who heralded the end of winter and the coming of spring but accommodated to the brutalizing circumstances of the four hundred years of the Turkish occupation.

It was, above all, because my parents named me after him that Saint Basil's Day became so important for my family. On the eve of that day, after returning from a late mass celebrating the advent and death of Agios Vasilios (he died on January 1), we would gather around our parents in the festive living room to perform the ritual of *Metanoia*, in which one by one we would kneel before them, kiss their extended hands holding a small gift, often a silver dollar, and beg their forgiveness for all the wrongs we had committed during the previous year. And after that, as we ate *klourakia* (glazed braided cookies with sesame seeds), my mother, a veritable repository of Greek folktales and songs she had learned as a child in her village in Thessaly, would tell us the story about Saint Basil's clandestine night visits to the villages of Greece throughout the four hundred years of the Turkish occupations to teach the children of the peasants the Greek language, which the Ottoman rulers forbade. At the end of her story she would sing about Saint Basil's return from Caesarea on New Year's to punish the wealthy for their indifference to the poor and to bring sweets and good tidings for the New Year to the wretched of the Greek earth.

Aghios Vasilis erchetai.
kai den mas katadechetai
apo, apo tin Kaisareia
sis archontissa kiria
vastaei kola kai charti
zacharokantio zimoti
des kai me, des kai me to palikari
to kalamari egrafe, tin moira tou tin elege
kai to charti omilei
Agie mou Agie Vasili.

(Saint Basil is coming
And he doesn't seem to have time for us [the wealthy]
from Caesarea
hear this, you aristocratic lady,
he holds paper in his hands
and hand kneaded sweets
paper and pen
and please pay attention to me [the brave young singer of the song]
the pen was writing, was narrating their fate
and the paper was speaking it
my Holy Basil.)

On New Year's Day my mother would awaken early in the morning to make the traditional *Vasilopita*, a huge egg and feta cheese pie under- and overlaid by multiple gossamer thin sheets of filo, in which she would hide a coin, as my father prepared a piglet (when there was enough money for such an extravagant dinner) for roasting. In mid-afternoon we would gather at the table to celebrate Saint Basil's Day, my birthday, and my name day all at once. After we had devoured the piglet, my mother brought the *Vasilopita* out, cut it into large triangles, and served each of us a piece. This moment was the climax of the glorious day's festivities. For according to the Saint Basil legend, the one who was given the piece of *Vasilopita* containing the coin would have good luck for the rest of that year.

As I lay on the cold ground of the tent in the dark, my mind in tatters, I hummed to myself the song my mother sang about Saint Basil—I had forgotten the words—and tried desperately to conjure his coming out of Caesarea and the Byzantine past to liberate me, his namesake, from my wretched captivity. But he was too distant in time and our occasions decisively different. No matter how intensely I tried, I couldn't conjure his holy image. It was too foreign. And so was the world I was trying to remember—the world of my childhood, of magical saviors like the Saint Basil my mother, especially, created for us. In the deepest recesses of my mind during that night of my twentieth birthday, modern armies that were tearing the world apart in the name of creating a better world, comrades in arms who were going after each other's jugulars, a civilized world that was becoming increasingly barbaric, clashed cacophonously with macrocephalic heads of benign Byzantine saints, enigmatic prayers capable of producing miracles, folk legends and songs promising positive resolutions of hopeless situations and a simple optimistic way of life. In that turbulent abyss I lost whatever faith I had previously had in the goodness of what my parents called "God's Creation."

The next day I signed up for an *Arbeitskommando*, as my Canadian friend had advised, and a few days later, full of anxiety about the place and nature of the labor I would be assigned to perform, was called to join a group of about sixty POWs, all Americans, who were to be marched out of the precincts of Stalag IV-B. Without being informed of our destination, we began at around nine in the morning our new and "final" journey in an easterly direction. This, I thought, ambiguously, was simultaneously ominous and hopeful, a movement closer to the volatile war zone of the Eastern front but also to where liberation by our Russian Allies was possible. Not too long after departing from Mühlberg, we saw road signs indicating that we were heading in the direction of Dresden. On seeing these, I became anxious. I was hoping, as I have said, that our Germans captors would assign us to a farm, where food was more readily accessible than in a city environment and we were likely to be treated more humanely. What kind of city was Dresden? Was it a military target? Had it been the victim of massive Allied bombings like the notorious one that, we had been told, had destroyed Hamburg? What kind of work would we be assigned to do in that city? Were the Russians close enough to unleash an assault on the city, as rumor had it? Were we, against our expectations, escaping the frying pan only to wind up in the fire in choosing to join the *Arbeitskommando*? These questions haunted me all along the long way until we arrived at the outskirts of Dresden.

As I gazed on the city before us, the anxious questions I was asking myself momentarily lost their force. Its beauty was awesome. The spires and domes of cathedrals and governmental and cultural buildings against a sky enflamed by a falling sun and the river winding through the city were breathtaking. The buildings were constructed of rust-colored stones, and their hybrid architecture was a combination of baroque, rococo, and eighteenth-century classical styles, all of which conveyed the aura of an old and venerable but also lively city that was defiantly indestructible, immune to the ravages of time and history. I reveled in the sense of permanence it exuded. Later I learned that it was called "the Florence of the Elbe" (a comparison between a northern European and Mediterranean culture replete with symbolic ambiguities). As we walked through this beautiful magisterial city, I saw little evidence that it had been bombed by the Allies. Nor did it seem to be a military city, one that had strategic value. I saw only a handful of soldiers and few installations of defense such as bunkers and antiaircraft batteries. Although I noticed that the city was crowded with refugees from the areas of the Eastern front, the citizens of Dresden seemed to be going about their everyday business as if their city were an oasis in a wasteland of war. I was astonished by the difference between Dresden and the other cities I had seen during our journey into the German interior. Despite my exhaustion, my hunger, my disappointment that our *Arbeitskommando* was not being taken to a farm, and my sense of having been compelled into an interior where there was no exit, I began to hope. Crossing the winding Elbe River over one of the beautiful baroque bridges that joined the western and eastern parts of the city offered us a magnificent view of its assuring erratic order. Perhaps, I thought, Dresden was the place to wait out the war with some degree of ease or at least with minimal bodily and spiritual pain. But that was not to be.

3. *Arbeitskommando*

What are the roots that clutch, what branches grow
Out of this stony rubbish?

T. S. ELIOT, *The Waste Land*

Our snail-paced journey through the center of Dresden brought us eventually to a nondescript suburb named Rabenau. I can't remember where precisely this suburb was in relation to the fabulous old city through which we had passed, though I think it was at the northwestern edge of Dresden. What I do remember is that it contained a number of small factories, one of which, we finally learned from our guards before being handed over to our new local ones, was our destination. It was a woodworking mill with three stories and a basement. The basement, we eventually learned, contained food supplies, mainly barrels of sauerkraut and bins of turnips and potatoes. The first floor was inhabited by a few German civilians, who were caretakers of or workers in the mill; the second contained the saw machines; and the third was our and our new home guards' living quarters. The last consisted of two sections, separated by a long corridor, one that housed the handful of guards and the other the prisoners who would operate the machines. This section of the floor was itself separated into two parts. One was a "dining room" containing four crude tables and benches on both side of a relatively large, barrel-shaped cast-iron stove, which was the source of whatever warmth we would feel during our captivity. On the far wall of this section of the room there was a series of compartmentalized shelves, each compartment containing a bowl, a spoon, and a tin water cup. The other section of the room was our sleeping quarters, which consisted of thirty double bunk beds with thin straw mattresses.

On entering our new quarters, I was too tired, too hungry, too eager, to sit or lie still after the grueling eight-hour march from Mühlberg to Rabenau in bitter cold weather to think about what living day after unending day in this confined, austere, and very primitive space would be like. I bracketed my increasing sense that I, like Candide, about whom I had read a couple years earlier in high school, was no more than an ignorant pawn in the hands of an inscrutable "higher cause," a god who felt no obligation to inform me, besides the patronizing Panglossian affirmation that "Whatever *is*, is right," of his unknown purpose and to explain why it entailed inflicting me and others like me with inordinate and seemingly unending bodily pain and mental anguish. Against my consciousness my belly said I was hungry; my legs said I was beat, and I was hoping no more than that our guards would give us food and let us retire to the adjacent sleeping quarters. But they were not about to oblige my wishes. Two of them, both in their late sixties or early seventies, wore the brownish green uniforms of the *Volksturm* (home guards) and carried rifles that seemed to date back to World War I, lined us up against the wall of the corridor at attention and took a roll call. Then, in a language consisting of broken English and simple German, they reminded us that we were prisoners of war and informed us that we would be working the saw machines downstairs from seven in the morning to seven in the evening; that they expected us not to waste time; that the lazy would be punished by withholding their food or being assigned to more difficult tasks; and less assertively, despite their intention, that Germany under their "beloved Führer" was going to win the war against the decadent British and American democracies (in that order).

After this information session, which was also part diatribe, we were led into the dining area and ordered to choose the utensil compartment that would become ours for the duration. We were then assigned to the table and the seats we would henceforth occupy. Shortly afterward, two quite old German civilians, who looked like retired bank employees re-developed into cooks, rolled in a cart carrying a huge steaming cauldron of some kind of soup and a pile of sliced black bread, which they distributed equally among the tables. Not having eaten that day and very little over the preceding days, we were ravenously hungry. But when we began eating, we were profoundly disappointed to find that the meal we were straining like dogs to assault consisted of an unseasoned soup containing a few diced turnips floating in hot water and a small slice of bread that tasted like sawdust. This and a cup of ersatz coffee in the morning, it turned out, would be our diet for the remainder of our stay in Rabenau. It was a far cry from what I had envisaged when I signed up to be a working *Kommando*. And it took its toll not only on our bodies but on our minds, indeed, as it will be seen, on our very beings.

After "dinner" we were advised by our guards to get some sleep because we would be aroused early in the morning to begin work in the sawmill below. Some of the prisoners gathered around the stove to absorb the little heat it was throwing off and to talk about their predicament. I went to the communal latrine—a room with a toilet and a long gutter—on the opposite side of the hallway from where the guards were quartered to relieve myself then returned to the sleeping quarters adjacent to the dining room. I chose a bunk, laid down on its rough and stale-smelling straw mattress in the hope of obliterating the nightmarish reality our higher cause had ordained for us. But nothing I imagined—my father and mother, my brothers and sister, Kathryn, the Sunapee Street gang, the books I had read in high school that I loved but struggled to hate—could efface its disconcerting immediacy. The world I left behind when I was captured had become by this time a realm of shadows—disembodied, fragmented, gossamer, unresponsive to my effort to bring them to corporeal presence. As I lay in my bunk that night early in the new year—terrifically hungry, cold, tired, alienated—I came to realize with a sense of finality that the new world I had been thrown into, a frightening violent world in which I was a disposable object at the mercy of the whim of humans whom circumstances had transformed into cruel masters, was the world I would henceforth inhabit, the home I would live in. What mattered, I decided—or thought I had decided—was bodily survival, and that entailed the obliteration of memory.

Sometime during this psychomachia I became old.

The next morning at five we were aroused by our guards, who walked up and down the rows between the bunks shouting, "Aufstehen! Aufstehen!" and prodding our sleeping bodies with their rifles. After undergoing the indignity of lining up at the communal latrine and then drinking a cup of ersatz coffee for breakfast, we were marched downstairs to the mill, where we were turned over to a civilian foreman, a fat and garrulous man who seemed to enjoy what he took to be the imperial role he was assigned to play. The empire over which his gaze presided was a bleak and dark space lighted dimly by a few overhanging bulbs and consisting of a number of saw machines operated by a huge fly belt extending from one end of the room to the other and huge piles of strips of old discarded wood. On the other side, a number of sawdust-covered windows faced a courtyard, where the civilian laborers in the compound spent their break periods.

When we had gathered around the imperious foreman, he explained in an elemental but imaginative English the operations of the factory at large and the purpose of the stacks of pre-used scraps of wood. And then he showed us how to operate the saw machines. The process was very simple. He assigned one group to the task of gluing the variously shaped scraps of old wood together into large rectangular boards. He assigned a second group to the saw machines that would cut these boards into small uniform strips. To a third group he assigned the job of re-gluing these strips into hollow, open-ended boxes, about two feet long. Clearly, these boxes were containers, but the foreman did not tell us what they were intended to hold. But it was not long before we realized that they were containers for artillery shells—that is to say, our labor would be contributing to the German war effort in violation of the Geneva Convention, which, we knew, prohibited the use of prisoners of war for that purpose.

When the foreman had finished his explanation and demonstrations, he assigned us to our respective jobs in the mill. I, whom he, in his glib and patronizing manner, identified as an intelligent, if decadent, young man by the broadness of my forehead, was assigned to operate one of the machines that sawed the recycled scraps of wood into the strips that formed the sides of the container, a task that required nothing more than pushing the wood along a preestablished line. We glued, sawed, re-glued, and stacked the finished products in even rows along the windowed wall all that day without respite, except to go to the bath room, under the supervision of our overseer. Another manifestation of the higher cause, I thought. And at six or seven in the evening, after what turned out to be an extremely boring and tiring day, our guards suddenly appeared to escort us back to our quarters. Once again we were served turnip soup and a small slice of black bread, which we later learned, after realizing that the lack of grain was a major problem for the German economy—and war effort—was made partially of the sawdust we produced downstairs.

Following dinner, some of the prisoners—more or less the same as the night before—gathered around the pot-bellied stove for warmth, camaraderie, and to dry out the morning's coffee grinds (and later on tea leaves when, on occasion, that luxury was granted us) for the purpose of turning them into smokable cigarettes. Others remained at the table collectively trying to read a German newspaper in the futile hope of acquiring some sense of the progress of the war. Still others—these few seemed to be the oldest (twenty-five to thirty years old)—retired to the sleeping quarters to bring their day to a close. I sat alone at the end of our table struggling to recollect the lines of a war poem I had read and been shaken by in my last year in high school. It was written by a disillusioned British soldier, whose name I didn't remember, during World War I. In this poem the soldier-poet turned the canonical lines of the Roman poet Horace, which I had also read in my Latin class, inside out:

> If in some smothering dream you too could pace
> Behind the wagon that we flung him in,
> And watch
> [something like his writhing white eyes . . .]
> and hear, at every jolt, the blood
> Come gargling from the froth-corrupted lungs.

I remember the words *obscene* and *vile*, the phrase "sores on innocent tongues."

> My friend, you would not tell with such high zest
> To children ardent for some desperate glory,
> The old Lie: Dulce et decorum est
> Pro Patria more. [Sweet and fitting it is / to die for the fatherland.]

This sequence of events became the undeviating and debilitating routine of our lives for the next long few weeks. We were aroused by the contemptuous shouts of our guards at five in the morning; we drank a cup of "coffee" with a piece of artificial bread (if we had the will to save some from the previous night); we worked the machines all day until seven in the evening; we ate the turnip, sometimes potato, soup and the black bread; we broke up into compatible groups to reminisce about the old days in the world, imagine the future after the war, or agonize over the conditions of our existence; we went to bed to come to terms with our private selves and, if we were strong, to sleep. As the days passed under this cruel regime, I began to be aware of the changes occurring in my body. My thighs became noticeably thinner, my ribs more visible, and my face gaunt. Sores kept breaking out on my hands and face, and my stomach, which seemed to have shriveled into a small ball, constantly ached.

One morning after breakfast the guards called us out into the hallway to announce a change. They told us that they had been informed by the higher authorities that a number of prisoners were needed to work in a lumber camp five or ten kilometers outside of Rabenau and asked for volunteers. They said this labor would be easier and more interesting than the work we were doing and those who volunteered would be given more food rations. About ten of the prisoners, desperate to escape the drudgery of the factory and jumping at the chance of eating better, risked the possibility that the guards were exaggerating the benefits and volunteered for this *Kommando*. But because that number wasn't sufficient, the guards chose another ten at random. Immediately afterward, they were marched away. Those of us remaining wondered what that labor would entail.

That night, on the return of the twenty, they told us that they had chosen or were assigned to a situation that was immensely more agonizing than working in the factory. On leaving the grounds of the factory, they were marched into the country in freezing weather, their frayed and minimal clothing inadequate to protect against its inclemency. After walking on an always ascending gravel road for about a half-hour, they came to a small rehabilitation compound by the roadside. There, they said, they were met by three Nazi soldiers, two Estonians and one Latvian, from a dreaded ss unit, who took over from the home guards. They were quite young, in their early twenties, recuperating from wounds received on the Eastern front. Although they were not German nationals, they were totally devoted to the Nazi cause and contemptuous of the ragged and motley Americans in their custody.

Under the aegis of these fastidious young soldiers, the prisoners resumed their uphill march until, a half-hour later, they arrived at their destination. It was a heavily wooded area at the base of a snow-covered mountain that, for some unknown purpose, was being cleared. Their job was to haul the huge logs that were shaped from the huge fir trees being felled on the mountainside down to a ramp bordered by a gravel road, where they were loaded onto trucks that bore them away. The task, they told us, was agonizingly difficult. Depending on the size of the log, four or six of them, with six-foot poles, would climb to the top of the clearing, slide the poles under the fallen and pruned tree, lift it off the ground, and carry it back down through the heavy snow to the ramp. Invariably, they said, the number of them assigned to each log was less than the number required to manage it without inordinately painful effort. Their ss guards, they said, were ruthless, even sadistic. They not only refused the men respite; they also, like Furies, unrelentingly harangued them about their degeneracy, their corruptness, their weakness, their lack of discipline, as they strained to carry their heavy burden. On occasion, to underscore their contemptuous opinion of Americans, the guards would punish those who faltered along the way by hitting them in the back with their rifle butts. It was impossible to survive for long under these conditions, they told us, especially given the little food the Germans gave them.

I listened to this account of my fellow prisoners' experience with great anxiety. Their treatment by their guards struck me as a form of torture. It was ludicrous to be grateful for the luck of not having been chosen for this dreadful labor—for being consigned to a slower death than the one facing this unfortunate group. But I was. I dreaded being exposed to the frigid January weather in inadequate clothing, the backbreaking labor and the relentless harangue of the fanatic guards the forest gang described. In the mill the temperature was more or less tolerable. Despite their mimicking of the military protocol of their superiors, the foreman and the guards were really civilians, and they were old, too preoccupied with demands of age to focus relentlessly on us. The work, though excruciatingly monotonous, was not arduous. And though the amount of food we were given was inadequate to nourish our bodies, our labor, unlike that of our unfortunate twenty, did not accelerate the rate of the biological process that atrophied it. Yet I was also, really for the first time, consciously angry at the inhumanity of our captors. And my awareness of this brutality was intensified by the fact that the work we were performing in the mill was in violation of the Geneva Convention. During the next few days, as the twenty who labored in the forest added to their tale of horror, my anger rose and, in the process of meditating on the conditions of our captivity, it turned into an amorphous—and, I also realized, irrational—desire to resist this oppression in some way.

One afternoon, not long after this insane impulse emerged, as I was running boards interminably through the saw machine, the saw began to vary its speed, as a result of which the wood would kick back to produce a deviance in the intended shape of the strip. I examined the machine from top to bottom but found nothing I could attribute the problem to. Then I looked across the room to the large fly belt that controlled all the machines and noticed that its motion too was erratic. I picked up a round steel bar about six inches long and an inch in diameter that was laying on the floor and, with, I think, the conscious intention of stabilizing the erratic motion of the machine, banged it against the gear under the machine. There was a loud noise, like the crack of a whip, on the other side of the room. I looked up and saw the huge belt fly off its wheels, and all the machines in the room abruptly stopped working.

Startled by the sudden noise and the accompanying silence, the foreman came running out of his office frantically agitated. Seeing the fly belt lying on the floor off the wheels and the machines at rest, he began screaming obscenities at us and demanding who was responsible for this act of subversion. For a moment my impulse was to play innocent and let the situation run its course. But then I realized that this choice would jeopardize my fellow workers. I decided, therefore, in fear and trembling, to tell the foreman exactly what happened—that I was trying to solve a problem—in the hope that this explanation would appease his rage and his suspicion that it was a deliberate act of sabotage. He looked steadily into my eyes for what seemed a very long time as if he were trying to evoke the truth I was trying to conceal. Then he told us to return to our quarters until the fly belt was repaired. Not knowing any of my fellow workers very well, I did not try to explain the ambiguous motives that drove me to that strange, unpremeditated act. Much later in the day we were recalled to our labor. I was relieved that the incident seemed not to have produced dire consequences. The next morning, as I was drinking my coffee, one of our guards came over to the table at which I was sitting to inform me that I had been reassigned to the forest crew.

Like so much else about my captivity, it is very difficult to convey the debilitating effect of this forced labor. At dawn, with virtually nothing in our stomachs and in bitter cold weather, our homeland security guards marched us out of the mill to the way station half the distance to the forest, where we picked up our ss guards bundled warmly in their heavy winter coats and then proceeded to our destination. On arriving, we were separated into teams of four or six and commenced the task of hauling the felled trees down the snow-covered mountainside to the ramp. We did this until one in the afternoon, when we broke for a half-hour to rest—and to eat whatever food we had preserved from the night before. Then we returned to our hard labor. Around five in the afternoon, when it began to turn dark, the guards rounded us up by the ramp, and we began our hour-long march back to the factory. We followed this deadly routine day in and day out, until it felt as if we were in a zone forever emptied of time. When, before being assigned to the forest crew, I was listening to the agonized accounts of those who had been working on the slope of the forest, I was horrified and felt empathy for them. But it wasn't happening to me. After being forced into participating in this torturous labor as our guards mocked our flailing efforts, I felt its intolerable pain in my body and soul. It was torture: the agony of my enervated body, one no longer strong enough to perform the task it was being forced to perform, compounded by the consciousness of my degradation.

What was intolerable about our labor in the forest was not simply the unbearable weight we carried down the mountainside and the climb back up in the thick snow. Nor was it the freezing temperature. (The sole of one of my boots had become separated from its binding, and the sustained pain of the cold in my toes was excruciating.) It was also the absolute necessity for, yet incredible difficulty of, lockstep timing on the part of the hauling team, especially under the cruel prodding of our guard. Often a misstep by one of us would throw the group off balance, and the log would fall to the ground, requiring the gigantic effort to relift it as the guard laughed and railed obscenities at our lack of teamwork. Like my bodily energy, the words at my command, which under normal conditions were capable of bringing relief to spiritual anguish, were utterly inadequate to ease my angry distress. Even the inclusive personifications that I used to rely on to enable me to ride through a crisis in my life, when my mind couldn't get its hands around the immensity of my mortal suffering—"Oh, God!" "Christ Almighty!" "Jesus!"—could not alleviate the sense of suffocation, of no exit, I felt under these infernal conditions.

One day during our half-hour break my team was sitting in the snow, our backs against unfelled trees at the upper edge of the clearing. We were eating the little bread we had saved from the night before. A few yards across the way our three ss guards were devouring the hot soup in their vacuum-sealed containers, one of them cruelly calling our attention to its steaming thickness. Trying hopelessly to avert our eyes and noses from that sight and smell, we began talking about the major league baseball teams for which we rooted. In the process one of my fellow teammates,

Aldo, a loquacious and all too self-important Italian from New York, who was a Giants fan, began jokingly to mock my loyalty to the insignificant Boston Braves. American baseball was as remote from my being in that context as the planet Pluto was from the Earth, but somehow—perhaps the combination of our guards' smugness and my interlocutor's know-it-all attitude—his misplaced assertiveness began to get under my skin. And in retaliation I shouted back at him something to the effect that he was an idiot for putting us on display to our torturers. This inaugurated an argument that caught the attention of our guards. One in particular, the diminutive Latvian with the manifest limp named Peter, who, more than the other two, took apparent pleasure in harassing us when our routine broke down, took this opportunity to launch an allegorical diatribe in English against our American decadence. Rising from his seated position and waving his rifle threateningly before our faces, he began screaming in broken English something to this effect: "You *Amerikaner, du bist ein* people of bastards. Your original German blood is become putrefied. *Juden, Schwarts*, aboriginal, Polish, Italian, Slav, *Griesche*, all these bloods in one sick body. That is why you cannot carry out a simple labor. That is why you fight with each other; that is why we will destroy your armies, we Aryans under our Führer."

As Peter railed against our decadent racial adulteration, he became more frenzied. Suddenly he turned in the direction of his comrades as if looking for something. Then he saw the two-handled tree saw, about six feet in length, lying upright along the trunk of the tree our guards were sitting under. He rushed over to the tree, picked up the saw, and returning, threw it violently to the snow-covered ground at our feet, shouting, "We will teach you *Amerikanische* swine how to work together." Picking up a two-headed ax that also lay against the tree, he began chopping into the trunk about a foot above the roots. After cutting a three- or four-inch deep wedge, he threw the ax down and commanded me and Aldo to pick up the saw and start sawing. I remember exchanging a glance with my fellow victim. Mine spoke of the horror about to ensue and pleaded something like mutual forgiveness. I couldn't decipher his. Then under the aegis of our little ss tyrant, we started sawing. Tired by a whole morning of hauling those heavy logs, we began slowly, tentatively trying to establish a rhythm that would make the process less straining to our psyches and easier on our weak bodies. But Peter, perceiving the implications of this movement, ordered us to saw faster. He wanted to force us to work against each other in a conflicting rhythm that would exhaust us physically and tear us apart spiritually. And he succeeded.

I cannot describe the pain my body and mind suffered in the process of the next quarter of an hour, which seemed like an eternity in a black hole. Although I remained silent, except for my heavy, rasping breathing, inside I was screaming in agony the whole time. When we had lost our rhythm and had to slow down to pick it up again, Peter would shout, "Fast! Fast! *Mach Schnell! Mach Schnell, Amerikanische* bastards," and jab his rifle butt into our backs in the vicinity of the kidney. The sharp physical pain, the acute exhaustion, the dreadful sense that this ordeal would never end . . . caged like a wild beast but no exit. Depleted of physical and emotional strength but no finality. A living death. It was torture in its most elemental and soul-destroying form.

Having sawed through about three-quarters of the tree under these conditions, Peter's comrades, who had initially enjoyed the spectacle, seemed to have become embarrassed by his frenzied excesses. To our exquisite relief one of them told him to desist and, when he resisted, pulled him away. They assigned two of the others of our team to finish the job at their pace. A few minutes later the accursed fir tree came crashing down toward the tree line. When the snow and debris had settled, the guards called us back to our labor as if what had come before was nothing out of the ordinary. As we marched back to the mill that night, the turmoil of my body and mind was exacerbated by an overwhelming question: how did I, whose world just a couple of months earlier had been open, free, and possible, end up in this endless hellish reality?

The greatest cruelty our German captors inflicted on us was the deprivation of adequate food. It not only atrophied our energy and made the forced labor in the forest intolerable. Even more terrible than this, it also reduced the desires that constituted our humanity to the single-minded yearning for food, mind into instinct, spirit into pure body. Hunger was at the heart of our suffering. Everything we thought, said, and did was oriented by this deprivation. In the forest, on the march back to the factory, in our quarters, especially in the communal areas frequented by our guards and the German civilians, my eyes always searched for anything that looked edible—weeds, grass, a premature dandelion, the discarded cores of the withered apples and strands of sauerkraut that seemed to be their daily fare. The hunger dehumanized us, turned our inner selves into single-minded wills committed to nothing more than survival, even at the expense of each other. How ironic, it seemed to me now, that I had actually volunteered for the *Arbeitskommando* in the hope of escaping the fate I had been warned against by the Canadian prisoner of war in Stalag IV-B! Because it involved the deprivation of food, the pain of hard labor, and the shame of degradation, our situation in the sawmill and the forest was worse than the situation of the long-timers, for whom, he had said, the knife blade was their armor.

As I have noted, our daily food rations consisted invariably of a bowl of watery soup, usually turnips and occasionally potatoes, and an inch-thick slice of ersatz bread, which was given to us in the evening after the day's work. Being always hungry, it was excruciatingly difficult to save some of the soup for the next morning and a little of the bread for the work break in the mill or the forest. But a few of us willed ourselves to do so. When the meal was over, we stored these meager but precious remains in the compartments allotted to us on the wall at the other side of the dining room. After an hour or so sitting around the tables to reminisce or around the stove to get warm, the lights were extinguished by our guards, and we retired to our dismal, louse-infested sleeping quarter for the night to recuperate as much energy and strength of mind as we could.

One morning—it must have been a week or two after the ordeal Aldo and I had undergone in the forest—when I went to my compartment to retrieve the small piece of bread I had stored there the night before, I found to my dismay that it was missing. I immediately attributed the theft to rats. But when, on our way to the forest, I mentioned this to the companion I was walking with, he confided to me that his compartment too had been raided on a couple of previous occasions. And it occurred to us that the thief might not have been a rat but one of our fellow prisoners. We were alarmed by the possibility but decided to let the matter go for the time being. If our surmise was the case, the act was indeed despicable, but given the conditions of our existence, it was also quite understandable. We hoped that another explanation, less terrible, would emerge in the meantime.

But this silence did not last long. One night we were all awakened from our golden sleep by a great commotion in the dining room. We rushed out to find out its cause, and as the lights came on, we saw, to our astonishment, a group of American prisoners holding down an emaciated young boy, about my age, one I had rarely noticed because he was so quiet and retiring, whom they had caught stealing a piece of bread from one of the compartments. They were, I recall, a group that worked in the mill and invariably sat around the central cast-iron stove after the evening meal, satellites of a short barrel-chested, round-faced, and self-righteously arrogant Texan with a long handlebar mustache who presided imperially over all its conversations. As the German guards, in various stages of undress looked on—for some reason they did not interfere, as if they had been already forewarned—the Texan informed us triumphantly that he and his buddies had been aware for some time that one of the American prisoners was raiding the compartments in the middle of the night when everyone was sound asleep, that they had suspected this fellow— I'll call him Rufe—to be the thief, and that they had laid a trap for him that night. Then he went into a tirade about this despicable American's betrayal of America and its Christian ideals, claiming that even our German captors would be appalled by the degeneracy of his loathsome acts. It had been decided by his group, he announced, that the miserable traitor—this "scumbag"—would run a gauntlet to pay for his contemptible un-American and un-Christian crimes. And the others seemed to concur or, like me, said nothing to oppose this grotesque judgment and punishment.

Along with a small minority I was, whatever my feelings about the enormity of the offense, horrified by the Texan's vengeful announcement.

It was cruel, barbaric, inhuman, and unworthy of people who professed to be Americans or Christians. But I was afraid and, perhaps, too confused to voice my instinctual opposition. The force and authority of this posse of vigilantes, especially the threatening demeanor of its arrogant and self-righteous leader, a virtual "Leatherstocking Nemesis," was overwhelming, and I, to my lasting shame, meekly succumbed. Orchestrated by the Texan and his followers, we American prisoners of the Nazi regime were herded out of the dining room into the narrow corridor beyond its entrance door and lined up on both its sides. The condemned man was then dragged kicking and screaming by the posse to the head of the double column. I had no intention of contributing to this barbaric form of justice, so I, inconspicuously as possible, remained at its tail end.

When everyone was in place, the Texan, who placed himself in a position to strike the first blow, raised his hand, and a grimly menacing silence ensued. Then, in a voice resonating with his vengeful justice, he said with an orotund drawl, "Brothers, our fellow American Rufe has committed the worst crime an American can commit. He not only stole our food, the precious food our bodies need to survive the ordeal of our captivity. In his despicable weakness this slimy little bastard also betrayed what's noble about Christian America to our enemy. We have to show the Germans that we're not degenerates, that he's a rotten apple in a big barrel of healthy apples. That's why we've got to make an example of him." Turning toward his frightened victim, he told Rufe that as soon as he gave the signal, the boy was to run through the gauntlet and take the punishment he rightfully deserved, adding that it might in the end save his "goddamned heathen soul." Then he raised his arm again like a starter at the gate of a dash, held it deliberately poised for a long instance, and rapidly brought it down to commence the process. But paralyzed by terror, Rufe didn't move. The Texan, who was standing on the right side of the aisle, raised his right arm, pulled it back, fist clenched, and smashed the victim full force in the face, drawing blood, then with all his force flung him forward to be pummeled similarly by the Texan's posse. Rufe fell to his knees, was shoved ahead, kicked in the butt, in his ribs, was lifted up and struck again in the face, fell, was pushed, kicked, and beaten down the long row, all the time pleading futilely for mercy, "Please don't, for Christ's sake!" By the time he had been propelled down to the end of the gauntlet line, where I and the others who had been reluctant to engage in this brutal act stood, his face was a bloody pulp, his body was limp, and he was whimpering in acute pain. There was no need to go on with the punishment. It had been executed. I was appalled, but it was an immense relief I felt. "Thank God," I thought, "for having been spared showing my open solidarity with the posse."

All this time our German guards were looking on silently at the spectacle. Were they sadistically enjoying it, a welcome break from the mind-numbing routine of guarding prisoners? Were they astonished by the in-humanity to which they were bearing witness? Were they taking pleasure in watching the ever-so-righteous Americans, who claimed they were saving the world from the barbarism of the Nazism? Had they been immu-nized to human suffering by the routinization of the violent excesses of Hitler's regime? I couldn't tell. Or rather, I was too distraught by what I had witnessed to draw a conclusion. Rufe was stealing what was priceless to us, especially those laboring in the forest. Without even that little bit of food we carried out there to sustain us through the unforeseeable fu-ture, we couldn't survive. Yet the cruel retributive punishment that was meted out to him by his fellow Americans was so clearly excessive. After all, he too was not simply hungry but starving. At a certain point wasn't it likely that all of us would have given way to the temptation to which he had succumbed? And wasn't it ironic that this form of punishment took precisely the form that, in the eyes of almost all modern Americans, their ancestors had claimed distinguished "our" civilization from the savagery of the barbarians they had vanquished at the beginning?

When the judgment of the American posse had been executed, our guards carried Rufe out into another part of the mill, presumably to take him to a hospital. That was the last we heard of him. He had come, and he had gone. Events rendered our wondering at his ultimate fate super-fluous. A week or so later the British and American air forces, en masse, firebombed Dresden.

4. In the Neighborhood of Zero

DRESDEN, FEBRUARY 13–14, 1945

Only that [materialist] historian will have the gift of fanning the spark of hope in the past who is firmly convinced that *even the dead* will not be safe from the enemy if he wins. And this enemy has not ceased to be victorious.

WALTER BENJAMIN, "On the Concept of History"

On the night of February 13 and the morning of February 14, 1945, the Allied air command undertook an air raid of Dresden, Germany, that utterly destroyed a hitherto unscathed city and killed many thousands of civilians, a huge number of refugees from the Eastern front, and British, American, and Russian prisoners of war. The number of human beings who died horrendous deaths in this less than twenty-four-hour period in a seven-year-long war has remained uncertain to this day, but the figure that has survived the many efforts by British and American official historians to downplay its literal and symbolic magnitude is in the vicinity of 100,000 to 135,000. And this horrific statistic is compounded by the kinds of death these Allied bombs rained down on this undefended and unexpecting city. The vast majority of the bombs dropped in the first and second raids, carried out by the British, were incendiaries, the result of which was a firestorm, the inordinate velocity of which brought the entire inner city down and produced massive death by incineration, suffocation, and asphyxiation to its inhabitants. The bombs in the third, unleashed by the Americans, were "ordinary" explosives, but they leveled what was still standing. As the last American bomber turned westward, Dresden, "the Florence of the Elbe," was on fire, crumbling to ashes, reduced to a wasteland populated by charred and mutilated and stinking bodies.

This singular event of World War II perpetrated by the Allied high command in London was systematically muted by the media of the "free world" and most of the histories of the war written by the victors in its aftermath in order to celebrate Western democracy—its humanity—over Western and later Eastern (Soviet) totalitarianism. Subsumed under the larger "global" story of victory against an evil that was infecting Western civilization, this terrific event was "localized," and the enormity of its calculated brutality—its terrorist goal—was, like Hiroshima and Nagaski, virtually obliterated from the West's cultural memory. The Allies justified their attack on this undefended city at the time by representing it as a strategic center for the German war effort against the Soviet Union on the Eastern front. The firebombing of Dresden, it was claimed, was intended to aid the Soviet army's defense of the homeland against the marauding German hordes in the East. Despite the fact that the Soviet army was at that time on the offensive, that rationalization, it seems, took hold and over the years since then became a historical truth. In thus viewing this singular temporal event from above—an event intensely lived by massive numbers of human beings below—these official histories enabled the forgetting of the firebombing of this defenseless city. In so doing, they tacitly put its horror out of play in the debates over later military actions undertaken by the United States in the period of the Cold War, the excessive violence of which might have been illuminated by the inhumanity of the bombing of Dresden—the mass slaughter perpetrated by Britain and the United States. I am referring, above all, to its scorched-earth policy (the use of napalm, herbicides, and other chemicals, the B-52 bombings) that killed and maimed over a million Vietnamese civilians, destroyed their land, and transformed an ancient rice culture into a population of refugees during the decade of the Vietnam War, all in the name of "saving Vietnam for the free world."

As far as I can remember, the only time in the past fifty years that bore witness to the reactivation of the firebombing of Dresden in the American (and British) cultural memory was in 1968, following the publication of the novel *Slaughterhouse-Five*, by the American author Kurt Vonnegut. Like me, Vonnegut was a member of 423rd Regiment of the 106th Division, was captured during the so-called Battle of the Bulge, was eventually assigned to a working *Kommando* in Dresden—a meat-packing slaughterhouse—and experienced the horrendous firebombing of Dresden. He was, in other words, like those of us who perished in the firestorm or miraculously "survived" it *there*—in the midst of the rain of terror. His novel, in other words, was intended to "bear witness"—in the Kierkegaardian sense of the phrase—to the firebombing. It was an autobiographical account from below the increasingly distanced gaze of the bombers of the helpless city, their commanders in the London Operations Room a couple of thousand miles away, and the official historians of this ruthlessly violent historical moment.

As a cursory look at the multitude of reminiscences of the Battle of Bulge and captivity posted on the Internet over the years by veterans of the ill-fated 106th Division testify, most, all too sadly, read their terrible experience of capture and imprisonment retrospectively, that is, in the triumphalist terms dictated by the official and popular representations of the war. The testimony of one John Kline, a member of the 106th, who was captured in the Battle of the Bulge, is utterly representative:

> The 106th Infantry Division was credited with a holding action that used much of the precious time of the German Offensive. Time was an important and vital ingredient in Hitler's plan to break through to the Meuse River and then go for Antwerp. The first three days of battle was vital and the 106th Infantry Division slowed his advance in the St. Vith area. By doing so the 106th played a large role in the final defeat of the German Army. The delay and extended battle used so much of the precious resources of the German Army that they were never again able to recoup and fight the style of war they had in earlier days. This delay in time was a big key in the final downfall of the German plans for their ARDENNES OFFENSIVE. The loss of their resources, both human and equipment, accelerated their final defeat and caused an early end to the long war in Europe.

In *Slaughterhouse-Five* Vonnegut, on the other hand, does not represent his division's disintegration in the face of the German onslaught that inaugurated the Battle of the Ardennes Forest in this ideologically warped language of heroism and victory. On the contrary, conscious of the power of official representations to mystify the minds of even those who suffered the horrors of such experiences, he emphasizes the abject defeat of the 106th. Nor does he rationalize the murderous firebombing of Dresden into a larger benign scenario: a prelude to the victory of the Allies in the European theater of operations. In the novel the bombing of Dresden culminates in unspeakable carnage, and its perpetration has all the characteristics of an act of terror. But when I read the novel at the time of its publication, I was, despite my anticipation, deeply disappointed. I felt there was something drastically missing in his representation—something essential in the event muffled by a narrative that was trying desperately to evoke this horrific essence by indirection or mediation.

Narrated by Vonnegut, the novel represents this cataclysmic event from the delayed fictive perspective of a young, rather nondescript soldier from a typical middle-class American town (Ilium, that is, Troy) in upstate New York, one Billy Pilgrim. Having returned after the war to his home, married the daughter of a wealthy optometrist, and become a well-to-do and prominent optometrist himself, a president of the local Lion's Club, he suddenly, in the 1960s, with the Vietnam War raging, undergoes a mental collapse. It takes the form of his remembering the experience of being captured in what came to be called the Battle of the Bulge and of the firebombing of Dresden in the tragicomic context of hallucinating a relationship with a people from outer space, the Tralfamadorians. At the time I understood and sympathized with my fellow survivor's motive for choosing this mode of indirection to represent a terrible moment of history that was unrepresentable:

> I nodded [to the narrator's interlocutor, the wife of one of his veteran buddies] that this was true. We had been foolish virgins in the war, right at the end of childhood.
>
> "But you're not going to write it that way, are you." This wasn't a question. It was an accusation.

"I—I don't know," I said.

"Well, I know," she said. "You'll pretend you were men instead of babies, and you'll be played in the movies by Frank Sinatra and John Wayne or some of those other glamorous, war-loving, dirty old men. And war will look just wonderful, so we'll have a lot more of them. And they'll be fought by babies like the babies upstairs."

So then I understood. It was war that made her so angry. She didn't want her babies or anybody else's babies killed in wars. And she thought wars were partly encouraged by books and movies.

So I held up my right hand and I made her a promise: "Mary," I said, "I don't think this book of mine is ever going to be finished. I must have written five thousand pages by now, and thrown them all away. If I ever do finish it, though, I give you my word of honor: there won't be a part for Frank Sinatra or John Wayne.

"I tell you what," I said, "I'll call it 'The Children's Crusade.'"

She was my friend after that.

For years I willfully avoided talking about my experience in Dresden. When my parents or brothers and sister or friends asked me to tell them about what had happened to me, I would invariably ward them off by saying in one way or another that "it was no big deal." I would not indulge them with war stories, nor could I face the awful task of telling the truth. I forced myself to forget that dreadful time, though that time always, sometimes ferociously, returned at night to haunt my sleep.

By the time of the publication of Vonnegut's novel—twenty years or so later—I, like him, no doubt, had come to terms with the great modern Jewish-German thinker Theodor Adorno's famous comment, echoing Walter Benjamin, on Auschwitz: "Cultural criticism finds itself faced with the final stage of the dialectic of culture and barbarism. To write poetry after Auschwitz is barbaric. And this corrodes even the knowledge of why it has become impossible to write poetry today." Nevertheless, Vonnegut's fictional representation, I couldn't help feeling, was incommensurable not only with my memory of that ghastly historical event but also, and above all, with my disconcerted sense of its global ethical significance. Despite my appreciation of his courage in retrieving this by now officially airbrushed human calamity, I felt, in fact, especially in the context of the shamefulness of the United States's intervention and conduct of the Vietnam War—not least, the obscene banality of the "body count"—that he somehow had trivialized its horror in the very process of attempting to bear witness to it. In locating the tragicomic plight of the hapless American Billy Pilgrim within the framework of a blackhumorous satire of small town, middle-class American life, seen from the wiser and wider perspective of a species from outer space, and in focusing on the impact of the firebombing on the young American innocents who were sucked into its undiscriminating vortex—a focus epitomized by the first part of the book's subtitle, "Or the Children's Crusade"—Vonnegut's mediated account left something fundamental and obvious about the event unsaid.

This unsaid part, I felt, was the irresistible reality that the firebombing of Dresden had been a calculated act of terror perpetrated by the Allies on an utterly unsuspecting and defenseless population of civilians. But even this way of putting it, for all its demystifying resonance, is inadequate because it is also contaminated by the abstract jargon commanded by the victors. The victims were living human beings—babies, children, women, men, young, old, mothers, fathers—most of whom happened to be on the "side" of the losers. In other words, I felt at the time, despite my better judgment (and certain principles of my "postmodern" intellectual perspective), that Vonnegut would have come closer to revealing the unspeakable truth of the history he wanted to bear witness to—the concealed history that began with the destruction of the 106th Division and culminated in the firebombing of Dresden—by pushing his representational art to its limits, that is, by failing to re-present this event's horrific singular reality.

All of the above is, of course, retrospective, the inevitable generalizations of one who, by the time he read *Slaughterhouse-Five*, had learned in some degree how to read history: the disjunctions between actual events and the way they are represented by the victors. In reality I had no idea that the bombing had occurred on February 13–14, Shrove Tuesday and

Ash Wednesday. I knew it was happening sometime in the winter because I was excruciatingly cold. I did not know that there were a great number of prisoners of war and refugees from the Eastern front in the city. I did not know how many died and were mutilated during the bombing. I knew nothing about the city's strategic value, though we had been told that it was an "open city" and from the looks of it on passing through to Rabenau surmised that it was neither a military garrison nor an operational center. I had no idea about the Allies' justification for the bombing of this beautiful and venerable city. I was *inter esse*, I would now put it: interested in the sense of being below—in the midst—ignorant of the workings of the world above that was making the decisions but now, more than ever in my life, acutely conscious of the reality that these decisions were affecting me—my body and soul—and all of the others who were in the midst of this horrendous storm.

Our *Arbeitskommando* had returned from another blustery day in the forest about an hour or so earlier, cold, exhausted, and excruciatingly hungry as usual but relieved to be "home," inside the sheltering walls of our prison house. It was around eight in the evening. We had eaten the slice of bread and bland turnip soup that was our daily fare and were gathered around the cast-iron barrel stove to absorb its heat. It was dark outside, but the night was relatively clear, the light of the moon revealing then concealing itself as the moving clouds passed slowly across its pale spotted face. I was sitting at the table in the mess room where I usually sat, as close to the stove as possible. I had taken my disintegrating shoes off to let the wet, cracked, and peeling skin of my bloated and corroding feet get some air.

Immediately in front of the stove sat the burly, mustached Texan who had organized the pogrom against Rufe. He was stirring the wet tea leaves that would become his next cigarette and, in his usual fashion, haranguing his buddies, on this occasion, which had been precipitated by the alleged theft of some of the tea leaves, about the un-Americanism of those "suckers" who violated the sacred laws of private property. As I sat there enjoying the comforting warmth of the stove and despite my awareness of the deadly, inexorable cyclical movement of our lives as prisoners, anticipating the temporary relief of the sleep that would obliterate the Texan and everything he stood for from my consciousness, I became vaguely aware of an unusual sound outside, a faint rumbling of some sort. At first I attributed it to a distant convoy of trucks, perhaps transporting soldiers or supplies to the Eastern front, which was not all that far from Dresden. It did not occur to me, so used to the idea were we, that the city was not a military target, that the rumbling might be the precursory signal of an Allied bombing raid. I returned from my momentary deflection to the Texan, who was now rolling the dried tea leaves into a cigarette.

He was informing his captive audience that the reason the 106th Division had surrendered so easily to the Germans was that its commanders had had to rely on too many foreigners from the North, those cowardly hybrids, mostly from southern Europe, who had come to the United States late as parasitical immigrants and so didn't feel the way "we" did about the American way of life—"we, who come from an older and purer Southern stock." I had heard this kind of vulgar diatribe before, though never in such an ironically revelatory context. The Texan's arrogance engaged my consciousness enough to drown out the distant rumbling. But when, no more than a minute later, the rumbling had become a louder drone coming from the sky, not the earth, it was impossible to mistake its source. We realized that the drone was coming from a large fleet of airplanes drawing near.

The Texan's harangue stopped in mid-sentence, and we sat silently waiting, hoping in the sudden stillness of the night that whatever was coming near would pass over us like Herod's hatchet men. Then all at once the sky lit up with search beams and flares crossing each other in seemingly delirious kaleidoscopic patterns, the night filled with the raucous screams of air-raid sirens and the sporadic barking of antiaircraft fire. Immediately afterward, the bombs began to fall, scream, explode, and the skyline of the city burst into red and yellow and orange flames.

Our guards, caught by surprise like us, came rushing into the room in various degrees of undress and, hysterically shouting obscenities, herded us at gunpoint down into the basement of the mill, the storehouse of the huge barrels of sauerkraut that was the daily fare of the German civilians who maintained the building and the grounds. In this utter darkness reeking with the smell of pickled cabbage, we sat out the infinite and horrendous time of the bombing, hoping desperately that it would end. We could see nothing, not even each other's faces; we could only hear the seemingly endless explosions and feel the old building above us shake precariously after each blast. Once again, I sat huddled in a fetal position, now under one of the barrels of sauerkraut, waiting breathlessly and anticipating the explosion that would blow us into oblivion.

The bombers kept coming, wave after wave after wave, relentlessly, their lethal bombs exploding in intervals and symmetrical rippling diminuendo patterns: what seemed to me, bizarrely, an infernal fugue orchestrated by a demonic presence hovering over the burning world, indifferent to sides, identities, differences:

Ba-doom, ba-doom, ba-boom, ba-doom, ba-doom, ba-doom
Ba-doom, ba-doom, ba-doom, ba-doom, ba-doom, ba-doom

Then:

Doom-ba, doom-ba, doom-ba, doom-ba, doom-ba, doom-ba
Doom-ba, doom-ba, doom-ba, doom-ba, doom-ba, doom-ba

At first I felt nothing but confused fright. The darkness, the unceasing roar of the invisible aircraft above, the inescapable din in the near distance, the shuddering building—all signaled my and my fellow prisoners' imminent violent deaths. It did not matter to me that these were "our" bombers, that they were penetrating deeply into the German interior, harbingers perhaps of the end of the war and victory over barbarism. They were, in this vulnerable suffocating space, inhuman killers, some kind of primal force turning the whole world upside down, as in the song that English girl had sung to me one night ages ago in Cheltenham. I put my forefingers in my ears to muffle this turbulent music, but its cruel cadence persisted in the ordered tremors of the cement floor I was sitting on. So did the felt thoughts this harmonious cacophony had triggered.

The bombing continued unabatedly. Under this pulverizing and death-dealing bombardment, my one desperate hope was that the mill would be spared because Rabenau was located in the outskirts of the city. Acutely attuned to the degree of the tremors precipitated by the explosions outside, I realized at a certain point, despite the incessant drone of the squadrons of bombers passing directly overhead, that the bombing was focused on the heart of the city. I could tell that bombs were falling in the precincts of the mill, but they seemed to be strays. Rabenau, I surmised with a certain degree of relief, was not a target. With this awareness that the vast majority of bombs were falling elsewhere, I began to feel that we might survive, and the suffocating image, coiled tightly around my mind, of being imminently buried alive in rubble, began to unwind.

Feeling less vulnerable, I then closed my blind eyes and tried to imagine what was happening in the heart of the undefended city under this tremendous and seemingly unending ferocious barrage of bombs, the devastation, the fate of its unsuspecting inhabitants. How many of the untold number of people living in Dresden had been going routinely about the process of living an ordinary winter evening when the bombing began, caught in train stations, trams, movie houses, theaters, dance halls, bars, churches, on an evening stroll, or returning from a visit with friends? Had there been time to find shelter from the relentless explosions of the falling bombs? Did the apartment houses in which the citizens of Dresden lived have air-raid shelters? Was there an adequate municipal home defense system like that I had seen on newsreels operating during the bombing of London by the German Luftwaffe? And what about all the prisoners of war in the city? My mind's eye envisaged the horror all of those people were suffering—though my vision of the carnage visited on the city by the bombers, it turned out later, was not even remotely close to the gruesome reality—and I tried to rationalize their vulnerability, the pain of their flesh and the suffering of their hearts and minds.

The people of Dresden were, after all, citizens of a nation led by a megalomaniac and a fanatic racist that had wreaked unspeakable havoc on the lives of millions of other human beings without moral constraint, not only combatants but also innocent civilians of neighboring nations and of racial minorities: systematic death in the gas chambers, mass executions, torture, mutilation, uprooting, starvation, forced labor, all in the name of the Aryan German race. Furthermore, this ferocious bombing of a German city so close to the Eastern front seemed now, in the wake of my feeling of reprieve, like a prophecy of victory and the annunciation of our freedom from captivity. But as much as I tried to impose this blame and this future on "them," the name wouldn't stick. Something inside me resisted my will to explain the horror, to blame its victims. The earlier image that had projected the bombers high above the city as killers, the murderous pawn of an inscrutable infernal presence, prevailed.

Painfully conscious that the many thousands of innocent people in the center of the city had been caught unaware, I couldn't help now, as the bombing continued relentlessly and with utter impunity, but imagine sudden, rampant, indiscriminate, violent carnage.

Ba-doom, ba-doom, ba-doom, ba-doom, ba-doom, ba-doom
Ba-doom, ba-doom, ba-doom, ba-doom, ba-doom, ba-doom

Nor could I repress the stirrings of guilt that it was *my* side—the defender of civilization—that was unleashing barbarism from long distance, or as I would put it now, from this new, highly abstract, and dehumanized technological vantage point. Caught and tossed in this emotional turmoil, like a broken branch of a tree in the turbulent winds of a hurricane, I waited desperately, as I had seemingly ages ago in the freight yard in Limburg, for the bombing to end. I ached to be relieved of the double but inseparably singular torture those bombers high overhead were inflicting on me, the dread of being buried alive or dismembered, and the acute moral confusion set on fire by my proximity to, indeed my sense of oneness with, the German citizens who were the ostensible targets of the Allied bombers. I remember at a certain point during that long ordeal someone striking a match—it must have been one of the German guards attempting to light a cigarette—the sudden flare of which, like a lightning flash careening in an instant across the sky—momentarily illuminating the cellar we inhabited. It was not the assuring image of my fellow human beings I saw in the lurid light of that instant, not the faces of those, condemned to the underworld, who would be redeemed by a hero wielding a golden bough as I had read in my childhood. It was, rather, as in the freight cars that had borne us across Germany into its depth, the spectral ghosts of an unredeemable infernal world, where light served the inscrutable powers of darkness.

When it had come to seem to my now time-warped mind that the bombing would continue forever, the bombs, as suddenly as they had started, stopped falling, and the building stopped shaking. The last Allied bomber, it seemed, had dropped its lethal load and turned west for its nine- or ten-hour return flight. A welcomed, if extremely tense, silence ensued. We heard no sirens, near and far, screaming out the all-clear signal. But after a few breathless minutes in the expectant silent dark it became clear that the horrific raid was over. It was around 10:30, shockingly less than an hour after the first bombs had begun exploding. We—Americans and Germans, prisoners and guards, friends and enemies—were all alive! We, all of us, had survived the carnage of what we surmised was an unusually heavy bombing raid. Even our relieved Volkssturm guards, in the immediate interim between the termination of the bombing and the return to the upper floors of the mill, were more friendly and solicitous, or so it seemed in the glow of renewed life after the certainty of death.

But this euphoria did not last long. Led by two guards carrying flashlights—the electric system had been destroyed during the bombing—we mounted in single file the two flights of steep stairs leading out of the cellar to the floor of our quarters. Upon arriving, we were stunned by what we encountered. The air in the room was extremely hot and so heavy and acrid with the smell of smoke we could barely breathe. And outside, through the few barred windows, we saw to our utter dismay that the whole city, as far as our eyes could see, was on fire, the flames, like innumerable forked tongues licking the night sky, shooting numerous streams of scattered fire high into the night, the chain of lurid light across the distant horizon, flickering tumultuously like an army of crazed satanic dancers celebrating the triumph of the god of hell. And a turbulent cloud of black smoke, heavy with debris and flashing intermittently—red, green, orange, white—hung like an agitated pall directly above the burning city. Even from this distance, the awesome spectacle being played out, silently to us, on the other side of the windows before our astonished eyes, was beyond the grasp of my imagination. I remember shivering uncontrollably in the face of this unnameable event. What I saw out there—its fury—just didn't belong in the domain of the human. And then I remembered that there were hundreds of thousands of people caught unaware in that gigantic and turbulent incinerator.

After a while our old guards, now enraged at what our airborne comrades had done to their undefended city—it was the venerable old Dresden, the *Altstadt* they called it, that apparently had been the senseless target of the bombers—ordered us away from the windows, all the while hurling abuses at us and threatening to take revenge as if we had unleashed the destructive angel that had descended savagely on Dresden. We were swinish barbarians, scum of the earth, cowardly apes, mindless murderers. At a certain moment during this verbal attack one of them, the mildest heretofore, raising his rifle and pointing its muzzle toward one of us—it may have been the Texan—shouted to his comrades that we all be taken down to the courtyard and executed for our crimes against humanity. This outburst was followed by a long uncertain silence. During that interval I tried desperately in my mind to disassociate myself from the perpetrators of the maelstrom. "It wasn't me, for Christ's sake, who did this! It was . . . it was . . . it was . . ." But I couldn't finish the thought. I was horrified by the irrational logic of the old man, but given the firestorm raging out there in the heart of city, what would I have concluded had I been him? I realized in my despairing turmoil that it was quite likely that the other guards would agree with him. The tense silence was broken when, fortunately, one of them reminded the agitated old man that such an action, however justified, was beyond their jurisdiction, and we were reprieved.

Ordering us to return to our usual evening pastime, the guards eagerly left the room, presumably to learn more about the consequences of the bombing and, perhaps, to receive instructions from a higher authority. A few minutes later we heard numerous voices, some angry, some frenzied, some excited, some wailing, emanating confusedly from the courtyard below. They were no doubt the voices of German civilians from the neighborhood who had had more immediate contact with the horrendous events outside, lamenting the catastrophe, mourning the dead, cursing the British air force, which had perpetrated the raid using primarily incendiary bombs, and informing our guards what they knew about the nature of the massive air raid, the extent of the damage, and the number of casualties.

We Americans, on the other hand, were not as unified as the Germans down below in the courtyard. Most of my fellow prisoners were elated. They had not only survived the bombing. They were also interpreting the air raid—so far into the interior of Germany and so clearly devastating—as proof of the rejuvenation of the Allies' war machine after the catastrophe in December, which had been underscored by our captors all through the next months, and, more tellingly, as testimony of the will of the Allies to bring the war to a victorious end.

"Hang in there, old buddies," our self-appointed leader, the Texan, drawled, "that firestorm out there should warm the cockles of your frozen butts. Those Krauts got what was coming to them. It won't be long now before the U.S. Army comes in to kick German ass. Let's just hope that our guys get here before the fucking Russkis. Burn, baby, burn, burn, burn, burn!"

A few of us, however, were not so gloating. One of my friends in the working command, a frail and emaciated fellow with whom I often teamed up in the agonizing process of hauling logs in the forest—a Midwesterner from a Chicago suburb who was about my age—protested. "Maybe I'm out of line about this, but I've got to say, Tex, that you're sounding like a heartless bastard. Yeah, I want the war to end too, to go home. Believe me, I'm sick to fucking death of this eternal waiting in this godawful limbo. But shit, man, those are real human beings burning alive out there!" And I, caught up in his agonized outrage, added, "Yeah, God damn it, they're civilians—mothers and fathers, children, babies—not soldiers. And Dresden, for Christ's sake, we all should know by now it's an open city, a hospital city, an undefended city. Sure, the Germans have been using us, against the Geneva Conventions, for their war effort. But do you think that justifies what's happening out there? . . . That killing fire? And our bombers up in the sky, safe and sound . . . and those help-less people down below, they weren't even warned to take shelter. Jesus, man, it's not all that simple . . . We—"

As I was groping stumblingly for a language that was beyond my grasp—searching futilely into the recesses of my mind for words adequate to the horror being enacted under the horizon of turbulent fire raging before our eyes, words circulating around the act of thinking—Tex, raising his clenched fist, seemingly with the Word in it, angrily interrupted: "You fucking Greaseball traitor! Who the fuck do you think you are talking about our cause in that degrading way?" Turning to his friends, he added with scorn: "That's what's gone wrong in the U.S. of A., old buddies. Our biggest mistake was to let crud of his ilk—fucking cowards, fucking un-grateful, dark-skinned bastards—into our country. If it was up to me—" Suddenly, as Tex's coarse diatribe began taking on a voluminous and tur-bulent rage—and I was imagining running another one of his gauntlets—we heard the roar of aircraft overhead. A moment later—it was around 1:30 in the morning—we saw green and then red flares light up the sky. And then bombs, massive numbers of them, began to fall on the fatally wounded city again.

This time, for a brief but grotesque few minutes, we had a view of what was happening in that dreadful interior. The bombers, wave after wave after wave—they were British Lancasters, maybe close to a thousand of them—were coming in for their bombing runs at an astoundingly low altitude, a sign of their virtual immunity. There seemed to be no German fighter planes to resist the attackers nor any substantial antiaircraft fire. The sky was lit up in multicolored turbulent patterns by flares released by the bombers. And the bombs they were dropping were mostly incen-diaries, some timed to explode above the buildings, others exploding on impact. It was unbelievable—a madman's hallucination in which all the reference points were vanishing. Everything that was familiar to us, ev-erything human, was being transformed into something unnameable, grotesquely bestial. The city out there was like the world of a painting by one Hieronymus Bosch I had seen and was captivated and appalled by in an art book when I was in high school.

Ca-boom, ca-boom, ca-boom, ca-boom, ca-boom
Ca-boom, ca-boom, ca-boom, ca-boom, ca-boom

And then, as I was watching this surreal spectacle in entranced horror, it occurred to me that the survivors of the first raid—those who had had time to find shelter—were now, thinking the bombing had ended, back in the shattered streets of the burning city, salvaging the remains of their worldly possessions or assisting the fire brigades in the task of dampening the unholy conflagration. "How could this be happening?" I thought. "Who was responsible for this destruction, this mass murder? What race of demons could be so utterly inhuman, so careless, so mindless, so indifferent to the pain, the suffering, the death, of innocent living beings, to be able to unleash this kind of annihilating violence I'm witnessing?" And then I thought, "This carnage isn't being perpetrated by demons but by human beings, in fact, by human beings who claim to have achieved the heights of civilization." A shudder ran through my body. They were *my* people.

Returning to the prisoners' quarters after the second attack began, our guards herded us back down into the cellar of the sawmill, now extremely hot and smelling heavily of sweat and sauerkraut, where we waited for what a headquarters commander would call "the show" to end. The same clamorous silence, the same shaking of the building, the same anticipation of a direct hit, the same terror, the same paucity of words . . . And again, up there, down here; height, depth; distance, proximity: the image of that bizarre moment in Herman Melville's *Moby-Dick* when Father Mapple, having climbed up into his pulpit and dragged the rope ladder into it, "was deposited within, leaving him impregnable in his little Quebec," and from that commanding height haranguing with lunatic rationality his congregation of errant sailors—"mariners, renegades, and castaways"—down below:

> But oh! shipmates on the starboard hand of every woe, there is a sure delight; and higher the top of the delight, than the bottom of the woe is deep. Is not the main-truck higher than the kelson is low? Delight is to him—a far, far upward, and inward delight—who against the proud gods and

commodores of this earth, ever stands forth his own inexorable self. Delight is to him whose strong arms yet support him, when the ship of this base treacherous world has gone down beneath him. Delight is to him who gives no quarter in the truth, and kills, burns, and destroys all sin though he pluck it out from under the robes of Senators and Judges. Delight—top-gallant delight is to him who acknowledges no law or lord, but the Lord his God, and is only a patriot to heaven. Delight is to him, whom all the waves and billows of the seas of the boisterous mob can never shake from this sure Keel of the Ages. And eternal delight and deliciousness will be his, who coming to lay him down, can say with his final breath—O Father—chiefly known to me by Thy rod—mortal or immortal, here I die, I have striven to be Thine, more than to be this world's, or mine own. Yet this is nothing; I leave eternity to Thee; for what is man that he should live out the lifetime of his God?

"What about us bastards down here?" I screamed in my mind to the bombers passing overhead, sullenly defiant, roaring, relentless—and utterly immune—like pterodactyls dropping their loads from their anuses. For that's what we down here were in: a world of shit. Under this interminable and ferocious barrage I couldn't discriminate between its victims.

Many years later, still haunted by that appalling moment during that second incendiary raid on Dresden and struggling intermittently to articulate in words the feeling its furor precipitated, I found the image I had been searching for all those years that would "tell" my story far more truthfully than all the words I had been able to muster in the aftermath. It was in the 1960s, the Vietnam War was escalating, and I was teaching at the State University of New York at Binghamton. It came to me out of nowhere, unsolicited, as a black epiphany. I was at that time, or so I thought, as far in time and mind from World War II, the firebombing of Dresden, and that particular dread-provoking moment as I could be. I was teaching a course on existential literature—the novels and plays of Jean-Paul Sartre, Albert Camus, Simone de Beauvoir, Friedrich Dürrenmatt, Eugène Ionesco, Samuel Beckett—and trying to think aloud what Sartre meant by what seemed to me to be his reversal of the traditional

Western philosophical notion that "essence precedes existence" to read "existence precedes essence." As I pondered that epochal metamorphosis, it occurred to me that "essence" is an other-worldly principle that will devastate any existent thing that refuses to conform to its ordering mandate: above/below. Suddenly I remembered that fiery night in Dresden and, by an uncanny association, a moment a few years later, when, in college, I was reading a book by Søren Kierkegaard, the great Christian existentialist Dane who, against Hegel and his dialectical theory of universal history, spoke on behalf of the people down below. It was an episode in that book in which Kierkegaard recalls a scene from his childhood. In it Søren, like Isaac trailing the patriarch Abraham, is trying to keep up with his austere and tempestuous father, who, on an unannounced errand, ferociously presses forward against a strong bitingly resistant mountain wind through the high scrub of a desolate Danish moor. All at once the father stops, raises his clenched fist, and to the astonishment of the boy, starts shaking it fiercely against the all-encompassing turbulent sky.

The bombers kept coming, and the explosions intensified. Unlike the first raid, during which the explosions generated something like an infernal contrapuntal music, this one, from the beginning and for reasons I couldn't fathom, was devoid of pattern and precipitated a sheer maleficent cacophony. As I sat in a corner of the cellar curled up in my fetal position and raging at that indifferent—or was it sadistic?—world above, a number of explosions nearby rocked our building so violently that I was certain it was going to collapse on top of us. There was utter silence in the expectant room. My heart was pounding hard and as erratically as the detonations outside:

Ca-boom, ca-boom, boom, boom, boom, ca-boom, ca-boom
Boom, ca-boom, ca-boom, boom, boom, ca-boom, boom, ca-boom
boom

I felt warm wetness flowing down my thighs. My life, I was sure, was about to come to its violent and invisible end. I tried to make my peace with the God I had more or less abandoned long before but couldn't address him by name, not, however, without remembering what my mother had often said to me when I had committed an act she thought was damnable: "It's all right, Vasili, I will bear your sin before God's eyes: *ta matia tou Theou.*" But the mill, miraculously it seemed, held together, and the sound of explosions receded.

Eventually—it seemed, as in the first raid that night, like an eternity—there was silence. The British bombers had, we thought, finished the job of destroying the city and were now returning to their home bases in distant England, where they would be greeted by their superiors with triumphant enthusiasm: "Good show, mates, bloody good show!" It was around 2:00 a.m., unbelievably less than a half-hour after the beginning of the assault. We down here, under the swirling pall of fire, debris, and smoke I imagined outside—I mean those of us in the mill and on the fringes of the attack—had once again survived. Most of my American comrades seemed elated, not simply at having come through unscathed but, as before, over the thought that the bombing meant the imminent end of the war. Some, however, seemed less assured of the morality of the bombing than they had after the first raid. Be that as it may, as for me, I was stunned. I was still alive but so wiped out, so drained of spirit, that being alive didn't seem to matter all that much anymore. I felt inanimate, empty of the quick of life, as if I existed in a dead present devoid of a future.

After the second bombing had terminated and the roar of the last Lancaster had faded away—as in the case of the earlier one, I don't remember hearing all-clear sirens—our guards led us back to our quarters, where, in the agitated lurid multicolored light cast by the blazing city, we underwent the same kind of abuse and the same threats they had inflicted on us after the first raid. But the catastrophic situation was uppermost in their minds. They seemed to have lost contact with the authorities and were uncertain about how to proceed. There was no question at that time of night and under those conditions of imposing on us the usual routine. They were far more interested in the damage inflicted by the bombs that had fallen in the immediate vicinity of the factory and learning about what was happening in the center of the city. Eventually they ordered us down into the courtyard to stand ready to help rescue work should that prove necessary. Despite the winter night, it was extremely hot and strangely turbulent, as if we were on the edge of a tropical storm. We spent the rest of the night and part of the next morning searching for bodies in the unbearably hot smoking rubble of a few apartment buildings in the vicinity of the mill that had been destroyed by stray bombs. Fortunately we found none. It was the consensus of our guards that the people in the neighborhood had evacuated the buildings in time to escape.

Shortly after dawn and under the volatile shadow of an immensely turbulent smoke-filled sky—it was Ash Wednesday, around 10:30 in the morning—we returned to the sawmill, where we were told to await further orders. I was physically and emotionally exhausted. My mind was like the sky in T. S. Eliot's poem, a "patient etherized upon a table." All I can remember about that interim is my sense of being in a living hell yet curiously glad that I wasn't dead. Somewhere in the deepest recesses of my numbed mind, I felt a relief from the tumultuous anticipation of immediate annihilation. It was over. It was over. What earthly good would another assault on the city do the Allies? We could now return to dying slowly.

Then as suddenly as before—it was around noon—and without the warning of the air-raid sirens, the roar of aircraft overhead once more, low in the sky, confident of their immunity coming in to finish off the city that had been finished off during the second raid the night before. We looked out the barred windows and saw a vast armada of American B-17 bombers—Flying Fortresses, in the vulgar vernacular of the American military command—maybe a thousand or more, accompanied by an escort of hundreds of P-51 fighter planes. And in utter disbelief, though not with the same attitude, we Americans watched another bombing of the already devastated city—massive, violent, relentless, pulverizing—recommence.

CA-BOOM, CA-BOOM, CA-BOOM, CA-BOOM, CA-BOOM
Ca-boom, ca-boom, ca-boom
Ca-BOOM
Ca-boom
CA-boom, ca-boom
Ca-boom, CA-BOOM CA-BOOM, ca-boom

This time the bombs that rained down on the mutilated body of the dying, if not already dead, city were not incendiaries; they were high-tonnage explosives, each of which, it seemed, pulverized an already destroyed whole city block on impact. As I watched this spectacle of immense destructive power in astonishment, I couldn't help remembering with grim irony the response of my father, always in awe, despite his otherwise critical consciousness, of the achievements of a godless humanity, by which he really meant God-driven American man, to a streamline locomotive engine in motion, a passenger airplane in flight thousands of feet above, a suspension bridge over a wide river, the speaking image emanating from a television tube, or even a jackhammer breaking up a cement sidewalk. On such occasions he would exclaim in wonder, ostensibly to me but really to himself—it was invariably in his native Greek; his English was inadequate to the task of expressing his feelings about such amazing things—"Adhes, Vasili! Adhes ti efkiaksan oi keratadhes!" ("Look, Billy! Look what those horned ones have made!") At a much later time I would call my father's response to the sort of powerful and awe-provoking machinery that instigated it the "technological sublime." And I would understand my own astonishment at the chaos of sight and sound produced by the men, machines, weapons—and frame of mind—overhead, that dreadful spectacle before my eyes that my imagination couldn't contain, to say nothing about process, as the mad fulfillment of its logic.

Once again our guards drove us away from the windows and down into the cellar to wait out the bombing. Once again the same intense heat, the same ground shaking, the same din of silence, the same seeming annihilation of time, the same expectation of instant death, the same terror—and the same absence of language, the same bitter sense that, in the omniscient eyes of those up there releasing their lethal weapons of massive destruction over our heads, we, all of us, down there under their furious gaze were invisible: nonbeings, nothings, nobodies. The only difference between this raid and the earlier ones to me was that I couldn't rationalize the perpetrators, couldn't blame the British for the immense violence out there. These were Americans, *my* people indeed:

I know what you'd say to me, if somehow I got you to see me. You'd tell me, in that obscenely corrupt language of yours, about the "Big Picture": "Keep your eyes on the Big Picture, young man. When you see what's happening in terms of that Big Picture, you'll understand." But I don't give a good fuck about your Big Picture. How do you see the Big Picture? Who sees the Big Picture? Where do you have to be to see the Big Picture? What I'm seeing—from down here—is not a picture; it's fire and destruction and chaos and death. Mass murder. My eyes are scorched. I can't ... I don't want to see the Big Picture. Stick the Big Picture up your ass.

As before, this third attack on the city by the American air force seemed as if it would go on forever—wave after wave, the increasing drone, seemingly unending. But in fact, it ended about a half-hour after the first blockbusters began to explode on the helpless city. And once again, miraculously, we had survived, at least bodily. We remained in the hot and fetid cellar of the sawmill for a couple more long hours, and then, when our guards were certain the raid was over, we returned to our quarters again, only to encounter a daylight dimmed to near darkness by the thick and turbulent cloud of black smoke and debris that hung over the city and to breathe the acrid air of a fatally wounded and contaminated world.

I can no longer recall what happened during the next few days. What I do remember is that my mind and body were enervated by the horrific violence and that I really didn't care, in my torpid state, whether I had survived or not. I tried desperately to imagine that the war was drawing to a close, that our rescue from captivity was imminent. I tried to think of a coming reunion with my mother and father, my sister and brothers, Kathryn, my Sunapee Street friends, but the acrid stench of destruction and death intervened. A radical change had occurred in the way I looked at the world. It was the same world I had always seen, but now it was somehow fearfully different. The familiar had becomes unfamiliar, the ordinary extraordinary, the normal estranged. I was *dislocated*. The guiding points of reference had suddenly disintegrated, and, awaking, I found myself, like Dante in the beginning of the *Inferno*, lost in a wilderness of pain:

Midway in our life's journey, I went astray
From the right road and woke to find myself
Alone in a dark woods.

But there was no Virgil to guide me toward the light, indeed, no light. Instead, I now saw what was always there before my eyes but invisible to them. I saw the skull beneath the skin, the nothingness that pulsed beneath every something. This world we inhabited was now a living hell, we were the ghostly damned, and there seemed to be no exist.

This was something like the state of mind I was in, when, on the third or fourth day after the firebombing of Dresden, our guards assigned me along with several other prisoners to a working *Kommando* intended to assist in the massive cleanup of the destroyed but still burning city. What I encountered in its smoldering rubble was unspeakable—so absolutely terrible that it left me literally speechless. No words at my command could name that horror. "It" was an event the singularity of which shattered the last vestige of my complacent conditioned notion that words were at my "command" for the purpose of "commanding" events.

It was then—during those few mind-shattering days in the abyssal heart of the darkness of what was once a city of light—"the Florence of the Elbe"—that I realized with utter finality, however intuitively, something that became forever afterward a constant of my waking life: that language was not a transparent instrument, as I had been led to believe by the culture I grew up in, particularly the media and the schools. It was not simply a matter of learning with the shock of recognition that there was no relationship between words and the things or events they would represent, that words were utterly inadequate to the "reality" to which they were supposed to refer. In the abominable, all-encompassing shatter of that devastated city, I couldn't escape feeling that words were also a means of deception. At best words served in some insidiously seductive way to give comfort in the face of, to provide the means of escape from, the terror of the unnameability of our being in the world: "a pillow for our heads," as I was to learn not too much later in reading Samuel Beckett's great novel *Watt*, which conveys this terrific dread aroused by the encounter with the nothingness of being in the logorrhea of the absurd: "Looking at a pot, for example, or thinking of a pot, at one of Mr. Knott's pots, of one of Mr. Knott's pots, it was in vain that Watt said, Pot, pot. Well perhaps not quite in vain, but very nearly. For it was not a pot, the more he looked, the more he reflected, the more he felt sure of that, that it was not a pot at all. It resembled a pot, it was almost a pot, but it was not a pot of which one could say, Pot, pot, and be comforted." At worst words were a masquerade, a surreptitious inscription on our innocent minds of a system of values, an ideology—a "Big Picture"—by an elite that made us the willing agents of the power of its makers. During those dreadful days, in short, I came to realize that I no longer knew what was real. The familiar terrain into which our world's language had mapped the phenomena of being had irrevocably changed.

On that third or fourth day after the bombing, the eight or nine of us who had been randomly picked for the job were marshaled into the saw-mill courtyard by our guards and told that we were to proceed into the heart of Dresden to search the ruins for the bodies of the victims of the Allies' destruction of their undefended city. We were told that the *Alt-stadt*, the old inner city we had passed through on our arrival in Dresden over an eternal month before, had been utterly destroyed, that thousands upon thousands of civilians had died horrendous deaths during the raids—incinerated in the firestorm, blown apart by bombs, buried alive in the rubble, asphyxiated in their cellars and shelters by carbon monoxide—that the survivors, though in shock, were ready to stand by the Führer and the Fatherland against the marauders and murderers who had perpetrated this savage act, and that if any of them attacked us, we would not be protected. Then we were marched off toward the old city on the other side of the Elbe River.

At that time I was too preoccupied with the immediate unknown to pay any attention to what I and my companions looked like to any of the German civilians who stopped to gaze at us as we shuffled, forlorn and silent, down the right side of the road, two abreast, toward the bridge and the shattered city. But I was extremely conscious of being *looked at* and of feeling the knifelike gaze of those eyes down into the marrow of my now visible bones. On the one hand, we must have appeared, in our emaciated physical state, our faltering and uncoordinated motion and motley dress, to some of these survivors, those who were sufficiently distant from the devastation, as ghostly apparitions or members of a species from another planet, the appropriate denizens of the charred infernal city overhung by a thick brownish gray pall of smoke. On the other hand, we must have seemed to others, those survivors who had been in the midst of the firebombing, to be the real—the satanic—avatars of the seemingly civilized human species that had unleashed the infernal conflagration that had consumed their innocent children, wives, husbands, and neighbors.

A half-hour after leaving the factory, we arrived at the bridge on the Elbe (I can't remember its name, if I ever did know it) that we had crossed from the opposite direction a month or so before. We had passed bombed and burned-out areas on the way in, but the panorama that lay before us across the river was unbelievably horrific. There was no building of the majestic city—apartment houses, government and business office buildings, churches, theaters, restaurants, movie houses—still standing as far as the eye could see. No well-groomed trees that once lined its streets and avenues. Only the uneven, jagged edges, like the stumps of broken teeth, of the buildings' foundations, the reddish brown litter of the stony chaotic rubble into which the upper stories and their baroque ornamentation had been reduced, here and there smoking fires still burning. Nor was there any clear sense of the paved streets that once bestowed order on the lives of the city's inhabitants and enabled them to communicate with each other, that, as I would say now, made a space where a multitude of people had gathered into a polis. We walked through a rubble-cluttered, thick blanket of gray and black ash and an undecidable acrid and nauseating smell that pervaded the air we breathed. What had struck me on the way in as a city endowed by time with extraordinary beauty, a unique diversity and grace, resonant depth and dignity, was now, in the wake of the firebombing by the Allied air force, a leveled and smoldering wasteland—"A heap of broken images"—and the abyssal source of an unappeasable because unnameable terror:

> And I will show you something different from either
> Your shadow at the morning striding behind you
> Or your shadow at evening rising to meet you;
> I will show you fear in a handful of dust.

As we neared the edge of the inner city, where we were to join the many other prisoner of war *Kommandos* that had also been assigned the dreadful task of excavating the ruins for the dead, the nauseating stench became increasingly intolerable. When we first encountered the odor on the way in, we had attributed it to burning wood, metal, minerals, rubber—anything but its real origin. But on entering the densely populated vicinity of death, we found that out with a vengeance. It was the putrefying flesh of dead human beings, at least forty in this instance, stacked in a huge pile one on top of the other—children, women, and men, old and young—in random fashion and in various stages of decomposition at the foot of a mountain of rubble. No doubt they had been dragged out of the ruins earlier. Nearby a number of horse-drawn wooden trough-shaped wagons, like those we had seen in the fields carrying hay or firewood on our journey to the stalag after being taken prisoners, were standing by. Our first job, we were told by our guards, who were now wearing handkerchiefs over their noses, was to load these rotting corpses into the wagons, which would then carry them to their mass burial somewhere beyond the borders of the city. And at the end of a couple of rifle barrels, we broke up into pairs and began our unholy labor.

My partner, who was a prisoner with whom I had not become well acquainted, and I looked at each other, shrugged our shoulders in resignation, and walked toward the pile of corpses. The smell of the decomposing bodies was overpowering. We hesitated, and the guards shouted obscenities at us, threatening to blow our brains out on the spot if we disobeyed. In their outraged eyes we were the alter egos of those monsters that had bombed their city and slaughtered their fellow German citizens, now stacked haphazardly, like garbage, in a mound of fetid flesh.

Reeling in the thick odor of obscene death and swallowing our saliva, we picked up one of the bodies, a middle-aged, clearly once handsome woman dressed in a black fur coat and a black hat with long green feathers angling back from the red silk band at its base. She was wearing black silk stockings and one black patent leather shoe. Her face was blue, its decomposing skin pocked with running open sores. A strand of gray-streaked black hair fell across her nose and parted lips to her chin, and her eyes were open, staring in fright, it seemed, at some dreadful thing hurrying near. Her twisted body in rigor mortis, along with our lack of strength and the rubble-covered ground we traversed, made it difficult to carry. We dropped our lifeless burden twice before managing to convey it to one of the waiting wagons, where we heaved it headlong onto the manure-covered wooden floor. As I stood there catching my breath and choking on the curdle rising from my nauseated stomach, before beginning a second round, the phrase "ashes to ashes, dust to dust" penetrated my clouded mind like a raucous laugh. I envisioned this corroding bag of bones dressed to the hilt before her sudden death. From the opulence of the outfit she was wearing, I imagined that she had been on her way to or back from a theater or a concert hall or maybe a church when the firebombs began to explode around her. What was it that burst into her head when her world came to this sudden apocalyptic close? I couldn't imagine it. "Battery dead."

But our unrelenting guard allowed us no time to philosophize. "Schnell, Americanische schweinhunden!" he shouted, prodding us with the barrel of his rifle. The next cadaver we raised from the rotting pile of dead was that of a young boy, about ten or eleven years old. He was wearing a mud-spattered and torn green jacket with a red swastika on the lapel, suggesting his membership in the Hitler Youth, but he was bare from the belly down to his toes. He had thick blond, straw-like hair, and his face was a blotchy yellowish gray and decomposing. His blue eyes, like the woman's, were wide open, staring at nothing. His right arm was missing, and from the stump at his shoulder there issued a thick streak of dried blood caked on his stiff tunic and even stiffer body below his waist. I was appalled at the horror of this sight and the events that must have preceded it. But this time, despite the nauseating stench emanating for the boy's body, I had the presence of mind to pull the lids down over his open eyes. Maybe it was compassion—as if I were the someone else I hoped would close my eyes should sudden death have prevented me from doing it myself. But maybe it was my guilt, the desire to escape that dead boy's knife-piercing blue-eyed gaze. I don't know. It was all so much more than I could comprehend. Holding our breath as long as we could to avoid the pestilential odor of decaying flesh, we picked the boy's corpse up, carried it over to the wagon, and heaved it in on top of the woman's body.

Returning to the mound of bodies, the next corpse we chose was utterly featureless. It was a shriveled human skeleton covered by a thin layer of seared skin, some of which was turning into liquid. It could have been an adult or child, male or female. It was impossible to tell. Its emaciated skull was hairless, and it had no eyes, only sockets, like two black holes with no bottoms. Whatever its gender or age, it was clear that this human being had been incinerated in the firebombing. Taking hold of its feet to pick the thing up, the pressure of my hands broke the crisply charred skin, releasing a putrid yellow liquid. We dropped our burden and looked pleadingly at our guard in the hope of being miraculously reprieved. In response he shouted furiously at us in German—"Schnell! Schnell!"—as he brought his rifle off his shoulder and aimed it at us. Picking the corpse up again, we carried it over to the wagon and added to its ghastly content. The horse neighed.

And that's the way it went for the rest of that interminable day. When our pallbearer *Kommando* had transferred the dead bodies of that mound into the waiting wagons, we were led away to another mound a few blocks farther on, where we were forced to repeat the horrific process. And after that another, then another, until it was dark and we were returned to the sawmill in Rabenau. It's impossible to convey, even vaguely, the acutely painful and confused feelings that ravaged my very being throughout that day. I had thought, when we were locked up in the suffocating boxcars heading into the interior of Germany, that I had experienced the absolute ultimate in psychological anguish, that nothing could exceed that agony. But I had been sorely mistaken. Immediately I was outraged at the vengeful cruelty of our guards. Their eye-for-an-eye response to the Allied bombers' destruction of their undefended city was inhuman. They were like animals at bay lashing out instinctively and blindly with tooth and claw at anyone associated with their murderous attackers. But deeper in my being, I felt something more fundamental, something that, as I have hinted at, had its faint origins at the time of my capture. No matter how strongly I tried to repress it, it assumed an irresistible presence in my mind while we were in the cellar of the mill as the helpless city was being laid waste and its people murdered by our combined Allied air forces. It was on one level the gnawing sense of guilty complicity with the perpetrators of this murderous firebombing of the defenseless city and its inhabitants and, on another, of identifying with the victims. The difference between me and the human beings whose corpses I had helped to load indiscrimi-nately into the wagons for mass burial all that dreadful day was that I had survived the fire and destruction and they had not, that I was alive and they were dead. I was, I suppose, grateful for that but not enough to erase my sense of community with them. It was that agonizingly paradoxical feeling I had felt before of having been dislocated, forcibly expelled from my side by my "side," into the unfamiliar precincts of the other, the feel-ing that we down here in this world of death and destruction—German civilians, refugees from the Eastern front, Allied prisoners of war—were not only worthless and expendable to those up there who had unleashed their deadly firebombs on us but also that, as such nobodies, we, each in our own way—by death or defeat or marginalization—had been deprived of our voices, our own stories. Worst of all was the feeling—one that had become increasingly acute and troubling since the commencement of my infernal journey—that I was *not* a nobody; that I *was*, in fact, some-body; that I bled, like those storybook heroes we were taught in school to venerate, when I was cut, that I suffered in spirit when I experienced loss and joy when I experienced gain.

Our *Kommando* was ordered into the city twice more after the first nightmarish encounter. My memory of those two days in the midst of fire and smoke, destruction and desolation, death and putrefaction, and in my case, profound confusion, despair, and hopelessness, have been blurred by the corrosions of time. And nothing my will can manage to do is able to penetrate that geological wreckage to drag that time, *in illo tempore* one might say ironically, back out into the light of the present. But two separate incidents remain to this day, like frozen fossils, deeply and precisely inscribed in the matrix of my mind. Were they real events? Or were they nightmare images conjured—seared—into my deracinated mind in the aftermath of that lunatic real time? I don't know. For a long time to come after *that* time, when the world itself seemed to have self-destructed and become itself a hallucination, I found it difficult to distinguish the real from the unreal. Nothing henceforth seemed normal, which is not only to say that everything seemed abnormal but also that what was normal was the nothing, the hole, the zero, at the bottom of being.

On both those days, I recall, our *Kommando* was assigned the task of searching for bodies that had perished under the debris of the collapsed buildings of a densely populated area of the inner city that, because of the smoldering fires, had not been penetrable by fire brigades, rescue squads, or salvage teams. This entailed moving the rubble—mounds of jagged blocks of masonry, twisted steel girders, brown stone cornices and disfigured statuary, clumps of shattered bricks, shards of broken glass, broken furniture, charred wood—that blocked the entrances and exits of the city's disintegrated buildings. It was not only backbreaking labor, especially for us prisoners of war, who were weak from malnutrition, but precarious as well, because moving one piece of scrap wedged in a mound of rubble might have unleashed a torrent of heavy debris capable of burying the searchers alive.

My group, which consisted of five prisoners, had cleared a path from what seemed to have been a street to an entrance of a roofless structure open to the heavy dull sky that may have been a bank or an office building of five or six stories and had entered the main interior, whose floor had caved in by a bomb blast or maybe under the pressure of the vacuum created by the firestorm. Many of the huge fragments of the tiled floor were tipped upward, some downward toward the basement. Our guards ordered us into that fragile pit to search for bodies. They threw a rope down along one of the more sturdy fragments, and we, one at a time, lowered ourselves ever so carefully, and in numbing fear, down to the subterranean level. We found a large chamber, heavy with the acrid smell of melted metal, the floor of which was covered by several inches of ash, dust, and debris. There was, however, no sign of life or death.

On the opposite side there were a number of broken wooden benches and a sort of counter, suggesting that the chamber had served as a lounge of some sort or, more likely, as an air-raid shelter. In the middle of the wall, between the row of benches, a huge jagged hole had been blasted open somehow or other. As we walked slowly and cautiously toward the entrance, we smelled the now common but still intolerable smell of death and putrefaction. At the opening we found a narrow underground corridor about twenty-five yards long. The searchers who had been given flashlights by our guards leading the way, we walked single file into the darkness. Suddenly the leader of the column stopped, exclaiming in horror, "Jesus Christ Almighty! Look at this!" We crowded in. The tunnel opened up into another smaller room. Sitting there on the floor, huddled together, we saw, in the lurid light of the flashlights, ten or twelve corpses of various ages and sexes, shriveled to their bones, their skins in the last stages of decomposition. They were all dressed as if they were about to go home after a day's work or out on the town, but their clothes seemed to be many sizes larger than their withered bodies. It was a grotesque tableau vivant. What a horrible death! I thought, though I couldn't tell from their disfigured appearance how they had died, except that it had been sudden and instantaneous. I guessed it had been a combination of asphyxiation and a wave of unimaginably hot air (carbon monoxide), not fire, caused by the firestorm triggered by the incendiary bombs that had destroyed the city.

We sent one of the search group back out to report our discovery to the German guards. Returning a few minutes later with several strands of heavy rope that the guards had passed down to him, he told us to harness each corpse to the ropes so it could be dragged up out of its tomb for burial. One by one, over the next hour or so, we roped the dead, who after the appropriate signal was given, were then, aided by the searchers all the way, slowly pulled out of the tunnel from above. I was positioned at the bottom of the diagonal shard of concrete floor on which we laid the cadavers. By the time each had arrived, it had been mangled beyond recognition by the gruesome ride across the jagged floor. One especially got to me, an old man, fetid beyond endurance, whose shrunken head, thick gold-rimmed glasses dangling from one charred ear, was adorned with thick disheveled gray hair like a lion's mane. In my mind this disintegrating skeletal carcass had been a scholar—one of Plato's philosopher kings my beautiful Latin teacher used to rave about in high school.

By the time all the bodies had been dragged up into the light of day and stacked in a neat pile, it was getting dark. Like us, our guards, too, were sick to death of this ghoulish task and eager for respite. Not long afterward, having failed to find a "hearse" to remove the bodies to a graveyard for burial, we were assembled for the march back to the sawmill in Rabenau. The bodies could wait until the next day. They were dead, after all. As we crossed over the bridge spanning the beautiful Elbe, I looked back on the devastated city, still burning in some places. The sky, heavy with a thick layer of smoke, was an infernal red. "'Unreal City . . . ,'" I thought with a shudder, remembering with great bitterness and sorrow the poem by T. S. Eliot that was so fashionable to quote when, a thousand years before, I was in high school.

The second incident occurred in the late afternoon of the following day. We had spent the entire morning and part of the afternoon at the difficult task of clearing debris at another site in the city not too far from the building in which we had found the corpses the day before. Under the relentlessly vengeful gaze of the German guards, our minds had not been given any respite from their abuse or our bodies from the forced labor they imposed on us. All through the day we lifted heavy broken stones, masonry, tangled steel, wooden beams, fallen statuary, and carried the wreckage to designated places next to previously cleared streets, where, like the piled-up bodies the day before, it would eventually be carted away to some unknown destination. To make matters worse, we were also verbally lashed by a number of German civilians, survivors of the firebombing, who apparently had lived in that area. Having pleaded futilely with the officials overseeing the site for permission to search their former homes in the hope of salvaging whatever remained of their belongings, they were taking their rage, their frustration, their despair, their sorrow, out on us. Cordoned off from the salvage area, they shouted abuses and on several occasions threw stones at us.

By that time I was so exhausted that my arms and my legs were trembling, and my head was spinning. I thought my body would give way at any moment. But even more painful was the excruciating sense of degradation I felt under the justified assault—the tongue-lashing, whose sting on the skin of my mind hurt as much as a whip on the skin of my body—of both our guards and the angry civilians. I knew I didn't deserve this demoralizing fate, yet I also knew I did. We were, after all, not innocent civilians but comrades of the British and Americans who had reduced this city to a wasteland and had murdered virtually its entire population. There was no reprieve, no way out: the dreadful feeling, once more, of being caught inside an eternal time warp in which fire and smoke and ruin, guilt and crisis and spiritual turbulence, were everlasting, a zero zone, like that dreaded hell—*oi kolasis*—my mother told us about as children to remind us of where we would go if we did not obey God's Ten Commandments, but that we had soon come to realize was just a cautionary myth.

It was late in the afternoon. Up to that point our *Kommando* had found no bodies. It seemed as if the occupants of the buildings to which we were clearing a way had escaped to another underground bomb shelter. Many parts of the city, we had gathered from our experience on the previous day and the conversations between the guards and civilians we had overheard, were connected by a network of tunnels. Somewhere in that maze, no doubt, they had been incinerated or blown into oblivion by the hot turbulent winds of the firestorm. While lifting a large fragment of a wooden beam that lay diagonally across two large pieces of masonry that were holding each other up, we spotted the hand of a child sticking out of the V-shaped space between them. A gold ring adorned one of the delicate fingers, which were clenched in a fist. Two of the searchers gently pulled one of the pieces of jagged masonry aside. There, curled up in a fetal position on a mound of debris, was a young girl, about twelve or thirteen years old. She was wearing an unbuttoned black coat and a red velvet dress opened at the neck. A long gold necklace dangled across one of her small adolescent breasts. She had long dark blonde hair pleated and rolled up into a bun. Her face was fair and exquisitely beautiful. She seemed to be asleep, like the princess in the storybook waiting to be brought back to life by the kiss of a prince. One of the searchers picked her hand up to take her pulse and after a few seconds dropped it. She was dead. Because her body was still intact, we guessed that she had died very recently.

On seeing the inert body of this beautiful young girl, whom death had not allowed the time to mature into a woman, I was filled with profound sorrow. How many more like this innocent child had suffered the same inexplicable and ruthlessly violent death? But then I realized that there was something that didn't ring true about this emotion. It was too general, too sentimental, too dependent on storytelling. It made a personified Death the always immune murderer of the countless innocent children like this one who had suffered terrible deaths during the firebombing of the city, whereas in reality the murders was committed by the British and American bombers who had been sent on and guide through this mission by the Allied military commanders hovering over their map of Europe in an operations room a thousand and more kilometers away, pushing model aircraft—the target of their deadly game, Dresden—with long cue sticks toward their doomed destination. My sorrow became contaminated with anger over the utter senselessness—and the incredible insensitivity—of these callous perpetrators of this very real apocalypse.

Suddenly, without premeditation, I picked the dead girl up in my arms in a wild protective gesture and then, awakened by the utter futility of my impulsive act, felt at a loss about what to do with my lifeless burden. I looked around at my comrades, at our guards, at the smoldering waste of the city in a state of turbulent confusion. Then I looked at the girl's face. Its features—fair, delicate, oval shaped, high cheekbones, catlike eyes, and petite—bore an uncanny resemblance to Kathryn. For an instance all the borders that separated and distinguished "us" from "them" were down. It seemed like the end of something, the reduction of Everything to nothing, the All to a "zero zone," but also, in a way—it was so faint an impulse—that I could not fathom then, a beginning. And without warning I began to sob uncontrollably as I rocked the dead girl cradled in my arms in the midst of those ruins.

Our German guards and my comrades were taken aback momentarily by my erratic, not to say unmanly, behavior and in that state of surprise said nothing until my crying had run its course. We were, I can imagine, a grotesque still life—I, holding the dead girl in my arms staring out vacantly beyond our immediate desolate location; the motley German *Volksturm* guards, uncertain about what to do; the *Kommando* of American prisoners, embarrassed at my emotional breakdown (retrospectively, I was grateful that Tex was not one of them); the venerable city below a sickly grayish yellow pall of smoke lying in ashes all around us as far as our eyes could see.

Then suddenly, without warning, the silence was broken by shouts: "Es ist Verboten! Es ist Verboten! Nein! Nein!" They were coming from a small group of German policemen standing some distance away from the *Kommando* on this side of an area across the street that had been cordoned off to prevent civilians from entering the salvage and search area. No sooner than we heard these commands, I found myself, the dead girl's limp body still in my arms, face to face with a middle-aged woman who, unseen by the policemen until it was too late, had slipped through the roped-off area and come to where we were standing. Her long blonde hair was disheveled. She was wearing a long black, mud-caked silk skirt and an oversized Wehrmacht officer's jacket buttoned up to the neck, the swastika above the chest pocket somehow glowing. In her right hand she was holding a red flower in a gesture that seemed absurdly like an offering. Her black eyes, ringed by the shadows of fatigue, were blazing. She looked piercingly into mine. Without saying a single word, she spit, full force, into my face. She then grabbed the dead girl out of my arms.

By this time two of the policemen had arrived at the scene. One rescued the dead body of the child; the other took hold of the flailing woman and led her away. With that acute sting of her fiery spit, the last vestige of my identity as an American—the image by which I had hitherto lived my life—curdled up and withered into ash. In that instant—it was a decisive-limit situation—I too had become a zero zone.

Too stunned to be able to think clearly, I passed the next hour or so in a kind of stumbling trance. It was only when we were crossing the bridge over the Elbe on our return to Rabenau that I began to think of the implications of what had happened. Who was that young girl? What was she doing when she was caught unaware by the bombing? Why was she alone? How had she survived so long? What was shouting in her young and innocent mind in the throes of premature death? And that fierce woman, like a hallucinated vengeful Fury . . . was she the girl's mother? A demented mother who, having lost her child in the bombing, was claiming this one as her own? An angry Nazi sympathizer? The soldier's jacket? That red flower in her fist? . . . And on and on. I was bewildered. I wanted desperately to know. But there were no answers, no possibility of ever learning their stories, no fifth and final act.

It was at first as if a monstrous demon, as in a painting by Goya, had brought his huge clenched cosmic fist crashing down on the stage of the world out of spite or caprice. But as the horror of these last few days came rushing tumultuously into my head, that capricious demon—that Saturn—and his devastating mythical cosmic fist reverted back to their original state: the strategic Allied air force and the thousands upon thousands of pounds of incendiary bombs it had dropped indiscriminately on an unprotected city of innocent civilians. Despite my effort to rationalize the carnage perpetrated by our side—this was a just war that had been initiated by an evil regime—I couldn't, as before, make my argument take hold. I had experienced a vaguely defined evil for which there simply was no justification. I couldn't formulate the feeling of anger and frustration I felt then, but it was persistent, a haunting specter, to the end of the war and many years thereafter. And it had to do precisely with bearing witness to, remembering, indeed re-membering, those thousands upon thousands of innocent lives that our incendiary bombs had wiped out—dismembered—and deprived of their stories in less than twenty-four hours.

5. Interlude

A gaze blank and pitiless as the sun,
Is moving its slow thighs, while all about it
Reel shadows of the indignant desert birds.

W. B. YEATS, "The Second Coming"

On the morning after our third—or was it the fourth?—excursion into Dresden to search the ruins of the city for the dead, our guards informed us that our assignment had been terminated and that we were to take up our duties where we had left off. I was at first immensely relieved to hear this because the horrors I had experienced those few days exceeded my ability to assimilate them. But it was, given the options, a hollow reprieve. I was hoping anxiously that at least I would rejoin the group working in the sawmill, but, as I expected, I was reassigned to the *Kommando* that was hauling logs in the forest beyond Rabenau. We did not know why we were withdrawn from the nauseous task in the inner city in favor of the mill and the forest. But from the increased pressure our ss guards put on us to be more productive, we inferred that the Soviet army had made a breakthrough and was closing in on Dresden. We in the forest *Kommando* were certain that the logs we were carrying down to the ramp and loading on to trucks were being used to build roadblocks. On returning to the forest, therefore, we undertook this forced labor with a different perspective from our earlier one. Our working conditions were more difficult, the ss guards more ruthless, and the food we were given was even less sustaining than before the destruction of Dresden. But there was a new aura in the air we breathed, an unspoken but palpable expectation of an imminent radical change in our lives. It was for me fraught with frightening ambiguity, but unlike the previous period in the forest, it was nevertheless somehow sustaining. A future had opened up, not necessarily the hope of a happy ending, though many of my fellow prisoners, I surmised, felt that above all, but simply the sheer sense of possibility where before there was only suffocating hopelessness. The devastation of Dresden had thrown me tangentially off the mind-numbing treadmill, off the recurring and eroding circle, into the zone of anxiety-provoking yet interesting uncertainty. How would our German guards treat us when the Russians attacked the city? Would we survive the attack? Would the Russians liberate us? How would we be returned to the American lines? How would my story end? I was acutely hungry and weak in body. I was bitter. I was angry. I was terrified. I was profoundly anxious. I was haunted by the ghosts of the multitudinous dead I had borne witness to on the previous days. Yet I was strangely elated.

When I returned to the forest, it was mid-February. We labored on that slope day after interminable day for another three or four weeks. The winter had become a little milder, but the work was more intense and the recuperating ss guards more vicious and demanding. The years have ground down the edges of the particulars of that time of my captivity. What I remember, besides this flickering uncanny sense of elation—of *being alive* in the midst of death and annihilation—was, above all, being hungry. After the firebombing of Dresden, our food rations, which initially had been far from adequate, were cut in half, the turnip soup tasting more watery and the meager slice of bread more like sawdust. Watching our guards eating their creamy potato soup, their thick black pumpernickel bread, and above all their apples, however withered, during the break period was torture. During the previous period in the forest I had not attended to my body. I knew that I had lost considerable weight and that my strength, especially in my arms and legs, had been radically depleted, but I would always deflect my attention away from the image of my body, no doubt from fear of not recognizing myself. Soon after returning to the forest *Kommando*, however, my hunger having become overwhelming, I began to take notice of its contours, the protruding bones of my ankles, my knees, and, most disturbing, my hips. I was skin and bone.

One evening, after we had returned to the sawmill and had eaten our meager fare, one of our guards came over to the table where I was sitting to say that the foreman of the mill had assigned me the job of cleaning the civilian workers' toilet facility on the other side of the courtyard and that I would be excused from the forest *Kommando* the next day. The foreman was a civilian, one of the few Germans who had shown me some degree of sympathy earlier when I was working at the saw machine. He used to call me jokingly "die Schnecke," the snail or slug. This kind of break in our routine was not especially unusual. It had happened before but not to me. I was pleased by this unexpected summons. It meant, as I had learned from others who had been similarly "chosen," a day of reprieve from the torture of lifting and carrying logs that weighed more than our physical strength could endure. Not least, it also meant a separation from the group—an individualization—that opened up the possibility of being treated like a human being, which to me meant receiving the gift of a scrap of food.

Early the next morning, after I had dressed and had my breakfast "coffee," one of the old guards led me off to the civilian side of the mill, where he handed me over to the foreman, a portly middle-aged man dressed in a long blue denim coat, with hanging jowls and a big belly, who seemed to take pride in his sense of humor. He greeted me with playful contempt as "die Amerikanische Schnecke." Then, after pantomiming a figure in extreme slow motion, he gave me the bucket and other cleaning utensils he had gathered together and led me to the latrine area, a long narrow corridor on the ground floor of the mill lined by a common metal toilet trough and a number of private stalls, and told me what I was supposed to do, all the while joking at my bizarre appearance. I couldn't quite understand his German except for the recurrence of the word *Schnecke*, but he seemed to be saying that I looked not like the mythical American of the New World—the pioneer, the trailblazer, the redeemer of mankind—but like the lowliest, most miserable and laughable slug that nature had ever suffered to crawl on this earth. I, in turn, tolerated his bantering. Whatever his real feelings—and there was something about his demeanor that suggested some degree of amused sympathy—his good nature was patronizing and utterly degrading, in a way more inhumane than the outright cruelty of our ss guards in the forest. But I was starving, my emaciated body and soul crying out to be fed, so I accepted his benign crudity in the hope that my toleration of his joking, would, like a hungry dog's accommodation of a teasing master's whim, be rewarded.

After he left I began the onerous task. The metal latrine stank heavily of stale urine, and the white toilet bowls in the stalls were coated by a yellowish brown substance. A short while later I became nauseated and desperately in need of fresh air. I walked rapidly down the corridor toward the exit opening up into the courtyard. As I was about to reach the door, I passed by a large mirror above a washstand and saw my reflection fleetingly, like a dark cloud passing across the moon. I stopped, turned back, and looked into the mirror. I was startled by what I saw. It was not me. Or if it was, it was my shadow, my ghost. Its face was gaunt, yellowish, like the color of the corroded enamel in the toilet bowls. It had listless brown hair, long, unkempt, and shaggy, that fell haphazardly over a pair of dull brown eyes sunk deep into their sockets. It had a short beard of sorts, strangely uneven in length, which gave prominence to the bones of its emaciated cheeks. And it looked terribly old. Yet it was a familiar face. Its shadowy contours hinted at the youthful handsome face it once was. But this resemblance exacerbated the strangeness of the face that was looking steadily back at me.

Appalled by what I saw—or was it the penetrating gaze of the apparition in the mirror?—I tore my tattered green jacket off and then my shirt to see more of this phantom, this incubus, that seemed to have taken over my being. The estrangement became final. I saw to my horror a destitute body. All the bones that had once endowed my torso with an attractive grace—Kathryn, among other girls, I remembered in acute anguish, would often tell me my body resembled that of an ancient Greek statue—seemed now an obscene travesty of their former splendor. The apparition's collarbone, its joints, its descending ribs, its hip bones, protruded grotesquely out of the sallow skin that covered them. It was not a human body I saw before me; it was a bag of rattling bones.

Suddenly I remembered the little "old guy" in our *Kommando*, Mc-Dooley (or something like that), who a little earlier—a week or so before the bombing of Dresden—had died, we were told by our guards, of tuberculosis, but as we all knew, if it was that dreaded disease, it was exacerbated by acute malnutrition. Slight of build, quite short, with a mouselike face, a balding head, and protruding teeth, he was around thirty years old, no more than five or ten years older than me, but he looked and acted as though he were a ghostly old man. I had felt sorry for him when I saw him shuffling from the dining table to his bunk after supper, but I was also always frightened by his undeviating hollow gaze. Now in my inflamed imagination he looked like the thing I saw in the mirror. "No!" I kept saying to myself as I ran my calloused hand up and down my ribs. "No! That's not me! That can't be me. Bill! Bill! Bill! I'm Bill Spanos! Vasilis!" I kept repeating, "I'm not that! Not *that*!"

In this state of terror I threw my clothes back on, ran back to the latrine, where I had left the bucket of detergent and brushes, and began scrubbing the corroded trough with all the energy I could muster out of my depleted body. It was as if that apparition had inscribed itself deeply in all its grotesqueness into the very matrix of my mind and I was hysterically trying to scour it away.

I worked at this real and symbolic task for the rest of the day, taking breaks every so often to renew my flagging strength, only to be revisited in that interim by the haunting apparition in the mirror and, like Sisyphus in the Greek myth—I didn't know then that he would be turned into a collective image of the plight of modern man in the wake of the war—compelled by its spectral force to return to my interminable and fruitless labor. The foreman came back on a couple of occasions to check on my progress and, seeing that the toilet facilities were markedly cleaner, each time nodded his head with surprise and self-satisfaction as he muttered, "Gut. Gut." In the late afternoon, as night was falling, he returned once more to inspect my work and, approving the results, gave me a slice of real bread as a reward for my accomplishment. He then brought me back to the prisoners' quarters, where, at the entrance, he bid me fare-well, not without expressing feigned astonishment at what a slug could do if it were treated wisely—I was no Sisyphus to this antithetical agent of the "Big Picture"—and promising to remember me should another such task arise.

That promise was, in fact, fulfilled shortly thereafter. In the meantime I rejoined the *Arbeitskommando* in the forest, where I resumed the ago-nizing labor of hauling logs on an empty stomach under the relentless and cruel prodding of our recuperating ss guards. Now, however, the or-deal was exacerbated by the frightening specter I had seen staring blankly at me from the mirror in the latrine. To make matters worse, we were in-undated by a welter of contradictory rumors about the progress of the war "out there" that were coming rampantly from everywhere and no-where. We could tell from the erratic behavior of our guards that some-thing portentous was happening in the world, but we hadn't the slight-est idea what that was. Some of the rumors suggested that the German army had retaliated on both the Western and Eastern fronts and driven the American and British armies back to the Atlantic coast and the So-viet army into Russian territory. Others suggested that the Nazi com-mand had developed a megabomb capable of destroying the entire pop-ulation of a country in a single explosion and was preparing to unleash it without warning against London and New York at any moment. Most hinted that both the American and British armies in the West and the So-viets in the East were moving inexorably toward Berlin and that the fall of Germany was imminent, a matter of days. However portentous these "larger matters" seemed—these issues pertaining to the life and death of nations—what mattered above all to most of us, certainly to me, at that time was the inexorable and persistent presence of hunger, the gnaw-ing sensation of lack and the insatiable desire for food at the center of my being that emanated outward to saturate my body right down to my capillaries. This is not to say that I was trivializing the world at war "out there." In keeping with my nagging sense of being the blameless victim of that "larger world"—or to put this feeling positively, with my emerging awareness that I possessed a self, maybe even the hubris of an upstart—

it is to say, rather, that the circumstances of our existence made me feel strangely but forcefully larger than life. I was in my mind somehow like Tantalus, forever reaching for the sustenance that the merciless Olympian gods forever kept from his grasp.

It was now early March, and, mercifully, the weather had modulated in the direction of spring. The pall of smoke rising mournfully from the burned city had dissipated, and the sun, though still pallid, was occasionally visible. It was a little warmer, the snow in the forest was beginning to melt, and here and there by the side of the road we traversed hiking back and forth between the mill and the forest, we saw occasional clusters of green grass, dandelions, and other herbs and weeds struggling to break out of the iron hold of winter. But these signs of spring were not so much harbingers of good things to come, although the sheer thought of being warm again was something we didn't discount. They represented, rather, the possibility of supplementing our meager meals. To this end I made it a strategic point, as we lined up for the hike back to the sawmill after the day's work, to place myself at the end of the column. My intention was to break rank, after our ss guards had handed us over to our older and more tolerant home guards, to grab and stuff a fistful of dandelion leaves into my pocket when the occasion warranted without being detected.

This desperate strategy worked, more or less, for a few days. When once in a while I saw a patch of green, seeming to me like a tree bearing golden fruit in Paradise, at the edge of the road, I would leap out of line, take hold of its tuft, sever the leaves from their root, and hide the precious loot in my corroding jacket pocket as I hurried back to my place in the marching column. At suppertime I would add the dandelion leaves—sometimes they were only blades of grass or other unknown weeds, but that finally didn't matter—to the always lukewarm turnip or potato soup, stir them until they were wilted, and then, as if I were a Roman emperor lying on a divan, partake of the luxurious feast. Eventually, however, a few of my fellow prisoners, apparently thinking that I had discovered the elixir of life in whatever I was putting into my bowl, began to follow suit. At first our old guards were amused by the ludicrousness of our animal-like antics, perhaps underscoring their sustaining negative image of American self-reliance, and tolerated them as long as they didn't delay the march home. But soon, when these occasional interruptions became excessive and the column's progress began to slow down markedly, their amusement turned into vicious anger, and they forbade them, warning us that anyone stepping out of line would be shot on the spot.

And so it went for a couple more uncertain weeks. Our food rations continued to decrease, the contradictory rumors escalated wildly, the ss guards in the forest became increasingly vicious, and our home guards grew more excitable. And spring was crouching, ready to spring. We, too, were on edge, more dislocated, more volatile, more attuned to the unknown future. We were waiting for the something—its heart beating, beating, beating, everywhere in the void around us—we knew now that "it" was soon going to break out. It was in this frame of mind that I found myself—this confused sense of acute hunger and ominous expectation, underscored by the haunting specter of the face I had seen in the mirror in the latrine, which would suddenly metamorphose into the dead girl buried in the rubble in Dresden—when, to my surprise, the foreman's earlier promise was "fulfilled."

One evening late in March or early April, after we had eaten and were sitting at the dining tables exchanging the rumors we had heard or invented that day, one of our guards came into the prisoners' quarters to ask which one of us was *die Schnecke*. When I raised my hand, he laughed sardonically, saying something to the effect that he expected as much but that, in the end, we could all answer to this name. He then informed me that instead of going out with the forest *Kommando* the next morning, I was to report to the foreman, Herr Klaus, who had some unannounced task in store for me. I had mixed feelings about this turn. I did not want to be the captive object of his degrading banter, nor if he was going to assign me to clean the latrine again, did I want to confront that apparition in the mirror. On the other hand, his gesture meant a reprieve from the forest and the ferocious barking of the ss guards. More important, he was, or so it seemed to my destitute being, singling me out—not any American prisoner of war, not an empty abstraction, but *me*—Bill Spanos— in all my singularity. I felt I would *be* somebody for a while. And besides, there was, at the other end of the day, likely to be that thick slice of real black bread.

The next morning, after the forest *Kommando* left the sawmill, the guard who had informed me of my election the night before led me down to the floor housing the machinery, my old workplace, where I was handed over to the foreman, who, as before, was wearing his long denim work coat. He greeted me, as I expected, with the same jovial irony he had used on the earlier occasion—"Die Americanische Schnecke ist hier, ja? Aber wie viel?" And then, ordering me to follow him, he led me, like Virgil leading Dante, down a flight of stairs, flashlight in hand, into the large basement of the mill, the terrible underworld where we had sat through the fire-bombing of Dresden. The room, damp and filled with the overpowering but familiar smell of sauerkraut, was pitch dark, except for the shifting beam of the foreman's flashlight, whose illumination and concealment of the cellar's various contents rendered them a volatile sequence of halluci-natory images. Eventually the foreman found the light switch and turned it on. One side of the room was a morass, cluttered by parts of disman-tled saw machines, saw blades, tables, chairs, discarded lamps, window blinds. The other side was lined with a number of large wooden barrels containing the sauerkraut. In a combination of German, English, and bodily gestures Herr Kraus informed me that some officials of the war effort were coming to inspect the mill soon and that my labor for the day was to organize the debris on one side of the room and to sweep and mop the entire basement floor.

After explaining my job in greater detail and showing me where the cleaning equipment was, he led me over to the barrels. Opening the lid of one of them, he reached down into it, pulled out a fistful of dripping yel-low pickled cabbage and, flaunting it under my nose, added with a grin, as if it were in fact an invitation rather than a prohibition, that eating any of "diese Scheisse" was "verboten." In response I made a facial gesture in-dicating that I found the smell of the sauerkraut revolting, though in re-ality it was, to my hungry nose, as enticing as the aroma of my mother's *fasoladha*. The foreman laughed slyly, as if he were a partner in a tale he, but not I, knew the ending of. Telling me he would be back in a couple of hours to check on my progress, he walked across the room to the cellar door, opened it as if to leave, but instead turned and gazed at me in silence for a few seconds. Then, grinning and pointing his finger at me, he said, "Remember, *meine Schnecke, diese Sauerkraut ist verboten*," and walked out.

I was relieved to be alone at last. The jovial German foreman troubled me. Was he sympathetic with my destitute condition, a basically good man who in his own way was being friendly? Or was he contemptuous of it, an evil spirit who was sadistically mocking me, maybe even seducing me into a catastrophic trap? Why had he focused my attention on the barrels of sauerkraut? Was he, like the devil, tempting me to commit the rash act he had forbidden? To escape this unpleasant ambiguity, I plunged into the task he had set for me with all my will. For hours, it seemed, I picked up scraps and sorted them into neat piles, moved the furniture that cluttered the cellar into rows, wiped the thick layer of dust from all the surfaces. But the very existence of food in the room was overwhelming. I worked feverishly in the hope of obliterating its acutely tempting presence from my consciousness, but, exacerbated by its odor, which was strong enough to taste, it persisted in flapping its huge wings. "That promise," I thought, "was it a trap? What would they do to me if they caught me stealing some of their sauerkraut?" I knew that the food the German civilians were eating was being rationed, that despite the foreman's cavalier reference to the sauerkraut as "shit," it was a precious staple of the civilian workers' diet. "Would they beat me? Would they shoot me? Or would they understand how it feels to be as hungry as I am and show me mercy?" I was, like Tantalus, tormented by the proximity, the *thereness* of the sauerkraut yet its unreachable distance. A couple of times I walked over to the barrels fiercely tempted to risk everything for a mouthful of its content, but each time the image of being caught in the act flashed through my mind, and I willed myself to return to my labor.

Sometime late in the morning, as I was agonizing over this terrible dilemma, the foreman returned to inspect my work. I was both relieved by his bringing my ordeal to its end yet furious at him for making my decision for me. He looked around the room, running his fingers over various surfaces and nodding his approval at what I had accomplished. Then, as if it were the real goal of his visit, he walked over to the barrels of sauerkraut, opened up the lid of one of them, and peered into it. Finding apparently that all was well with its precious contents, he looked at me with his piercing black eyes and seemingly malevolent grin and said, "*Gut! Gut! Schnecke,* you do good *Arbeit, und* you obey *das landrecht,* how you say, *das* rule of the land. *Ja, Ja!*" But I had the distinct impression that he didn't mean exactly what he was saying, that he was in fact somehow disappointed, but I wasn't sure about what. Had he invited me down here to a feast and was disappointed to find that I had not given him the peculiar satisfaction he had hoped to get for his benign gesture? Or was he disappointed that I had not succumbed to the tempting bait he had laid out for me?

The reprieve, if that's what one could call it, however, was short lived. As I was pondering over these ambiguities, the foreman announced that he had to attend to affairs in the sawmill. My American comrades who were working upstairs, he said, were being careless about the settings of the saw machines, and as a result, the sizes of the pieces of wood they were sawing were turning out to be imperfect. I was to go on cleaning the cellar until he returned later in the afternoon to take me back to the prisoners' quarters. Catching my eye, he looked over to the barrels of sauerkraut and smiled. Although he said nothing, I had the eerie feeling once again that he was tempting me.

After he left, this time without stopping ominously at the door, I returned to my labor—and my agonizing dilemma—with a vengeance. To deflect my mind from the barrels of sauerkraut as I worked, I concentrated on my previous visits to the cellar—on the dark breathless hours during the bombing of Dresden when the whole world seemed on the verge of caving in on us, on the horror of what we were imagining was happening in the old city, on our repeated reprieves. Then, when I had exhausted those memories, I turned my mind on the witness I had borne in the ruins of the city—the piles of incinerated and decaying bodies, the asphyxiated corpses in the basement of the building, the dead young girl in my arms, and the angry woman, red flower in hand, who spat in my face.

But it was a losing battle. I found myself, against my entire will, drawing closer and closer toward my ruin. The acrid smell of the sauerkraut was to me what the exquisite song of the Sirens was to Odysseus. But there was nothing that could stop the ears of my hunger, not even the thought of execution. "Fuck it!" I shouted to myself. "Fuck it! It doesn't matter. What will be, will be! I'm going to eat some of that *Scheisse!*"

I walked over to one of the forbidden barrels—the one the foreman had singled out—opened the lid, grabbed a fistful of sauerkraut, and shoved it into my mouth. The taste was pungent but exquisite and immediately gratifying. Tears filled my eyes, but I couldn't tell whether they were induced by the fumes of the sauerkraut or the acute pleasure that comes from the sudden, long withheld satisfaction of an intense desire. Before swallowing what was already there, I grabbed another handful and stuffed it into my churning mouth as the limp strands of yellow cabbage dripped down my chin onto the floor. Then another and yet another. Nothing did matter except the gratification of my craving hunger. In the throes of this orgy I forgot my situation—the war, my captivity, the foreman's ominous warning, my fear of being caught. I had stepped out of the world and into a free-floating eternity, a voluptuous Elysium overflowing with the smell and taste of pickled cabbage.

After I had swallowed several mouthfuls, my delirium still unabated, it occurred to me with irrepressible force that instant gratification was just not enough to satiate my aroused desire. I would confiscate some of this food of the gods for later consumption. But how? Clearly, I couldn't carry it out of the cellar in a container, as if it were a Holy Grail invisible to the eyes of the infidel. The only option was to convey it on my person. But that too seemed impossible because the sauerkraut was wet and soggy and would drip through my pants or jacket pockets. Then, with what seemed the clarity of a visionary, I remembered that the pants I was wearing were not the fatigues I had worn in combat. Those had been shredded long before and had been replaced—I can't remember when or how—by a pair of heavy British jump pants that, unlike American military wear, had pockets just above the knees that were lined with leather. Without further consideration I reached into the barrel, pulled out another handful of the slimy sauerkraut, squeezed the liquid out of it, and deposited the precious load into one of the pockets of my pants. I was euphoric. What a wonderful gift the foreman had bestowed on me!

But suddenly, after the third or fourth fistful, I saw to my dismay dark wet stains on the exterior of the thigh pockets. In that moment, as I ransacked my awakened mind for a solution, I was shocked by a loud crack from the other side of the cellar. Looking up, my heart beating wildly, I saw the outline of the foreman's body, a long thick cane in his hand, standing still by the open door. He was looking at me with eyes that seemed capable of turning me into stone. To avoid his lethal gaze I looked down at the stained bulges at my knees and suddenly woke up to the reality I had obliterated. I saw in that instant the absurdity of the scene—it was like an image of Charlie Chaplin slipping on a banana peel—but also its horror. I had fallen into the satanic foreman's trap, and I would most likely have to pay for my weakness—or stupid courage—with my life. That, it struck me, was the end of the story he knew but I didn't. How had it happened? As I was standing there frozen by the bright light of his Medusan eye, the foreman slowly, methodically, silently, walked across the room, holding his cane high as if he were about to strike. When he arrived, he stopped in front of me. I closed my eyes and waited for the crashing blow. In that eternal instant of blackness I saw the cane he held metamorphose into a squad of rifles aimed at my heart. But it didn't fall. I opened my eyes and looked into the foreman's grim face, at first in terror and then with a sheepish grin, as if to say that I had, in my ignorance, misinterpreted his directives. He glared back sullenly—and then, like a thunderclap, broke out into raucous laughter, as his ample belly shook in tune with its convulsions. I had been spared once again.

After his laughter subsided and he had regained his composure, the foreman, shaking his head and sighing, as if I were a hopeless case, said, "*Ach, Schnecke,* you are just like everybody else . . . *Alles* . . . no different," and then in a lighter tone, pushing his cane into my belly, "and you will pay for your lack of willpower tomorrow"—or so I interpreted his German. He ordered me to return the sauerkraut in my pockets to the barrels then, prodding me playfully with his cane all the way, led me out of that underworld. When we arrived at the door of the prisoners' quarters, he said to me, "Guten abend, kind." Taken aback by this startling termination of the day, I was left speechless. I knew then that what had happened in the cellar would remain our mutual secret. And I was immensely grateful to him. But try as I might, I couldn't find the words to reply. He, on the other hand, pinching his nose with his thumb and forefinger and pointing with his cane to the stains on my knee pockets, as if to say that I should do something about the offensive smell of the pickled cabbage, opened the door of the compound, stepped to one side, and smiled that ambiguous smile as I passed through. And I, remembering the promise he had made the first time, was left to ponder its meaning.

The next day I rejoined my *Kommando* and worked in the forest for the next two weeks or so. As the foreman had predicted, I did indeed pay for my lack of willpower with an excruciatingly severe case of diarrhea that made me weaker than I was before. But this discomfort was nothing compared to the dislocating impact of events that were unfolding in the world immediately outside our narrow confines and beyond—or to be more accurate, of the rumors that were now circulating, like the turbulent winds heralding the coming storm, in the forest and in our prisoners' quarters. The Americans, it was being whispered, had crossed the Rhine River, and the Soviet armies had crossed the Oder, had taken Vienna, and were pounding at the eastern gates of Dresden. Both armies were racing toward Berlin. It was also rumored that a pact had been signed by President Franklin Roosevelt, Prime Minister Winston Churchill, and Chairman Joseph Stalin that divided up the people of Europe, like the spoils of war, suggesting, among other disturbing possibilities, a rift between the Allied forces. On the other hand, we were hearing daily from our guards that the German armies had counterattacked in the West and in the East and had driven the United States and British armies back across the Rhine and the Soviets back across the Oder River.

Again, as during the firebombing of Dresden and in its immediate aftermath, I had throughout all this vexing time the palpable sense that something was imminent, an immense unknown event that would affect our lives in a decisive way. Again, too, I had the disconcerting feeling that we were nothing more than the nameless victims of a powerful presence, invisible, unnameable, unknowable, beyond our comprehension: "the collateral damage" of a higher cause, in the banal language of expertise spawned by the war. But *there*, all-seeing, indifferent, inexorable. In the midst of the tumult of that time I was dislocated as never before. I didn't know what to think. Was the war about to end? Would it go on until we perished from the brutally cruel conditions of our existence? If the war ended, what then? Would we survive such an anarchic world without boundaries? It was frightening to contemplate any of these possibilities.

One evening in the middle of April, having returned from the forest and eaten our meager fare, our guards, to makes matter worse, gathered us into the dining room and announced triumphantly that our president of the United States, Franklin Delano Roosevelt, "ist tod" and that, in the aftermath of his death, the leaders of the Allies were struggling for power over the direction of the war. As a consequence, the Allied war machine had fallen into turmoil and was beginning to disintegrate. We were stunned by this news. We didn't want to believe it. We wanted to think it was simply propaganda. But we weren't at all sure. What did we know about the raging world outside the suffocating confines of this little factory in the infernal depths of Germany? The wings of the ominous absent presence of the cataclysmic event we had been anticipating were beating louder.

Two or three days later, before dawn and without advance notice or explanation, our guards roused us out of sleep at gunpoint, evacuated us from the sawmill in great haste, and led us to a highway on the outskirts of Rabenau heading south toward Czechoslovakia. There we joined a huge column of prisoners, four or five hundred, who for an unknown reason were being marched out of the pending war zone toward an unknown destination. In the distance to the east we heard the steady rumble of massive artillery fire. We knew that the Soviet army was advancing on the already dead city of Dresden. "And what rough beast, its hour come at last, / Slouches towards Bethlehem to be born?"

6. Persephone and the Beast

April is the cruelest month, breeding
Lilacs out of the dead land, mixing
Memory and desire, stirring
Dull roots with spring rain.
Winter kept us warm, covering
Earth in forgetful snow, feeding
A little life with dried tubers.

T. S. ELIOT, *The Waste Land*

As in the case of the destruction of Dresden, I find it impossible to represent the experience I underwent in the closing days of the war and of my captivity in a way that would be adequate to its surreality. But for different reasons. Both experiences were unspeakable in their incommensurability with everything we had been given to understand as civilization. They simply defied accommodation to the language of Western rationality. But the firebombing of Dresden was utterly singular in its irrational rationality, an event that revealed to me decisively the latent contradiction, the violence, inhering in the very benign logic of the Western—democratic, humanist, capitalist—narrative of civilization. It evoked, and still does, something akin to, but more terrible than, the "vision" to which, according to Marlow in Joseph Conrad's *Heart of Darkness*, Kurtz must have borne witness as he cried out his last resonant words:

It was as though a veil had been rent. I saw on that ivory face the expression of somber pride, of ruthless power, of craven terror—of an intense and hopeless despair. Did he live his life again in every detail of desire, temptation and surrender during that supreme moment of complete knowledge? He cried in a whisper at some image, at some vision—he cried out twice, a cry that was no more than a breath:

"The Horror! The Horror!"

My experience during the last days of the war was no less irrational, no less the antithesis of what I had been led by my schoolteachers to believe constituted civilization, but it was played out not in the singular terms of horror as such but in the more general terms of a horror I felt to be somehow farcical. At that time I was not sophisticated enough, indeed too ignorant, to explain the difference I felt in an acutely palpable way. It was not until several years after the war, when, in college under the GI Bill of Rights, I began to read the existentialists—the journals of Søren Kierkegaard, the novels of Jean-Paul Sartre, Albert Camus, Simone de Beauvois, and André Malraux, Samuel Beckett, Günter Grass, and the plays of Eugène Ionesco, Jean Genet, Jean Tardieu, and Harold Pinter—that I found a language that was more commensurable, at least in theory, to that surreal world I entered in crossing over into Czechoslovakia as the war was coming to its nightmarish end. In some deeply felt way all these writers were struggling, against the official historians' monumentalizing account, to articulate the world-shattering consequences of this civilizational cataclysm.

It was, to appropriate the ambivalent directives of this later language, an absurd—an unworlded—world, one in which not only "God was dead," bereft of a shaping principle of presence, but also in which everything became possible, an upside-down world that mocked the old one but was also announcing in the silent ironic language of the absurd the advent of a new one. It was, in a much later language, a "zero zone," in which all the boundaries had collapsed. The war had disclosed to me that the venerable old world, like Dresden itself, was a laughably corrupt and jerry-built edifice, but it also enabled alternative visions of the human city that had previously been precluded by the monumental solemnities attributed to the old one. The world I was thrust into during that cruelest of months— I was like a fetus resisting the labor of the womb of time—was, according to the official histories of the West, a world liberated from tyranny. That was in some sense true, but for me in the midst of it—and however prematurely and reluctantly, awakened to intimations of my mortality— liberation was far more complicated. Bereft of a prospect, I was above all frightened at what lay immediately ahead. But at the same time, and despite the precariousness of my situation and the acts of inhumanity to which I had borne witness, I couldn't repress the strange elation at being alive in the midst of the death and destruction wrought earlier in the smoldering ruins in Dresden, the uncanny feeling, however amorphous it was, that the boundless conditions that instigated this fright also instigated hope and the will to live, a strange, rootless, but persistent joy.

The column our *Kommando* joined on being evacuated from the factory in Rabenau consisted of prisoners of war from every nation of the Western Hemisphere, though most were British and Americans. It was a motley multitude, a ragtag army of specters or scarecrows, depending on one's point of view, displaying all the outward signs of severe deprivation. And yet, it seemed to me, we exuded a curious volatility in our abjectness, no doubt the effect of our anticipation of liberation. Our journey south was overseen by a surprisingly small number of guards, mostly old men belonging to the *Volksturm*, who carried rifles from the World War I era. And unlike their counterparts when we first arrived in Dresden, they seemed reluctant to fulfill a task that was taking them away from their homes and families at a time when they were being immediately threatened.

As our column moved south, like a gigantic wounded caterpillar, its body was increasingly swelled by other small groups of prisoners pouring into the main highway from tributary streets and roads. We had no sure idea why we had been evacuated and where we were going. Nor, it seemed, did our guards. Our puppet masters had either abandoned us or the strings with which they had hitherto manipulated our movements had somehow been cut. Or maybe they had simply gone mad. All we knew was that we knew nothing. The void surrounded us as if it were an invading presence.

Not long after our *Kommando* joined the column, and in the process of asking the prisoners we met anxiously who they were, where they had come from, what they thought our destination was, what they knew about the status of the war in the West and the East, I made the acquaintance of a young Greek American, about my age. His name was Aris, short for Aristotle, and he was born and grew up in Chicago. In recounting his life, it became clear to me that except for the fact that he had lived in a ghetto of a densely populated Midwestern city, his life as a Greek American was quite similar to mine. He too had suffered the indignities and degradations of ethnic prejudice, had rebelled against his immigrant parents' Old World culture in his desire to feel at home in the New World, and had struggled futilely to reconcile the claims of both worlds on his identity. But what I found most likable about Aris was his playfully ironic attitude toward the cause he was serving. He was not, like so many of the Greek Americans I grew up with, an unquestioning enthusiast of the American way of life. Nor did he believe that the United States's purpose for entering the war was to save the world for democracy. But unlike me, he had a sense of humor that not only prevented these reservations from getting under his skin but also allowed him to put them in a positive light.

Aris, like me, had been taken prisoner of war in the Battle of the Ardennes Forest in December, but the horrendous journey into the interior of Germany had brought him in the end to Leipzig, where he joined an *Arbeitskommando* assigned to repair bombed-out train tracks in the railroad yards of that city. When I met him, he looked even more emaciated than I did at the time I had seen my reflection in the mirror of the sawmill latrine in Rabenau. He was also coughing up blood, which made me suspect that he had tuberculosis or a severe case of walking pneumonia. But he played down his illness, and I, not knowing what else to do, went along with him, though I couldn't help but remember the fate of my fellow inmate McDooley.

We walked all that day, maybe thirty or thirty-five kilometers, passing a city we heard the German guards call Teplitz, without food or water, stopping frequently along the way to pick up more small groups of prisoners. At dusk we were led off the highway onto a country road that terminated a short time later at what seemed to be an abandoned stone quarry near which a small river flowed. Aris and I were lucky enough to find squatting space in an open shed covered by a corrugated tin roof. We had water to drink that night but no food. To pass the time of the night, we amplified our stories. I was never a gregarious person. Throughout my childhood and adolescence I was acutely shy, even afraid of people, and tended to avoid intimate contact with them. For reasons beyond my comprehension, though I felt it had to do with my alien status, I was never able to will myself to belong. My friends called me "a loner." Throughout the months of my captivity, when I felt irremediably cut off from my family, feeling lost, desperately lonely, and in need of the comfort of companionship, I had not made any close friends. In fact, I felt distant from all of my fellow prisoners and alienated from some. It felt good, therefore, to find a kindred spirit in the midst of this chaos, where things were falling apart and the center wasn't holding. Aris's words of remembrance were a stay, a gossamer thread that bound me to sanity.

Early the next morning, after a sleepless night, our guards announced that we would be receiving a bread ration before moving on to our still unknown destination. I don't know where the bread came from—it was probably brought into the quarry by truck during the night. Nor do I recall how it was distributed, except that I was involved in passing half-loaves of this dark ersatz bread down a long line from an unknown source and that somehow at the end of the process and in Aris's behalf, who was desperately in need of rest, I had managed to come away with two half-loaves, rather than the one I was allotted. What I do remember vividly was the aftermath of this distribution.

As we sat in the corner of our shelter feasting ravenously on the bread, we were suddenly accosted by two prisoners of war much older than us. The clothes they wore indicated they were British, not Americans. One of them dropped to his knees in front of me, while the other remained standing, anxiously it seemed, at the edge of the shelter. Aris and I were surprised by this unexpected and ominous visitation. But before we had a chance to ask the reason for their visit, the kneeling one—he was redheaded—suddenly raised one of his hairy freckled arms, pressed a knife blade concealed under his forefinger into my neck, and, in a seething whisper delivered in a very thick Scottish accent, accused me—"you grrimy lital Yankee bawstad!"—of stealing his comrade's share of the bread and demanded its return.

I was astounded by this accusation but even more frightened by the pressure of the knifepoint on the skin of my throat. I tried to explain to him that I had gotten the second portion of bread for my friend, who was too sick and exhausted to stand in the bread line, that if I had stolen this bread it was from the Germans, not from him and his friend. "Why, for Christ's sake, would I steal bread out of the mouth of one of my fellow prisoners?" But he wasn't listening. He was, it seemed to me, inexorably intent on extorting the bread from us even if he had to cut my throat to do it. I was shaken by the ferocity of his fiery gaze, but I was also outraged by his animal-like assault and for an instant had the urge to resist. But when Aris saw this, he said to me, "Give him the bread, Bill. You're not going to change his mind." This interruption disintegrated whatever will to resist I had. I thrust the remainder of my portion violently into the Scotchman's midriff. "Take the goddamned thing. I hope you choke on it," I said. He shoved it into his field jacket pocket and pulled the knife away for my neck. Then he looked intently at Aris for a moment as if to say something, but apparently changing his mind, he turned to his companion, who seemed anxious, and with a gesture of his head indicated that it was time to leave.

I was appalled by and fiercely angry at our British visitors. I couldn't understand why victims of oppression would want to victimize their fellow victims. They were human predators who had committed an unforgivable act. But then I remembered what the Canadian soldier in Stalag IV-B had said to me about the psychological state of hungry prisoners of war, and my rage began to abate. Did our visitors extort the bread at knifepoint out of sheer malevolence or corruption? Or was it an undiscriminating act of desperation triggered by mind-blinding hunger? But why, then, hadn't I or Aris had the same urge? As I was formulating this question, I remembered that my attacker, strangely, had not demanded the other half-loaf that Aris was holding. And suddenly it struck me like a blow to the solar plexus that perhaps in managing to acquire that second half-loaf, I had been, in some way beyond my capacity to determine, guilty of precisely the crime the Scotchman was accusing me of, that I had indeed stolen the bread out of his comrade's mouth or, if not his comrade's, then out of the mouth of some other one of my starving fellow victims. I was utterly baffled at what at first had seemed so simple. This memory of the Scotchman's equivocal gesture, like a stone thrown into a still body of water, set ripples in motion in my consciousness that resonated outward in ever-expanding circles to encompass the war itself and then faded away into nothingness. What remained in my otherwise bewildered mind was, rightly or wrongly, the strong conviction that if we were going to survive, we would have to escape from what seemed to me the doomed column, a column that for all I knew was heading nowhere.

That evening, after another long day without food on the road going south, our cumbersome, snail-paced march was brought to a halt by the muffled rumbling of heavy and sustained artillery fire in the distance. The order came down from somewhere that we were to remain at this point of our progress for the duration of the night. With this decisive evidence that a major military action was under way in the vicinity, coupled with our guards' anxious indecisiveness, the rumors intensified, and our expectations became more uncertain. The Soviets were mounting their final attack against the German army in the East. The war, we were quite sure now, was ending. What would happen to us? Would our volatile German guards abandon the column? Would they order a mass execution? Because of the ferocity of the Germans' hatred of the racially inferior "Bolshevik Slavs"—I remembered the fiercely pleading eyes of the gaunt Russian prisoner in the stalag outside of Limburg reaching his hand toward me through barbed wire as we marched back to the freight yard—I had by this time come to believe that there were no longer, if there ever were, rules of engagement that would deter the vengeful fury of the Soviet victors. On the other hand, thanks to the previous evidence of ideological differences and the increasingly persistent rumors of growing tension between the Western capitalist and Eastern communist allies—the "gis" and the "Russkis"—I had also come to fear that the Soviet army would do little to repatriate us once the war was over. There were, as far as I could tell, no signs of the American and British armies in the immediate West. We were in a kind of no-man's-land without promise. Above all, however, I was excruciatingly aware of the gnawing in my stomach that, in its unrelenting immediacy, minimized the imperatives, if it did not entirely overpower my consciousness of, the "larger" issues.

It was in this desperate frame of mind, as daylight began to fade, that I broached the questionable idea of escape to Aris. I tried to persuade him—as much as I was trying to persuade myself—that we were not going to make it if we remained attached to the column like parasites on its dying body. Between the volatile unpredictability of our fellow prisoners and the nervousness of our guards, who, besides, were in no position to alleviate our hunger, and the certain knowledge that we were starving, we were sure to lose our struggle to survive. We had no other choice but to try to make a break. If, eventually, we fell into the hands of the Russians, so be it. We'd be better off under them than remaining captives of the Germans, who were becoming increasingly desperate. Our chances of being repatriated would be far greater under their jurisdiction than if we remained with the column.

Aris was not convinced by my argument, but on the other hand, he didn't reject it outright. Like me, he felt that at best the alternatives were not real ones, that they were equally positive and negative. Whatever we decided to do, the consequence was as likely to bring us down as it was to raise us up. It was Aris's need for food that tipped the balance in my favor. Not long afterward, as the pale sun began to set, we decided to risk the break. Earlier we had seen a pair of German peasants, maybe husband and wife, working in a newly plowed field on the elevated horizon overlooking the road we were sitting on. We guessed from their repeated motions in silhouette—reaching into cloth sacks, pulling something out, and then bending to bury it into the earth—that they were planting seed potatoes. So we decided that our first project after taking leave of the column was to raid that potato field.

Escaping, if that's what one would call it, was not difficult because, as I have said, our guards were few and far between, and they seemed, under the constant echoing of the artillery in the distance, more preoccupied with their own imminent fates than with ours. When the sun had set, leaving only a purplish glow on the horizon, and the mass of prisoners were settling down along both sides of the road for the night, Aris and I left the column, as if to find a place to relieve ourselves. Crossing the road, we entered a sparsely wooded area where we hid behind a clump of bushes ostensibly to piss but really to look back at the column of prisoners to see if we were being observed by our guards. Satisfied that there were none in sight, we began climbing up the hillside. On arriving at the crest of the incline, we found to our delight that we had been right. It was indeed a newly planted potato field. Digging into the soft black earth with our fingers, we pulled out a couple of small reddish potatoes, wiped the dirt off on our pants, and immediately began chewing them to appease our intense hunger. Eating ravenously as we dug into the earth, unplanting the seedling potatoes and stuffing them into our pockets, we virtually forgot the perilous circumstances of our occasion.

Suddenly, as we were euphorically harvesting these spoils on our knees, we heard the crackling of gunfire coming from the direction of the column in the road. We realized then that we were offering the viewer below the same silhouetted figures on the horizon that the peasant planters had offered to us. (When I now recall this moment, it is strangely the image of a row of Indians on horseback silhouetted against the evening sky in view of the white settlers in the wagon train below in John Ford's westerns that I see.) Rising, we began running in the southerly direction from which the distant booming of the artillery was coming. But the dozen or so potatoes I had stuffed in my thigh pockets were too heavy, and I began to stumble clumsily, all the while recalling the catastrophic scene of the theft of the sauerkraut, though now devoid of the foreman to rely on for redemption. Having rid himself of his harvest, Aris, irritated by my time-wasting idiocy, urged me to do the same. But I was reluctant to obey him, despite the sustained gunfire. I tried once more, frantically, to run but fell again after a few steps. Finally, convinced that running with the potatoes in my pockets was impossible, I gave up and reluctantly unloaded my precious cargo.

After several minutes of hard running, we became breathless and were compelled to stop and rest. We noted with great relief that the gunfire had ceased and hoped that this meant that we had gotten out of the range of the rifles. But it also occurred to us that this cease-fire meant that the shooters were now pursuing us. Realizing that there was no other alternative, we decided to keep moving in the direction of the artillery fire, hoping that our guards were too preoccupied with their own precarious situation to be concerned about two escaped prisoners. It was dark now and difficult to see behind and ahead of us. Nevertheless, we decided to keep going until we were sure that we were not being pursued. Guided by the muffled reverberations of the artillery fire, we made our way slowly through wooded areas and pastureland toward the south until we were utterly exhausted. It was now deep into the night. Sure at last that we were not being followed, we decided to wait until the morning before resuming our journey into the beckoning and threatening unknown future. We lay down on the damp earth under a tree, curled up together, and left each other to pursue his own imagined future as the echoing bombardment in the distance continued.

Lying there tangled up in my tumultuous thoughts, the immediate silence of the night underscoring the enigmatic language of the reverberating artillery fire in the distance, I couldn't help but envision our deracinated plight in the mocking image of the anxious and bewildered New Testament shepherds guided by the star of Bethlehem toward the manger where Christ, the Savior, was being born. But then I realized that this derisive image itself was nothing more than a new version, triggered by the unceasing thunder of exploding artillery shells in the distance, of the ambiguous, seemingly indifferent and cruel cosmic puppeteer dangling all of us down below from his unapproachable and impregnable fortress above that had haunted me from the time of my captivity, through the firebombing of Dresden and its aftermath among its smoldering ruins, to our sudden evacuation of the sawmill in Rabenau, when those puppet strings seemed to have been cut or the puppeteer had gone mad. I was too anxious to sleep that night in the abysmal middle of nowhere. I tried to control my anxiety by willing my parents, my brothers, my sister, my boyhood friends, my Kathryn, my Claire, into the kaleidoscope of my mind. But the undecipherable language of the explosions in the distance interfered. What prevailed, despite my efforts to establish reference points, was the spectral enigma of tomorrow.

Just before dawn I woke Aris to tell him that it was time to take the dreaded plunge. He agreed. We relieved ourselves and, having decided the night before to follow our initial instinct, began walking once again in the direction of the cannonading, which was still going on, although now only intermittently. As we slogged cautiously through the wet fields some distance from but parallel to the road below, we passed neat small farmhouses that seemed to us, in our destitution, like beckoning remnants of refuge in a world that had fallen apart, even though we knew that their inhabitants, under the menace of the guns, were as unhomed as we were. Eventually the farmhouses gave way to residential houses. And then, about a mile or two in the distance, we saw from the summit of the hill we had climbed the panorama of a small city, the city, it occurred to us, that must have been the destination of the prisoners of war who had been evacuated from Dresden. It didn't offer the comforting prospect of a noble or even picturesque order in which every detail, live or inert, took its proper place within the larger whole, as in certain landscape paintings I had seen that represented distant scenes from such an elevated vantage point. It was, on the contrary, a panorama of utter chaos, a grotesque travesty of the measured and settled uniformity the Western world identifies with civilization. The center of the city was in turmoil, clogged with throngs of civilians and soldiers, passenger cars, horse-drawn wagons, oxcarts, commercial trucks, army transports, all in silent turbulent motion and seemingly going nowhere. And all along the eastern edge of the city heavy smoke was rising high into the gray spring sky and settling into a dark pall. It seemed to us a time of de-creation. Not knowing what else to do, we began our slow decent toward the maelstrom. As we were doing so, we noticed that the bombardment had ceased.

Arriving at the bottom of the incline, we came across an unpaved country road, no doubt one that the peasants in the area used to bring their fruits, vegetables, and livestock to market. Because it was empty, we followed it toward the city. Eventually we encountered a paved two-lane highway that crossed diagonally over the gravel road. At the meeting of the two, we saw a sign on a pole pointing toward the city, which read "Brux, 10 kilometers." It was then that we realized we were in the German Sudetenland from which the Nazis had launched World War II in 1939. This, I remembered, was the area of Czechoslovakia that Chamberlain and Deladier, with the support of the German majority in the region clamoring for union with Germany, ceded to Hitler at Munich. Given the confusion in the city we had seen from above, we were surprised to find that the highway leading in and out of the city was empty and wondered why it bore few signs of traffic. At the same time we were relieved and decided, come what may, to follow it into town.

About five or six kilometers later, under the ominous silence of the guns, we arrived at last at the circumference of the war zone. The streets and avenues were clogged with clamorous traffic. Everyone and everything—men, women, beasts, trucks, automobiles, carts—were moving slowly, discordantly, and frantically in a southwesterly direction. It was clear to us that the city was being evacuated not only by the German troops but also, strangely, by a large, seemingly frightened portion of the population and that the civilians and the soldiers were vying for the right of way. We entered the disintegrating city in fear and trembling. So desperately intent were its inhabitants on flight, however, that no one, to our great relief, paid attention to us. We were, it seemed, entirely on our own.

It took us a while to adjust to this unexpected turn in the itinerary that had brought us so suddenly out of captivity into liberation with a vengeance. We were sure now that the artillery fire we had been hearing all this time had come from the attacking Soviets and that the German army on the Eastern front had suffered a decisive defeat and was in chaotic retreat. It was very possible, we thought with tentative elation, that the war was over or about to come to its end. But then what? Our world, a world of nobodies, had finally collided with the other, larger substantial world—the world that counted. We seemed to have been propelled into another zero zone or, even worse, caught in a furious vortex that was disintegrating everything "they" had built and sucking every chip of the debris, big and small, high and low, down into its pulverizing centerless center.

When we entered the city, we had seen hundreds of Czechoslovakian flags—blue, white, and red—hanging out of the upper windows of tenement buildings. And we had inferred that these had been displayed by the inhabitants as proof of their identity as Czechs, hoping by this symbolic avowal to be spared the terrible fate the German Czechs, who had urged Hitler to incorporate the Sudetenland into Germany, anticipated at the hands of the conquering Soviet army. These Russian soldiers, we had learned incrementally during the time of our captivity, were thirsty for revenge. They had borne witness over a cataclysmic five-year period of unremitting war to the invasion and devastation of their mother country by invaders who had flaunted the international rules of warfare in the name of the Aryan people's war against communism and the inferior Slavic race and had ruthlessly and brutally slaughtered many millions of their fellow soldiers and civilians, including prisoners. I saw all this degradation and cruelty perpetrated by the German command earlier that winter in the hollow stare of that living corpse as we filed by the open-air barbed wire enclosure that housed only Russian prisoners of war on our way back to the railroad yard in Limburg. We were pretty certain, therefore, that the German exodus from the city was not simply a flight in the face of the imminent arrival of the Soviet troops. The German soldiers and civilian refugees were moving in a southwesterly direction, which made us think that the American and British forces advancing from the West were now close by and that the multitude of German civilians and soldiers fleeing from Brux were intent on surrendering to and seeking refuge with them. In the midst of this violent intrusion of the outside world, which had always been a haunting but invisible presence, into our isolated inside world, Aris and I decided that our best choice was to go with the flow.

We joined the crowd somewhere in the middle of the city as it was making its way toward the main highway out of it. We walked silently, our hearts in our mouths, for a while by the side of a ragged group of civilians trying as best we could to keep a low profile. No one seemed to notice us, or if they did, they didn't care. We were relieved by this indifference. With luck we'd soon be back in Allied hands. Not long afterward, as we were indulging in this fragile hope, a number of German army trucks conveying soldiers began to force their way from behind us through the throng, blasting their horns to clear a path. In the tumult one of the trucks pulled up beside us, and two young armed German soldiers—they were, I noticed, no older than we were—jumped off and began making their way toward us. My first reaction was a sinking despair. So this was the end of our escape? We would be taken back into German custody and then . . . But to our surprise they were not hostile when they reached us. They were, in fact, as disoriented, even frightened, as we were. They asked us anxiously and hurriedly in broken English who we were, where we had come from, where we were going. We told them that we were American prisoners of war, that we had been evacuated from Dresden and then let loose as the Russian army began attacking this city, that we had assumed the war was over and were trying to find our way back to American lines. On hearing us through, they didn't assume the demeanor of authority as we expected; rather, they invited us—in a way that seemed as much a plea—to board their truck, which was headed toward a town named Komotini, some thirty or so kilometers southwest of Brux, which, they thought, the American army had reached in its drive eastward. Their intention, they said, without referring to their motives, was to surrender to the American army.

For a moment I felt a vindictive exuberance at the bizarre irony of this startling invitation. Our captors were begging us to become theirs. They thought they would be safer in the hands of the Americans than they would be if they fell to the Russians, and Aris and I were their intermediaries. But then, looking at these defeated—I would now say demythologized—young German soldiers, the situation suddenly underwent a strange sea change. They metamorphosed before my eyes into two forlorn boys, no less overwhelmed and dislocated by events beyond their control than we were. In the midst of this deranged world we were all comrades, lost and desperately seeking together a way out of the same seemingly labyrinthine predicament we had been driven into.

Our German interlocutors informed us that the highway heading toward Komotini was no more than a kilometer from our present position and that when we got there we'd be free to travel at the normal speed. Relieved to think that we were at last on our way to the American lines and liberation from the agony of uncertainty, we accepted their invitation. When we had all climbed aboard, the troop carrier resumed its bullying effort to clear a path for itself through the swarming crowd of civilians and foot soldiers. Our progress through the city was slow and, despite the claims of privilege and urgency made by the soldier driver in the cab, was met occasionally by angry resistance. But we were making some headway. All the while our anxious new young friends were prying us with questions about the war in the West, where and how we were taken prisoners, and where we had spent our captivity in Germany. When we told them that we had been evacuated from Dresden after the bombing, their questions became even more eager and intense. To them, it seemed, the destruction of the city was still a rumor. Was it really true that the entire city had been burned down to the ground? Had everyone in the city been killed in the firebombing? Did the Americans and British use a new kind of bomb that caused a tornado of fire? Had the Russians persuaded the Americans to destroy the undefended city? Or was all this Nazi propaganda intended to inspire them to fight to the death against the murderous Russian barbarians on the Eastern front?

As they were struggling to ask these questions in a mixture of German, English, and French and we to answer them, our truck approached a large hospital on the front lawn on which a multitude of wounded soldiers in various degrees of mutilation were lying on stretchers apparently waiting to be evacuated. Suddenly we saw a middle-aged German officer in dress uniform wearing the ss insignia running toward us brandishing a Lugar and shouting commands to stop. The truck came to a halt. In a loud angry voice he asked one of the soldiers, pointing to Aris and me, who we were and why we were riding in a German military vehicle. Without waiting for an answer, he ordered us at gunpoint to get out of the truck. It was clear that he was commandeering it in behalf of the wounded soldiers on the hospital lawn. We got off the truck and stood there waiting. Frozen by the muzzle of the pistol in my face, I foresaw this moment as the end of our infernal journey. But once more fate, or rather the exigencies of the immediate situation, intervened. Looking at us for a while as if he were deliberating, the ss officer then pointed his Lugar in the direction of the ragged flow of traffic and waved us on as if he were flicking fleas off his immaculate jacket. Then turning to the young soldiers who had befriended us, he ordered them sharply to board as many of the wounded as the carrier could bear. Aris and I left without a word. We were grateful that we had survived another crisis but at the same time no more certain about anything than we were before we had been invited to board the truck.

On the way we passed a substantial number of wood-framed buildings that looked like German army barracks that had been recently abandoned. We eventually arrived at the intersection between the city street we were following and the highway heading toward Komotini. The highway too was clogged with anxious civilian refugees, carts, wagons, and cars bearing their belongings and German army trucks carrying exhausted and defeated soldiers, but traffic was moving faster. Instead of merging with the column, however, we stopped by the roadside to evaluate the situation. I was, perversely no doubt, reluctant to join the mass of humanity headed toward Komotini. It was still a long way off. And after all, the information that the American army had advanced to that point was only a rumor. More decisively, I was feeling weak and excruciatingly hungry, not to say anxious about Aris's progressively deteriorating condition. We had eaten nothing since those small raw potatoes several days earlier and were utterly exhausted. Our chances, I thought, of finding food and a place to rest in a city that was being evacuated by many of its inhabitants and by the German military were pretty good. Then I remembered the military barracks we had seen a short way back. Conjuring in my mind a cornucopia of food and drink abandoned by the routed German army as if it were real, I suggested to Aris—it was actually more a resolution than a suggestion—that we return there to explore the possibilities those "empty" barracks offered. Aris was ambivalent. Returning to American custody was uppermost in his mind, but he too was hungry and far weaker than I was. So he capitulated to my urging. Abandoning the advancing retreating column, we headed back in the direction of the barracks.

It was by this time late in the afternoon. The guns in the distance had ceased firing. A portentous silence, exacerbated by the grinding engines of slow-moving vehicles, hung over the doomed city. On our arrival at the compound our original guess was confirmed. It was indeed a group of two-storied army barracks, built on an incline, that had been abandoned by their inhabitants. Cautiously opening the upper-level door of one of the buildings, we entered a large room containing a row of cots on both sides. At the far end of the room we saw a stand full of stacked rifles with cartridge boxes at one side. The room was in complete disarray. Most of the cots were unmade. Army uniforms—shirts, jackets, caps, pants, boots, dress bayonets—were scattered all over the floor. Had their owners changed into civilian clothes before departing? Several pistols lay on footlockers. Magazines, newspapers, letters, envelopes, photographs, lay strewn on the cots, footlockers, and floor. All this disorder was testimony to the suddenness of the evacuation. And the absent presence of its former inhabitants, exacerbated by the debris of a former world, reawakened in me, poignantly, the sense that they were human beings before they were soldiers.

What struck us immediately with physical force on entering the abandoned barrack, however, was not this unsoldierly disorder but the tantalizing aroma of recently cooked food. Like a couple of sniffing stray dogs, we began searching for its invisible source, but to our disappointment and wonder we found no visible signs of it. Just as we were about to give up the hunt, however, I happened to look out of one the windows overlooking a sort of fenced-in courtyard. There below, like a mirage, I saw a huge round vat on rollers—a field kitchen—that was half-filled with what looked like a thick creamy white soup. It couldn't have been abandoned more than an hour earlier because its contents were still steaming. Finding the door leading to the lower level, we rushed stumblingly down the stairs into the courtyard. The steaming vat, like the sudden appearance of the Holy Grail in the vicinity of the Castle Perilous to crazed Parsifal, beckoned as if it were inviting us into the promised land of milk and honey. But what the chalice that had appeared to us contained was neither wine nor milk and honey; it was several gallons of a hot rice soup the spicy aroma of which, to us, was infinitely more enticing than the wine sought after by the knights of the Round Table and, for that matter, the ambrosial nectar that inebriated the Olympian gods. We mounted the ladder blocks on each side, bent over the rim of the vat so our faces were inches away from its thick, white liquid content. And as our noses bathed voluptuously in the exquisitely pungent smell, we shoveled fistfuls of the steaming rice into our ravenous mouths. The sauerkraut in the cellar of the factory in Rabenau was as dung compared to this ethereal taste.

As we were wallowing in the vat, the roar of low-flying aircraft, accompanied by the chatter of machine-gun fire, shattered the silence. Looking up, we saw a number of Soviet fighter planes—maybe a squadron of MIGs—strafing the city and the highway leading out of it. We were startled. But this danger didn't deter us from the mesmerizing vat. We plunged back into it, gorging ourselves on the rice as the fighters flew overhead in what seemed like incoherent patterns, firing bursts and dropping an occasional bomb on some unknown or maybe random target. The MIGs' targets, we thought, were primarily concentrations of German troops still in the city or on the highway in flight.

Suddenly, however, one of them came screaming in toward us, strafing the ground ahead. We dove under the vat just as the bullets started to tear up the earth in the courtyard, shattering the walls and windows of the barracks. After making its pass, the fighter banked full circle and came in again, firing mercilessly and disintegrating everything in its path. Curled up tight to provide the smallest possible target, we were petrified, waiting with our stomachs in our mouths, for the fighter's next run. The MIG's pilot, I thought, had spotted the army barracks and was intent on demolishing it. But after making its turn, it flew of tangentially to another target. We waited, huddled under the vat, for about five minutes. The strafing continued but not near us. Eventually we stood up, looked at each other for a moment as if to ask what we should do next, and then shrugging my shoulders, I said, "Fuck it, Aris!" and dove back into the rice. Aris followed, and we ate until we could keep no more of the rice down. When we were finished, we noticed that the fighters had withdrawn as suddenly, apparently, as they had appeared. Darkness was descending, and the helpless city was silent once again.

Aris and I went back into the barracks, found the shower room, stripped our dirty, louse-infested clothes off our grimy emaciated bodies, and for the first time in months, washed ourselves under the stream of falling cold and exhilarating water. Then, after putting our clothes back on, we armed ourselves with the Lugars that had been left behind by the fleeing Germans, picked out our respective cots, and without saying a word, laid down under the indifferent or malicious or angry sky to rest our weary bodies or, more accurately, to make the hopeless effort to make sense of the fractured events we had experienced that tumultuous day.

What my mind locked in on, as if it were the blind mouth of an infant seeking the nipple of its mother's breast, was the exorbitant pleasure I felt eating those first fistfuls of rice in the midst of dislocation, death, and destruction. This pleasure, I couldn't help but remark, was strangely as unspeakable as the horror I felt at seeing and smelling the pile of charred and rotting bodies on that first day in the inner city of Dresden after the firebombing. Try as I might, however, I couldn't make the connection between these stark antitheses overt. Nevertheless, I knew way down deep in my being that "it" was there—that there was a resolution in that mocking discord—and all through most of that night my unpracticed mind circle around the enigma like a moth around a lamp, until sometime before dawn I fell asleep.

Strange to say I can no more describe that pleasure of eating the rice now, sixty years later, than I can the horror of seeing and smelling those corpses in the ruins of Dresden. It will have to suffice to say that I remember that experience as I do the experience of the corpses almost as exactly as it happened that day in a foreign city when, in the midst of a gratuitous violence that made no sense to me, I, as a young boy, was awakening in astonishment to an awareness of my expendability—and to an anger at the world we young programmed soldiers, in our clumsy and tangled effort to articulate our sense of dignity and worth, referred to as "They," that amorphous body of the elect that, like the Pied Piper, played the tune to which we danced to our destruction. From that moment both experiences, so jarringly discordant, remained somehow interlocked in my mind. They are testimony to the fact that more than any other time in my life, this one seared into my very being the indissoluble belongingness of the soul and the body, pain and pleasure, living and dying, poiesis and excrement, the high and the low, elect and preterite—and my revulsion at all transcendental views of human being, interpretations of our existence from above, that represent them as hierarchical opposites, as a war in which it is the duty of the first term to annihilate the second.

It was not until several years later, however, when I was at Wesleyan University, that these recalcitrant antitheses "resolved" themselves into a "discordia concours." I was suffering from the spiritual turmoil—now, in the wake of the Vietnam War, reduced to "post-traumatic stress syndrome"—inflicted on my psyche by captivity, the carnage of Dresden, and the anarchy of its aftermath and struggling to make the volatile fragments cohere. It happened, paradoxically, when I came across T. S. Eliot's great Christian poem, *Four Quartets*, his own agonized "raid on the inarticulate" in the wake of World War II—his effort to come to terms with the civilizational catastrophe in a language that the war had rendered anachronistic. I am referring particularly to the deeply moving polyphonic lines from "East Coker," in which the poet, struggling to accommodate the carnal life of the lowly, "Earth feet, loam feet, lifted in country mirth," to the life of the soul, ends up (in my mind) imagining, in Edward Said's beautiful and resonant rendition, "'the whole consort dancing together' contrapuntally":

Keeping time,
Keeping the rhythm in their dancing
As in their living in the living seasons
The time of the seasons and the constellations

The time of milking and the time of harvest
The time of the coupling of man and woman
And that of beast. Feet rising and falling,
Eating and drinking. Dung and death.

On awakening from our troubled sleep early the next morning, Aris and I were immediately struck by the silence that pervaded the city beyond the barracks. The artillery guns were still silent, the sky was empty of aircraft, and the rumble of motors on the highway seemed to have markedly diminished. We were eager to discover what was happening out there in that ominous void waiting to be filled. But our stomachs, bloated by the rice soup we had devoured, had begun to feel the effects of our incontinent gorging the night before. We decided to remain in the barracks until the attack of diarrhea had run its course. Late in the afternoon, after my third or fourth sprint to the latrine, the silence was broken by the renewed roar of heavily laden trucks coming toward us from the direction of the inner city. Going outside, we were shocked to see down below a huge convey of Soviet troop carriers filled with soldiers entering the city from the East and moving slowly in the direction of Komotini. The slouching beast had arrived. We were both elated at the definitive end of our captivity and also anxious to learn the nature of this beast and the new dispensation it was announcing. It was April, the time of the return of Persephone to the world, but April was a cruel month. It wasn't easy to will her into being.

7. Love in the Ruins

It is Apollo who tranquilizes the individual by drawing boundary lines, and who, by enjoining again and again the practice of self-knowledge, reminds him of the holy, universal norms. But lest the Apollonian tendency freeze all form into Egyptian rigidity, and in attempting to prescribe its orbit to each particular wave inhibit the movement of the lake, the Dionysian flood tide periodically destroys all the circles in which the Apollonian will would confine Hellenism.

FRIEDRICH NIETZSCHE, *The Birth of Tragedy*

The events of my last few days in Brux were devoid of any logic and thus resist being reduced to a story. The city was now in an interregnum, between a world that had been utterly destroyed and one yet to be born. To me its name, Brux, for all practical purposes no longer referred to anything familiar. That world had been utterly estranged, had become overnight a no-man's-land—a "crippled zone," in Thomas Pynchon's resonant phrase. It was, in some primordial sense, no longer a city; it was a post-civilizational wilderness without borders, without physical and moral reference points. Those human beings who remained there no longer inhabited it; the war had transformed them into nomads. And virtually everything associated with the city, the very embodiment of civilization—identity, culture, law, order, beauty—seemed to have given way to its opposite: difference, nature, lawlessness, anarchy, ugliness. And we too, Aris and I, having been what I would now call decentered or unhomed, had become wanderers in the wilderness, devoid of identities, of direction, hunter-gatherers living off the destroyed land. Being in the midst of this estranged world was a frightening condition.

During those days in the interregnum I was profoundly struck and disoriented by the startling novelty, the singularity, of everything in the previous world I had taken for granted—from the clothing I wore to the traffic lights I obeyed at street intersections to the books I read to the laws binding people I lived by—and by their vulnerability. But I want to reiterate, the anxiety-provoking randomness of the events we experienced during those days were to me, in some inexplicable sense, also uncannily bound to a feeling of exhilaration. In being dislocated by my new awareness of the fragility of the civilization I had inherited from my elders, I also realized that its order had not arisen naturally, as if it had emerged fully developed from the womb of history in the fullness of time but was made by man—by European and American and Russian humanity. Even more provocative, I became vaguely but disturbingly aware that these European and American and Russian makers of our "civilization" were not ordinary people like us, flailing helplessly in the crippled zone, but a difficult to identify, though very real, "chosen" few and that despite the histories I had read in school, they had made the civilized world very badly. But there was for me some faint and ungraspable redemptive impulse buried in this dark awareness. What I was witnessing in confronting these singular and unnarratable events was not simply the end of the world as I had known it. It certainly was that. But it was also, in some indefinable visceral sense, a beginning.

It is the morning of our second day in the new world. Aris and I take another shower in freezing-cold water and then search the abandoned barracks for underwear and clothing to replace our rags. Aris discards his GI fatigue pants for a virtually new pair of oversized dark green woolen German army pants but decides to keep his GI tops and his green U.S. Army field jacket. I keep my English army trousers but exchange my filthy and crusted U.S. Army shirt for a new soft green sweater-like German Wehrmacht shirt, which is emblazoned on the left chest with a red Nazi swastika woven into the breast of a stylized eagle. With great relief we replace our dirty underwear with clean ones we find in the lockers and our dilapidated shoes with new, spit-polished German army boots. I go to the rifle rack at the far end of the barracks, pick up a long-sheathed bayonet, and fit it onto my belt. Then I pick up the black Lugar I had taken to bed with me. I look at it intently for a while and then check to see if it's loaded. When I find that it is, I shove it in my pants under my belt, hoping I'll never have to use it. Aris follows suit. We have no idea what to do next. It's six of one and a half-dozen of another, as Aris puts it to me. But something has to be done. After appropriating a couple of rucksacks hanging on pegs in the room, we head for the door. When we get there, we pause and we eye each other over with willed gravity and then burst out laughing without saying anything. We look like harlequins. But we are really fitting denizens of this absurd dying world that's also being reborn. So we cross the boundary and venture out into its emptied-out space.

The din of passing trucks in the near distance has continued unabated all through the night. We decide to make our entry into the new world not by returning to the highway going to Komotini but by taking a side street back into the center of the city in the vicinity of the hospital, where we had been evicted from the troop carrier by the German officer. As we walk, we notice once again the anomaly of welcoming Czech flags hanging out of the apartment windows of a city in the Sudetenland, testimony to the pervasive fear the triumphant conquerors instilled in the defeated natives. And then, on arriving at the conjunction between our street and the main artery leading out of the city, we see and hear the convoy of Soviet army trucks carrying troops in dingy gray, weather-beaten uniforms and artillery moving at a snail's pace in the direction of the highway to Komotini. I am immediately struck by the Red Star painted on the hood of every truck and especially by the occasional red flag bearing the hammer and sickle attached to the outside rear-view mirror of some of the trucks. I'm not sure why. They are powerful symbols of our liberation, but they also strike me as strangely foreign. I am momentarily disturbed by this ambiguity. I recall the marked difference our officers reiteratively insinuated in information sessions between our European and our Eastern allies during basic training and while we were preparing for combat in England. We were never allowed to forget that our Russian allies were communists. We enter the avenue and begin walking in the opposite direction from the movement of the trucks. Some of the soldiers in the trucks notice us but don't seem to pay attention. Most are boisterous, waving canteens at the people on the streets, singing Soviet marching songs, and shouting Russian words we can't make out but assume have something to do with the victory of the motherland.

A couple of blocks farther down we see two long lines of soldiers, rifles slung on their shoulders, extending from the artery on which the trucks are passing to an invisible source in the depths of one of the side streets. On coming closer, we are surprised to see that most of them are girls, no older than us, that they are combat soldiers who had clearly been fighting alongside their fellow males. We had seen British and American women in uniform, but they were not combat soldiers. This difference underscores my sense of the foreignness of the conquerors. The members of the first line are handing empty ten-gallon gasoline cans down to the source; those of the second line are handing full cans back to the slowly passing trucks, where they are taken over by a designated receiver. For a moment we think the women soldiers are replenishing the truck with gasoline. But then, remembering the joyous singing and waving of canteens emanating from the passing convoy, we realize that the gas cans contain wine and that the hidden source is a liberated winery or a wine cellar.

As we watch this unexpected spectacle in troubled awe, one of the young female soldiers notices us, no doubt because of the outlandish clothing we are wearing. Breaking away from the line, she comes toward us. Her sudden gesture draws the attention of everyone in the vicinity, both in the lines and in the passing trucks, toward us, and it fills us with anxiety. She asks us something in Russian, which we take to mean "Who are you?" I tell her in English and then in German that we are Americans, "prisoners of war, *Kriegsgefangene.*" She seems to understand that and goes on to ask something else, which I can't fathom. But guessing that it might have something to do with what has brought us to this city, I say, drawing a finger in a perpendicular motion, "*Arbeitskommando* in Dresden." At hearing the word *Dresden*, her eyes light up, as if the sound I have uttered were magical, and she begins to talk animatedly and with great intensity. The soldier undergoes a transformation before my eyes. She becomes a pretty girl. I notice the curved shape of her full breasts protruding, ever so faintly and enticingly, behind her thick gray army shirt as she raises an arm as if to underscore her words, and I feel for an exquisite second the surge of sexual desire, that sweet and agonizing urge that the war and my captivity had obliterated from my young body. I try to decipher her words by attending to her bodily gestures. But the language barrier intervenes at this pregnant moment of border crossing. What does the word *Dresden* mean to her? What has it ignited in those shining black oriental eyes? Realizing the futility of communicating, she stops talking and throws up her hands in resignation. She looks at us, shrugs her shoulders, and smiles. Then, turning toward her companions in the line, she says something to one of them. A few seconds later she is handed a canteen full of wine, which she offers to me. "*Drink*," she says, and, as I take a sip, she adds with a cordial emphasis, "*Nastrovia*." I thank her for her kindness and pass the canteen to Aris. He drinks, and she—this beautiful, godlike apparition in a soldier's uniform—repeats the golden word.

Aris and I find ourselves in the far eastern edge of Brux. We're scavenging for food because we've finished the rice soup in the field kitchen. It's a warehouse district that's been destroyed, no doubt by the artillery fire we had heard as we were approaching the city a few days earlier. It's late in the afternoon, and the pale spring sun is beginning to descend behind the skeletons of the shattered buildings. The Czech flags are everywhere, though the remaining citizenry are more or less invisible. At the end of the empty street on which we've been walking, we turn the corner and see a forlorn old black mare harnessed to a small farmer's wagon, her bones protruding from her emaciated body. She's tethered to a street lamp and, between snorts, nibbles at debris in the gutter. We hurry over to the wagon and, finding it empty, look around in search of the owner. We notice a shattered wooden door facing us across the street big enough to accommodate a couple of large trucks. Crossing over to the other side, we enter the darkness, our Lugars in hand, and are immediately struck by a variety of pungent sweet smells. When our eyes become used to the dark, we realize that we have stumbled onto an apparently abandoned storehouse of bottled preserves—strawberry, raspberry, blueberry, orange, apricot, and others we had never seen before—that had partially escaped destruction. We call to find out if anyone is there but get no response. Then, putting our pistols back into our belts, we sit down amid the mountain of broken glass jars, open one that's still intact containing strawberry jam, and using our fingers as spoons, begin to eat. Despite the indigestion I have been suffering since devouring the immense quantity of rice in the barracks courtyard, this strawberry jam is the first taste of something sweet I have had since being captured. The sauerkraut in the cellar of the factory in Rabenau and the rice in the courtyard of the barracks had satisfied my hunger for food; this jam reminds me of feelings beyond bodily need and is rejuvenating.

When we are satiated, we return to the street outside. On looking at each other in the light of day, we both break out laughing. Our faces, like those of children who have raided their mother's cupboard—or dresser—are covered with garish red and blue streaks. For that lightning flash second the war subsides, and I feel like the invulnerable young boy I was before being dragged into this inferno with no seeming exit. But the horse's sudden whinny jolts me back into the reality of our situation, and we recommence our search for the owner of the horse and wagon. We walk up and down the street calling "Hello! Hello! *Wo bist du?*" but find no signs of anyone. When we are satisfied that the horse has been abandoned, we begin to plunder the demolished storehouse. Most of the jars are broken, and shards of glass make the scavenging difficult. But we do find a dozen or so bottles in the morass that are still intact, and we load them into the wagon. Then, realizing that it's getting dark outside, we untie the rope that tethers the wagon to the street lamp and climb into it. Only then does it occur to us that neither of us knows how to drive a horse-drawn wagon and that even if we did, we have nowhere to go with our loot.

The reins that are tied to the wagon seat suddenly remind me of a terrible moment in my childhood, my first and last encounter with a horse.

I was around eight or nine years old, and several of us were playing in the street in front of a long gray workers' apartment house that stood adjacent to a shoe shop in Newport. My mother had brought me on that Saturday afternoon to visit a friend, a *patriotissa*, who worked in the factory. At the intersection between the street on which we were playing and one heading perpendicularly up a steep incline, the mailman had parked his horse and buggy while he was delivering mail to the apartment dwellers. Always impatient with routine games, I enticed my companions to walk over to the wagon to admire the horse of the legendary mailman Charlie Jobes. Then, mimicking the latest cowboy hero of the Saturday afternoon western serials to prove my courage to one of the girls I was especially attracted to, I mounted the wagon, picked up the reins, and waving them up and down, shouted, "Giddy-ap! Giddy-ap!" Frightened by my foreign voice, the horse snorted and stamped for an instant and then, to my horror, reared and started to gallop up the hill. I kept shouting, "Whoa! Whoa!" but the horse wouldn't obey. Out of the corner of my eye I saw the mailman, who had just come out of one of the apartments, running at full speed beside the horse. He grabbed its bridle and after a terrific effort brought the frightened animal to stand. Then he reached up, pulled me down off the wagon, and commenced to spank me.

Recalling this traumatic scene and our lack of a specific destination, I suggest to Aris that we abandon our scheme. But he is unwilling. He is too exhausted to do any more walking. As for a destination, he suggests that we return to the abandoned army barracks for the time being. Realizing that there's no changing his mind, I exchange places with him, hoping that the language he uses to address the horse will be more magical than mine was. He picks up the reins and gently slaps them across the mare's rump, and to my astonishment, she begins to walk slowly. When we get to the end of the street, Aris pulls the mare's head to the right, and she responds. We turn into a severely damaged part of the city. There at the end of the block facing us, we see the bare back wall of a building, several stories high, that has been destroyed by artillery fire. On it, painted in blood-red letters at least ten feet long, we read, "HITLER IST TOT!" And above it a huge black swastika, a red slash running diagonally across it.

"The war must be over," I tell Aris in a subdued voice. He looks at me as if he were flicking a gnat off his nose and says, "So? What's that got to do with us?" I, looking at the graffiti and shaking my head, say, more to myself than him, "It's so crazy, man!"

We are somewhere in a residential section of the city, close to but hidden from the highway on which the Soviet troop carriers are slowly moving in a southwesterly direction toward Komotini. There is rubble everywhere, but the area has come through the shelling pretty much intact. The Czech flags hanging out the apartment windows above us are ubiquitous. Loud and cacophonous, the roar of the shifting gears coming from the near distance frightens our mare. Acutely attuned to the realities of the between world in which we are wandering aimlessly, we call her Persephone after the ancient Greek goddess who ruled in the underworld in the winter months and the upper world in the spring all because she ate the forbidden seeds of a pomegranate. As we sit in the cart agonizing over the question of our next move amid so much confusion, we hear a female voice calling from above. Looking up, we see two women, their heads leaning out the third-floor window of one of the apartments. For a moment we think they are trying to catch the attention of someone, perhaps a neighbor, in the street. Because there's no one in the vicinity, however, we soon realize that the voice is addressing us. "Kommen Sie! Kommen Sie!" one of them calls, beckoning with her finger, then pointing below to the entrance of the apartment building. We look at each other as if to say, "What the hell!" tether Persephone to a lamp pole, and enter the apartment house.

On ascending the three flights of stairs, we are greeted by the two comely women at the door of their apartment. They lead us into the living room and invite us to sit down on a divan. They appear to be somewhere between thirty-five and forty years old. One is thin, the other more portly. Both are very good-looking, and their clothing conceals well-built bodies. The thin one—her name is Brigitte—has hair the color of straw that is piled in a bun; the hair of the portly one—her name is Frieda—is dark brown and hangs loosely down her back. But they do not strike me, as I had thought at first, to be prostitutes. Both wear wedding rings and nondescript housedresses that come down below their knees. Their handsome faces are drawn, on the edge of being prematurely wrinkled, and they seem to express anxiety. As Brigitte prepares coffee, Frieda sits down beside us and begins nervously to explain their curious invitation. She speaks a little French and English, along with her German, and between them and much body language manages to convey to us something close to the pertinent information.

Frieda says at once that their husbands are German-Czech soldiers who have been fighting on the Eastern front, that they have heard nothing from them in several months and have all but concluded from the reports about the savage fighting there that they have been killed in the war or, worse than that, taken prisoners by the barbarian "Bolsheviks." Now that the war is over (it is in this offhand manner that our guess upon encountering the graffiti announcing the death of Hitler is corroborated), she says, they are terrified by the possibility that the Bolshevik occupiers will unleash a reign of terror against the Sudetenland Germans in revenge for the devastation of their own homeland by the Germans. It is already being rumored throughout the city, she says with great anxiety, that the Bolshevik soldiers are billeting themselves in German-Czech households, turning them into animal dens, and raping the women and even their children. They had been watching us from the window of their apartment all that day to determine who we were. Confused by the strange mismatched clothing we wore, they were for a long time uncertain about what to do. But when they saw Aris patting our horse's shaggy mane and heard him address her kindly as "old girl," they decided that we weren't vicious brutes and guessed we were probably British or American prisoners of war. On satisfying themselves that we at least weren't Russian, they decided to risk inviting us in and offering us their hospitality in return for our protection. When Brigitte returns with the coffee, she says almost pleadingly, "*Ja, unsere Herren, Schlafen sie, hier; couchez-vous ici avec nous*; sleep with us"—or something like that.

In response to this strange proposal we tell these women that we are, indeed, Americans—prisoners of war who had been evacuated from Dresden after the firebombing, marched into Czechoslovakia, and then abandoned to our own fates when the Soviet army attacked and overran the city. We are extremely grateful for their kind hospitality, but we are hardly in a position to protect them. I look down at the Lugar between my belt and my scrawny belly, lay my palm on the butt that juts out of my pants, and say to Brigitte with what must seem to her like a stupid grin, "I don't even know how to use this thing."

They both laugh. That doesn't matter, they assure us. What does matter is that we occupy the apartment. The Russians won't interfere with their American allies.

"Besides," I say, not at all certain that I am right, "what makes you think the Russian soldiers will come here to force themselves on you? They haven't been fighting all these years just to get a chance to rape German women. They're here to liberate Czechoslovakia from the tyranny of the Nazis, to bring peace, to begin rebuilding the world, to make it better than the one that the war has destroyed."

They look at each other, as if in disbelief and then turn toward us with faces that seem motherly. Frieda says, "*Ach, unsere Herren, ihr seid Kinder. Vous êtes enfantes*; you are children!"

I am not quite convinced that she is right, though her words make their mark. I tell her that the anxiety they feel as German women over their safety is understandable, given their circumstances. It's true that they are members of a defeated people, that all the laws have been annulled, and that now anything goes. But they must dwell on the bright, not the dark, possibilities of this in-between time. They must have faith in their fellow men, their empathy with those who suffer, especially the innocent. As I strain to articulate my confused thoughts in languages over which I have no command, I realize that I'm flailing. I look at Aris, who has said nothing all this time, and see that he is very tired and forlorn. I abruptly drop the issue and say to the German women, "Okay, if you really want us to stay with you, we will."

Night has fallen. I go down to the street where the cart is tethered, fill a rope bucket of straw, and put it around Persephone's head. Then I pick up an armful of jam jars and return to the apartment. The women have prepared a supper of soup, larded bread, and beer. We eat in the awkward silence. When the meal is over, they prepare baths, first for Aris and then for me. When we are refreshed, Brigitte leads me to her room, while Frieda shows Aris to hers. Brigitte hands me a pair of men's woolen pajamas. She says, "You will sleep in my bed," and leaves the room.

I try desperately, despite my awareness of the impossibility, to place this bizarre episode in the fractured morass of the events that have happened during the last few days. I think of the blue, white, and red Czech flags hanging out the windows, the terror in the faces of the civilians, the allusions to Russian brutality we had heard in training. What, I wonder, do these women expect of us? Do they want sex as well as protection? Do they think we want sex in payment for our protection? As I lay in Brigitte's bed baffled by these anxieties and wondering if she will return—and if she does, what I will do—the door of the bedroom opens. My eyes are closed, feigning sleep. I hear her footsteps coming toward the bed. There is a long pause—I can feel her gaze on my body—and then I feel her hand gently ruffling my shaggy hair, and in a sad whisper she repeats, "Ach, mein Herr, du bist ein Kind." She lies down beside me, her back toward my front. I can hear her suppressing sobs. But I say nothing. What, I ask myself, is there to say? Who is protecting whom?

We have parked Persephone on a side street and made our way to the center of the city, where a steady stream of Soviet troop carriers is passing through, while Soviet soldiers are leading German prisoners to some unknown destination. Anxious to get our bearings in the deterritorialized world we find ourselves in, we have ventured beyond the apartment to this tumultuous thoroughfare where we're likely to discover news of the outside world, not least the whereabouts of the American army. We are sitting at a sidewalk table of an abandoned *Gasthaus* that borders the main artery, observing the passing Russian soldiers in the hope of singling one out who looks as if he would be willing to talk with us.

As we look, we are suddenly accosted by two Russian soldiers who have closed in on us from the opposite direction of the traffic flow. They seem to be military police. One of them, a dour-looking middle-aged man with a long scar running down his cheek to his neck, who seems officious, stretches out his hand to us and asks for our "papers." We, of course, have none. He seems irritated, and from his reiteration of the word *Deutsche*, we infer that he thinks we are Germans in some kind of disguise. We tell him that we are American prisoners of war—"Amerikanische Kriegsgefangene." But he is not listening. He raises his right hand and puts his finger on the swastika and eagle on my shirt then turns to his companion, a much younger man, around our age, and says something to him. How can we explain our dress to these interrogators? How can we convince them that we are Americans, that we are their allies, that we have been fighting the same enemy? I am bewildered and feel helpless. In that moment I realize with the shock of recognition what I have felt increasingly from the time I was drafted into the army: that I, and in some sense all of us in this borderless zone, have become a *nobody*, that the war has robbed me of my identity, that I am utterly at the mercy of powers beyond my capacity to control or resist.

As I flounder among the shards of this vision, I suddenly remember my dog tags hanging around my neck. Pulling them up over my head and pointing to my name, I show them to the Russian soldier. "See here, my name, William V. Spanos; my serial number, 51269816 T43-4409; my mother's name, Mary S. Spanos; and my home address in the United States, 99 Sunapee Street, Newport, New Hampshire." I repeat that we are Americans, that we were captured in Belgium in late December, and that we were prisoners in the Dresden area until the Russian army began attacking the city. He examines the print on the dog tags closely then shows them to his comrade, who apparently can read some English. The young man nods his head and says something to his superior that I take to be a verification of my identity as an American. After a brief exchange, during which the younger soldier seems to be trying to convince the other that we are Americans or else—and this is more likely the case—that we and they are still on the same side, the older one scrutinizes my dog tags again then hands them back to me without further words. The younger one looks at us and smiles, then raising his right hand, makes the sign of victory with his first and second fingers. Is he referring to the victory of the Allies over the Germans and the promise of a new world order? Or more modestly and locally, is he referring to our success in warding off an incipient clash of ideological identities? I am not sure. What I am deeply struck by, once again, is the fragility of my identity. Who am I? An American soldier? A Greek American soldier? A soldier of the Allied forces? I feel as if I'm weightless, a disembodied ghost free-floating in a zone lacking gravity. I can't connect the name on my dog tags to the person who has shown it to the Russian soldier. What if I had lost them somewhere along the way? Is the solidity of my sense of self dependent on the name and the information inscribed on them?

With a gesture of his head our grave interlocutor signals to his younger comrade that it's time to depart. The young Russian soldier nods but hesitates. Then he turns to us and, through words from various languages and bodily gestures, informs us that there's a stalag on the outskirts of the city containing many British *Kriegsgefangene* who are waiting for the British and American military commands to send trucks or trains to transport them back to their lines. We thank him warmly for this heartening information. As the two Russians depart the younger smiles and once again raises his fingers in the V shape.

Aris and I are out on the streets in the vicinity of the city's main thoroughfare seeking further information about the prisoner of war camp housing a large contingency of British prisoners we have been told about. I have stripped my shirt of the embroidered eagle and swastika and made my American dog tags prominently visible. The Soviet army continues to pour through Brux toward an uncertain destination, though we think it is to meet the American army converging on the Elbe from the West— or what by this time has become for us, alas, an equally viable possibility, to prevent the Americans from proceeding beyond the river. The Russian soldiers are in high spirits. Some of them serve as guards of German prisoners of war. As we stand on the sidewalk watching the stream of trucks and men moving slowly in a southwesterly direction, we empathize with our Russian comrades' elation released by the end of the brutal war. But we also feel anxious over the symbolic significance of the opposing directions these Allied armies are taking. This is not because we are consciously concerned about a higher cause; it is because we are hoping for a smooth transition from vulnerability to security.

As we stand there waving our thumbs up to the Russian troops passing by in the trucks, the movement on the road comes to a temporary halt, probably the result of congestion ahead. During the pause we try to inaugurate a conversation with the foot soldiers in the street immediately in front of us who are guarding a number of German officers, some of them, strangely, in parade dress. Most of them are no older than us, and they exude the arrogance of victory. Or is it the joy of knowing they will still be alive tomorrow and the next day—and the next?

As we banter in our mutually unintelligible languages, one of the soldiers pulls a very imposing German officer out of the column and pushes him toward us. He looks as if he's around fifty years old and is wearing a clean, neatly tailored green army coat over a dress uniform. The coat is encircled by a wide black leather belt, on one side of which hangs an empty holster and on the other a sheathed ceremonial dagger. A silver swastika is inserted on its dark reddish brown wooden handle. The young Russian looks with mock disdain at the purely practical bayonet hanging from my pants belt then at the elegant dagger, indicating the multiple differences between them, and orders the prisoner to take his belt off and give it to me. I can see that the proud German officer of the master race is humiliated by the command of this nonentity—this young ignorant Russian soldier, a lowly private, no doubt a peasant and not least a Slav, degrading him in public, stripping him of the symbol of authority and power in front of a couple of ragamuffin vagabonds. I am acutely conscious of the irony of the reversal of power relations and sympathize with the young boy's arrogant order. But I raise my arms in front of me, palms out, in a gesture intended to show that I appreciated the Russian soldier's goodwill but that I really don't want the dagger. He pays no attention to my gesture, however. Instead, he grabs the German officer's belt buckle, undoes it, and throws it into my arms and motions to me to put it on. I am reluctant. The ornamental dagger is repellent to me. But I do, not wanting to disappoint my enthusiastic benefactor. He looks at the belt hanging loosely around my thin waist approvingly. Then he turns to his comrades and asks them to admire me too. He and his comrades have made me, like it or not, the symbol of the victory of the Allies over Germany. He gives us the V sign with his fingers, and we return it.

Aris and I are scavenging for food in the neighborhood of what was once a shopping area. As usual we have harnessed Persephone on a back street nearby. She is now wearing a red flower in her bridle that Aris has cut from a pot sitting on a windowsill. Persephone's poppy. Russian soldiers, old and young, men and women, are strolling errantly in the street and on the sidewalks. Some of them are drunk and volatile. Keeping a low profile, we watch intently. Despite the victory of the Allies, this dead space at the edge of Europe, where the West runs up against the East, is now as a matter of practical fact theirs, and we are foreign spectators. As much as I try to see it as an open, a neutral, zone, it seems to be quickly and inexorably reverting to the border world it was before the Germans were driven out.

As I contemplate this disturbing irony, a huge figure lurching unsteadily on the other side of the street enters our field of vision. He is a drunken Russian soldier, seemingly larger than life, holding a bottle of vodka by the neck with one hand and gesticulating with the other in tune with what seems to be a folk song he is singing in a loud and inebriated but engaging baritone voice. He stops before a large storefront window behind which a variety of musical instruments are on display. He pauses and then smashes his free fist through the plate glass, enters the shop, and come back out through the shattered window waving a saxophone in his bleeding hand. He puts the reed into his mouth and starts blowing. Like an Apollo strumming his golden lyre or a Gabriel blowing his horn, he seems to think his music is recuperating the shattered world. But the sound he manages to force out of the instrument is cacophonous, a series of screeches, high, like steel grinding on steel, and low, like the croaking of an army of frogs. To me he seems like the god of chaos, Dionysus, and the noise his horn makes the apocalyptic annunciation of the de-creation.

As Aris and I watch in awe, the diabolic Russian musician notices us, maybe even recognizes that we're Americans, and waving the saxophone, calls us over to the music shop before which he is standing. Despite our inability to understand a word he's saying, we realize that he's inviting— or ordering—us to enter the shop, choose an instrument, and join him in his celebration. Because we think his words are more an order than an invitation, we reluctantly enter the shop and begin to look around. Aris picks up a harmonica lying on a small display table near the window. I venture more deeply into the recesses of the abandoned shop and find a shelf of books all in German. One in particular attracts my attention. It's bound in soft, shiny pitch-black leather with red print on its spine. Coming closer, I pull it off the shelf and see, inscribed in the black leather, a blood red swastika and below it, also in blood red, the title and the author: *Mein Kampf*, Adolf Hitler. I open it up and notice that the opening words of each paragraph are printed in an elaborate ornamental red calligraphy unmistakably similar to that adorning the pages of medieval theological manuscripts. I am disconcerted by the juxtaposition, but for some inexplicable reason I put the book in my rucksack.

When we return to the street, we find our Gabriel vomiting in the gutter, the saxophone hanging around his neck and some comrades ministering to him. We are uncertain what to do. We have been somehow attracted to the Russian celebrant, his annunciation of what? . . . the end of an era? The beginning of a new one? The triumph of chaos? Aris is even disappointed that he can't accompany him with his newly acquired harmonica, which, of course, he can't play. But then, we realize, it isn't our show; we are simply peripheral spectators. So we take this opportunity to depart the shattered premises.

It is our last night in Brigitte and Frieda's apartment. Despite Aris's nonchalant, even playful, demeanor, I can tell from the melancholy clouding of his eyes and his persistent coughing that his health is deteriorating. And we both have had enough of the peculiar anxiety instigated by this in-between world, the strange fear that has no object. We have decided, therefore, to seek out the prisoner of war camp at the edge of the city, where, according to our Russian informants, a large number of Brits and Americans have stayed put to await repatriation to American and British lines. We have told our kind and solicitous German hosts of our intention, and they are saddened. Given the regimented austerity of their previous lives in a totalitarian country, they have been fascinated by the unpredictability—the errancy—of our boyish thinking and our actions. Or so it seems to me. They also have felt a certain sense of security by our presence. We have seemed to them, inexplicably, like a talismanic taboo to the frightening Russian occupiers. Above all, they have taken real delight in ministering to our needs. Yet they have understood our predicament in this volatile in-between world and concurred reluctantly with our decision to seek a path out of the chaos toward greater stability.

To celebrate this last sad night, the women have prepared a luxurious feast for us. The table is covered by a delicately embroidered, white linen tablecloth, matching napkins, colorful ceramic plates, and sets of intricately designed silverware, clearly brought out from the recesses of the apartment—and their owners' happier past—for this occasion, and it is adorned by the flickering light of two black candle stubs held in silver candlesticks. On this opulently laden table they have laid out the steaming dish of boiled smoked ham hocks and cabbage they have just prepared, two loaves of rye bread, and a small chocolate cake, which they had baked in the afternoon, covered with the strawberry preserves we confiscated from the warehouse, and four ornate porcelain steins full of beer, close to the last of their supply. In keeping with the festive occasion, they have discarded their usual drab housecoats, which concealed the flowing curves of their bodies, and have dressed themselves in clothing that accentuates them. Frieda wears a tight-fitting black dress adorned by red floral patterns with a plunging neckline that reveals her ample bosom. Brigitte wears a red silk blouse, also with a low, revealing neckline, and a long black skirt that is split on one side up to the middle of her thigh. We all know that the festivities ring hollow, that below the masquerade we are conscious of the dark reality of our immediate situation—ill health and the unpredictable void of the in-between on one side and, inextricably related, the inextinguishable anxiety of violence, of being conquered, on the other, not to say of the vulnerability of the displaced humanity of the shattered world beyond the apartment. And yet, to me at least, there is something about this apparently incongruous constellation—some symptomatic and finally unnameable reality struggling to be born—that overcomes the appalling reality of deprivation, loss, violence, and terror.

Aris and I and Brigitte and Frieda come from radically different cultures whose foreignness has been exacerbated by radically opposing political perspectives that have torn the world apart. The husband-soldiers of these two women, who had been fighting against (and probably been killed by) the Russians in the East—and indirectly, our comrades in the West, are ghostly presences at our festive table. We also come from different times. We are innocent children in their eyes, and they are experienced adults in ours. Nor for that matter do I really know Aris and he me. And I am tempted to say the same about Brigitte and Frieda, despite their being German-Czech. We are all strangers to each other. Yet as we partake of the food and drink, all the while struggling against the language barrier to communicate to each other by whatever means available to us, I sense that it is precisely these differences and boundaries that, paradoxically, have enabled us to achieve a different kind of community than the one we had been taught to idealize. During the few days in the boiling kettle into which we, like fish, have been thrown by the higher powers over which we have no control—since that time I have often understood this trite metaphor about crisis as the alchemical alembic that can turn the very anguish of finite life into something rich and strange without transforming the ingredients—we, down here in the midst of the appalling disintegration and confusion of the zero zone, have become a small community of aliens in defiance of the indifferent world above. Or so, in the face of tomorrow, I would like to think.

When dinner is over, we clean the table, and the women wash the dishes and return the venerable silverware to the recesses from which it has been resurrected for this unexpected occasion. It is late now, and we are all tired. The exuberant aura we managed to create during the evening has begun to wane, as if the charge that had energized our polyphonic voices is dissipating. Eventually silence takes over, and a sad solemnity sets in. Frieda takes Aris by the arm and, saying "Gute Nacht" to Brigitte and me, leads him across the kitchen into the hallway that opens up into her bedroom. Brigitte and I remain seated at the table in the dark as the guttering candles cast their feeble flickering beams of light across our faces. I am sad but also agitated. Although I have acknowledged what I have taken to be her unspoken wish not to sexualize our relationship during these days, I have been acutely aroused this evening by the indissoluble relationship between her knowing gentleness and the soft voluptuous grace of her mature body—her breasts vibrating faintly below the surface of her red silk blouse when she moves and the slit up the side of the close-fitting black skirt revealing her lithe thigh up close to her hip. I am confused, even guilty for harboring such unnatural feelings, especially for breaking the covenant to which we had tacitly agreed. I am her protector, not her predator. Besides, I say contemptuously to myself, she's twice as old as I am, old enough to be my mother, for Christ's sake . . . And yet she is *there*, in all her burnished beauty, like an offering.

She looks at me penetratingly, her dark green eyes, intensified by the shadows under them that time has produced, seeming to ask a question, the tenor of which I can't make out. I will myself to turn mine down and away from hers. Then she takes my hand and cups it between her rough palms—a gesture that sends a thrill of ecstatic pleasure all through my body—and asks me, with a knowing look, if I have ever made love to a woman before. I am acutely embarrassed and feel my face become warm. She smiles but does not allow me to escape her question. My impulse is to lie and say yes, but I know that she knows that I haven't. So I confess, "*Nein, Frau Brigitte, niemals*, I have never made love to a woman." She squeezes my hand, which is now sweating, and nods faintly, as if my admission confirms her intuition. A long silence ensues, during which she looks intently at me but seems to be elsewhere as well. Then she releases my hand, and kissing me on the forehead, she says softly that it's time to go to bed. I am relieved by her words. They alleviate the anxiety provoked by the thought of betraying our covenant. But I am also immensely disappointed.

She guides me into her bedroom and, as usual, returns to the kitchen while I undress and get into the pajamas she has left at the foot of the bed. When I am done, she knocks softly at the door and, without waiting for my response, reenters the bedroom. To my surprise she is still dressed. She walks over to the bed on which I am sitting and sits down beside me. Without saying a word, she looks gravely into my eyes and begins to unbutton her red blouse. She is not wearing a brassiere. When she is done, she takes my two hands into hers, pulls them up in front of her, and presses them against her full breasts. Her gesture takes my breath away, and I lose my bearings for a brief moment. I don't know whether to honor the covenant or abandon it, withdraw my hands or use them. But I recover and, tentatively taking the initiative, begin to fondle her breasts with my fingers. She heaves a sigh, which I take to be her abandonment of a last restraint or a resolution of a previous doubt, and I bend over to kiss her. As our lips meet, she parts them with her tongue and falls back on the pillow. I know I have crossed a boundary, but I'm still uncertain about where to go from there. I lay on top of her for a while, clinging to her body and by turns gently kissing her nipples, her neck, her lips, her hair, and wait expectantly for her final gift.

She, all the while, vacillates between responsiveness and passivity to my initiatives. I can't be sure that she wants me to consummate the momentum we have inaugurated—and somewhere in my disjointed mind I hope she doesn't. As I agonize over these conflicting possibilities, she suddenly, and with a kind of finality but gently, eases me off her body, reaches down, and takes her underwear off—they too are red—pulls up her skirt, spreads her legs, and says in a tender whisper, "Come into me." I hurriedly—and clumsily—take my pajamas off and enter her. The touch sends a wave of pleasure through my body as exquisite as the horror I had felt when, in the infernal miasma of Dresden, the outraged German woman had spit into my face. I shudder, and then I begin to thrust gently. I look into her darkened eyes with intensity, searching for the source of this astonishing pleasure, but in their glistening deep I see only flickering shadows obscuring my distorted face. As I gaze into her eyes, hers steadily focused on mine, I see her closed lips turn into an ever so faint smile I cannot read. For a second it speaks a quiet, long forgotten joy, but then it tells of a gentle and infinitely suffering sorrow. I come suddenly to a shuddering climax; she, under me, thrusting, moans quietly. And I am overpowered by a feeling I have never imagined possible. A joyous pain, like a flash of lightning in the dark. Then, my eyes closed, she pulls my head down on her soft breasts, and as I fall into the sleep of a momentary eternity—or rise out of my body into a momentary oblivion—I hear her say softly, more to herself than to me, "Ach, mein Kind, Willi . . ."

In the morning of the next day Aris and I said good-bye to Brigitte and Frieda. There were no lamentations, no beating of chests, no recriminations, no expressions of gratitude, no offerings of advice, no references to the future. Somehow we all must have felt that such human gestures were inappropriate in that pulverized world. Just simple and quiet handshakes and farewells, as if we were departing guests of a pension at which we had stayed a few days to recuperate our flagging energy. We consigned our old mare's fate to the women, not without invoking her new ironic name, and set out on foot like pilgrims to the stalag, a few kilometers outside the city limits, we had been told about by our Russian comrade. Like so many others on this infernal journey I was bound upon, these two German-Czech women, who seemed to me to be gifts of grace, had come and gone.

When Aris and I arrived at the stalag, we learned that the American and Soviet commands had arranged to evacuate the British and American prisoners of war it contained in exchange for Soviet prisoners liberated by the American army. Two or three days later, in the midst of great excitement and some uneasiness at a certain ill-defined hostility between the Americans and the Soviets that had set in, an old locomotive carrying a huge number of uncovered wooden freight wagons chugged into a siding near the stalag, and we boarded, not knowing our destination except that the train was headed west toward American lines.

Although our few days living with the German-Czech women had been a welcomed reprieve, an instant of translucent light in a dismal night, we were eager to escape from the chaos and uncertainty—the dark dread—of the terrible uncanny in-between world we had been thrown into after the firebombing of Dresden. I was sick to death of being forever in the infernal middle and, with the memory of the funereal pall of smoke hanging over the dead city, the mounds of rubble, the thick layer of ash under our feet, and the piles of putrefying bodies scourging my mind, I was longing desperately for closure, for the end of my seemingly interminable story. And this feeling was exacerbated by my realization that Aris's health, despite his courageous effort to conceal it, was deteriorating, that he was in need of medical attention. The boxcars were jammed with evacuees, around thirty-five or forty in each, and it seemed to me, the American officers in charge of the evacuation treated us with an impatience bordering on disdain. The conditions, I felt at the margins of my consciousness, were ironically reminiscent of those in the freight train that had inaugurated our infernal journey.

But I shrugged this feeling off in favor of the anticipation of return. It was, then, with unspeakable relief that I heard the locomotive hoot the signal of departure, the wheels grind under our boxcar and felt the lurch and shudder of the train as it began to move in a southwesterly direction. I was, I thought, going *home*.

8. Return

We shall not cease from exploration
And the end of all our exploring
Will be to arrive where we started
And know the place for the first time.

T. S. ELIOT, "Little Gidding," *Four Quartets*

The destination of the freight train that carried us out of the void of the Sudetenland, it turned out, was Pilsen, Czechoslovakia, a city about sixty or seventy kilometers south of Brux and west of Prague. It was, if I remember correctly, the official point south of Berlin at which the American army, reluctantly, halted its advance into the East in deference to the demands of the Soviet Union. My memory of the journey and the few days we remained in Pilsen is vague, no doubt because the focus of my interest was intensely anticipatory. I was impatient to escape the dread-provoking in-between world I had been buffeted back and forth in during the past few weeks but also to arrive at a place far away from its turbulent immediacy, somewhere where I could more easily fight the demon of the Dresden firestorm that had wrapped its coils around my uncomprehending mind. What I remember, above all, was my separation from Aris.

When the train reached its destination in the railroad yards in Pilsen, we were herded into U.S. Army trucks that bore us to a transit tent camp near the city's airport, where we underwent a rapid, mass-production process of "rehabilitation." During that time I had the feeling of anticlimax, an uneasy sense that we were not welcomed returning comrades but more like an unwanted burden, if not a desolate rabble of pariahs. Immediately on arrival, we were taken to a large barracks, where we were divested of our rags and deloused en masse. In the process I learned to my astonishment that I weighed 115 pounds, 53 pounds less than I weighed prior to my captivity. I also noticed for the first time that the skin of my emaciated body was unnaturally yellowish and was covered with tiny red and white blotches, testimony to its service as host and nourishment for a colony of lice over a long period of time. Then we were cursorily examined by teams of army doctors. I was informed that I had a mild but easily curable case of jaundice, the result of malnutrition, and frozen feet, "a bodily wound," one of them told me in a voice that seemed on the edge of mockery, "that was sure to earn you the purple heart" (as indeed, it eventually did). I was aware that this large-scale operation had been thrown together rapidly by the U.S. Army authorities, and I, conscious of the debilitated state of my body—it was the state of my mind that had been my concern up to this moment—was grateful for the attention we were getting. But somehow I couldn't ward off the suspicion that we former prisoners were second-class citizens precisely because we had been prisoners, not triumphant warriors.

Aris, we learned on the other hand, showed symptoms of a serious lung disease as well as malnutrition; he would have to be immediately hospitalized. A day later he was taken off to a hospital. I thanked him for his support and bid him good-bye, promising to look him up as soon as the occasion warranted. The day after, dressed in new khakis, field jacket, and army boots, I, along with about twenty-five or thirty former American prisoners of war, boarded a c-47, the U.S. Army cargo plane that had carried paratroopers during the war. It flew us to Camp Lucky Strike, somewhere in Normandy near the Atlantic coast. I never saw Aris again. He too had come and gone. Once again, I had the feeling that *my* story was being superseded—indeed obliterated—by a massive, nameless, and malignant force beyond my power to resist.

I spent about two weeks at Camp Lucky Strike in what the noncommissioned officers called "rehab." Ostensibly this meant eating unseasoned boiled chicken more or less three times a day. I don't recall being medically examined once during the entire two weeks. I do remember being marshaled along with a couple of hundred rehabilitees into a huge tent and "welcomed" back into the bosom of the U.S. Army by a captain in the information service. In the process he not only reminded us, in case we had forgotten it during the time of our captivity, of the United States's great victory over the forces of evil that had threatened to destroy "civilization as we know it," of the American people's perennial, divinely ordained, mission to save the "Old World" from its decadent self, of the vast number of young Americans who, "like our pioneers of old," willingly sacrificed their lives in the name of freedom and democracy—and to liberate those of us who had been taken prisoners of war. He said this as an apparent aside, but I couldn't help feel that it was at least one of his main points. Given the fact that I experienced the war primarily from the perspective of the Eastern front, I was also disturbed that in his self-congratulatory speech, the captain said nothing about the role that the millions of soldiers of the Soviet army played in the defeat of Nazi Germany. Despite my joy at being liberated, the captain's speech, precisely because its perspective was so monomaniacally American, was to me, somehow, speaking of a future for us—the masses of humanity—in which nothing essential was likely to change.

What I had caught a glimpse of in the corner of my eye in Brux—that the borders that had broken down were already being rebuilt, that another war was in the making—had returned to disturb my renewed joy for life. And then, irrepressibly insistent, there was the tremendous destruction of Dresden and its incinerated civilian population, who in that world below all causes—that zero zone—had become a place of neighbors. I felt a vague but urgent desire to ask—or was it to remind?—the captain about the firebombing of Dresden, but, of course, I repressed it. I even felt guilty for entertaining such a heretical thought. Moreover, I wasn't exactly sure what I would be asking about. And besides, who was I, a draftee, a common soldier, a liberated prisoner of war, to take on, to speak back to, the captain, this larger-than-life official of the upper world who at that moment struck me as the voice of a triumphant America?

During those two weeks at Camp Lucky Strike I ate compulsively to replenish my depleted body, savoring every bite of the enormous quantity of bland food we were given by recalling especially those times in the snow-filled forest outside of Dresden when we, with the torturous pain of hunger, watched our ss guards sadistically flaunt their thick potato soup, their apples, their thick slices of black bread. But I also ate compulsively to forget, to obliterate, the unspeakable horrors I had experienced. In that short time I regained a lot of the weight I had lost in captivity. But my body did not regain its original athletic shape. It became bloated, puffy, soft, undeveloped, and the color of my skin remained yellowish. Nor did my strength come back. I felt weak, always at the edge of being ill. I willed myself to take joy in returning to the living world from the horrific hell in which I had suffered in those previous five months. I was alive. In a little while I would be repatriated; I would be reunited with my mother and father, my brothers and sister, my schoolboy friends, my beloved Kathryn; I would be going *home*.

This effort at conjuring the joyful peace of civilized order and community helped on occasion. But there was always a lack at the bottom of my being, an absence epitomized by the memory of the sting of the old woman's spit. And nothing I willed could fill it. The world I had yearned for throughout my captivity now seemed unfamiliar, strange, awry. I felt somehow as if I no longer belonged to it. I overcame this dreadful feeling at times by telling myself that things would get better when I returned to the United States, to the bosom of my family, but I couldn't sustain this comforting image. And this insistent sense of alienation at a time when I should have been rejoicing in the familiar of the recuperated world made me, on occasion, terribly unhappy.

It was in this troubled state of mind and body that I received the announcement from one of the sergeants in charge of the group of former prisoners of war to which I belonged that we were to be repatriated to the United States for reunion with our families and then further rehabilitation at Fort Oglethorpe in Georgia. Early in June 1945 my unit was trucked to a French seaport on the coast of Normandy—I think it was Le Havre, but I'm not certain—where we boarded a battered old convoy ship whose destination was Boston, Massachusetts. I remember very little about that six- or seven-day voyage across the Atlantic, except that it was excruciatingly long and tedious. When we arrived, it was, it occurred to me with knowing irony, without fanfare. Indeed, from the moment we disembarked and boarded army trucks to our arrival several hours later at Fort Devens (the camp where I was initiated into the U.S. Army three years earlier), the return to our homeland was accomplished almost invisibly, I am now tempted to say clandestinely, though I realize that this way of putting it is an exaggeration. For the next two days we were processed army style: hurry up and wait. There were few heartfelt welcomes, few questions about our overseas units, the battles we had fought, our experiences in the aftermath of the war. The process was utterly methodical. It was, to me at least, despite the celebratory aura I sensed at the circumference of the confined space we inhabited, as if we were recruits undergoing the systematic procedure of initiation into the army in reverse.

On a Friday, around six in the afternoon, dressed in my newly pressed khakis and combat boots and carrying my duffel bag, I boarded an army bus that took me to Boston. My duffel bag contained a change of army clothes, fatigues, my Nazi officer's dagger, and the copy of *Mein Kampf*. Why I chose that thing to carry back to the United States with me I didn't know, though I suspect it was because, despite my conscious will to forget that dreadful vagabond in-between world from which I had recently escaped, I felt the need to remember it with the force of exigency. On arriving in Boston, I boarded a commercial carrier that drove me to Concord, New Hampshire, where I intended to take the Vermont Transit bus that once or twice a day, as I remembered, drove passengers to Newport, my hometown. Arriving in Concord around midnight, I discovered, to my great disappointment, that the last bus to Newport had left hours earlier and that the next one was not scheduled to depart until sometime late on Saturday morning. Extremely eager to bring my long, disorienting journey to its end, I thought at first that I'd hitchhike to Newport. But then I realized that somehow, in a way I couldn't quite fathom, I wasn't prepared for the reunion with my family. I decided, therefore, to stay in Concord that night.

Finding a diner that was open all night on the now dark and empty main street of the city, I walked in, took my army cap off, tucked it under my belt, and, sitting down on a stool at the counter, ordered a cup of coffee from the lone waitress. She was around forty or forty-five years old, good-looking but worn, and friendly, with a striking resemblance to Brigitte. After greeting me with a pleasant "Hi, soldier!" she asked me where I had come from and where I was going. I told her that I had just returned to the United States from Europe and was on my way home to Newport but, having missed my bus, wondered if I could wait the night out in her diner until morning. Glad to have my company, she assured me that I could. I was grateful to her but hoped that her invitation to stay would not entail serious conversation. I was very tired, but more than that, I was sort of down because I couldn't understand why I wasn't totally up about coming home. I wanted to sit alone quietly to work myself out of my depression. But the waitress took my reserve for something else, shyness maybe or disappointment at missing my bus, and, to cheer me up, tried to engage me in conversation about my experiences in Europe.

I didn't want to talk about the war. I couldn't turn the infernal journey I had taken from the Ardennes Forest to Limburg to Dresden to Brux into the kind of story I thought she expected from me. I had no story like that to tell. Still, I was grateful for her kindness—grateful too for reminding me of the "New Hampsha" accent that had vanished for so long out of my life—and reciprocated. But I didn't want to disappoint her by telling her I had been a prisoner in Germany, not one of the conquering heroes returning home from the second Great War. Instead, I assumed as best I could the expected stateside attitude of victory. Remembering the name that the catastrophe my division had suffered at the hands of the German army in the Ardennes Forest had come to be called, I told her that I had fought in the decisive Battle of the Bulge and that, after that, found it easy sailing until the end of war, a matter of a long-term mop-up exercise, the suicide of Adolf Hitler, the surrender of the German army, the meeting up with the Russian army on the Elbe River, and V-Day, as it was called. I hated myself for lying, but at that time—and for a very long time to come—I just couldn't face telling the truth or, rather, the morass in which "the truth" of the war, like a virus in the bloodstream, was dissolved. The only concession to that truth I made was to insist that it was the massive Russian counterattack in the East that had made the American and British victory in the West possible.

Sometime in the middle of the night, after drinking my third or fourth cup of coffee and smoking an entire pack of cigarettes, the waitress suddenly remembered that the truck driver who delivered the *Manchester Union* and the *Concord Monitor* to the villages in the vicinity of Concord invariably stopped at the diner for a cup of coffee before beginning the second phase of his delivery route. She was almost certain that Newport was on his itinerary. And if and when he came to the diner for that "cup of joe," she would ask him if he'd be willing to let me ride with him to Newport. That way, she said, I could be there even before the morning bus to my hometown left Concord. At around 4:30 in the morning the newspaper delivery man walked into the diner for his cup of coffee. On seeing him enter, the waitress greeted him enthusiastically then, introducing him to me, told him that I had just returned from Europe and was on my way home to Newport and asked if he'd be kind enough to give me a ride. He said he would be honored to deliver the young soldier right to his mother and father's doorsteps.

A few minutes later the driver picked up my duffel bag, carried it out of the diner, and tossed it into the back of the truck filled with taut bundles of newspapers. I expressed my gratitude to the waitress, not without a pang of guilt for not being open with her and, on the invitation of the driver, entered the cab. The dark was turning faintly light at its edges. He turned the ignition on, gunned the roaring motor with a certain flourish, as if to announce the difference of this trip, and we were off on the last forty-mile stretch of my long journey of return. We stopped often to drop off the bundles of newspapers at the occasional general store bordering the highway heading northwest and the local pharmacy in the two or three rural villages we drove through along the way. And I, eager to show my gratitude for his generosity, helped the driver carry the bundles into them. At the outset he asked me more or less the same questions the waitress had asked me and with the same expectation in his voice—how long I had been in Europe, where I had fought, what being in combat was like, where I was when Germany surrendered. And I couldn't help but answer them in the same reluctant way I had answered hers, despite feeling bad about it. After a while he realized that I wasn't in the mood to talk, so he left me to myself.

Gazing out the window of the cab as I churned inside, I began to take notice of the familiar New England landscape, its unpredictable jagged rises and declines, its huge glacial boulders rising out of the recently planted uneven fields, the great variety of wildflowers along the roadside, the play of dark shadows and shards of light in the depths of small but dense forests of firs, the ragged ancient stone fences that told eloquently of the resistant earth, so different from the passive flat red land of Georgia and the rolling wet black land of Indiana. These scenes of familiar variety eased my inexplicable anguish. And as we neared closer and closer to my destination, the familiarity became even more particular. The sandy beach at the northernmost point of Lake Sunapee, which had been the outer perimeter of my childhood consciousness; Sunapee Mountain, where I had skied before it was transformed into a ski resort; Birch Grove, where my parents' friends, the Evangelous (who owned an automobile), would take us on occasional Sundays in the summertime for swimming and a picnic; the town of Guild, where the parents of a girl I loved intensely from a distance in high school worked in the Dorr Woolen Mill; Lily Pond, where we went night fishing for catfish; the cemetery, where the Greek American families of Newport buried their dead; the Sugar River, where we went skating in the winter; the Newport Woolen Mill, which employed a third of the population of our town. But this increasingly intense, kaleidoscopic stream of familiar images suffered a terrific sea change when, at the crest of the knoll, the highway became my beloved and hated Sunapee Street, where I had lived my entire life before entering the army. At that climactic moment of return the chain of familiar images was interrupted, explosively, by a different relay—the rubble and ash of Dresden, the piles of charred corpses, the woman in black with one shoe; the young boy in the green jacket, bare from the waist down, with a missing arm; the incinerated corpse whose gender and age we could not determine; the shriveled bodies in evening finery of the civilians who had been asphyxiated and roasted by the heat of the firestorm in the tunnel under the city; the beautiful dead girl in the red skirt and the ferocious woman who had torn her out of my arms and spit in my face: the multitude of the dead, all my kin under the rain of that terror. I now think these violently antithetical chains of images colliding in my head as I drew near to my home were striving to transform a cacophony into polyphony. But at that time, and for a very long time thereafter, they were to me symptomatic of a wound in my very being that could never heal.

Then, as I was being tossed in that turbulence, on the lower side of the knoll, I saw my home, 99 Sunapee Street, Newport, New Hampshire—and, yes, the United States of America, earth, the galaxy of the Milky Way. "That's it! That's where I live!" I shouted to the driver, pointing ahead, my heart pounding furiously, to the small yellow and brown, two-storied house on the left side of the highway. "I'm home, the end of the line! This is where I get off!" The driver, shocked out of his own reverie by the sudden rupture of the silence, slammed the brakes, bringing the truck to a screeching halt. As I scrambled for the door, he got out of the cab, pulled my duffel bag out of the back of the truck, carried it across the road, and, as if he were delivering another bundle of newspapers, deposited it on the porch landing at the top of the staircase of the house. Turning to me, he said in an air of Yankee humor but with a certain care, "Well, soldier, I've delivered you to your parents' doorstep just like I said I would. I hope I've brought them good news." I smiled, sensing his meaning, thanked him for what he had done for me, and said good-bye.

It was about six in the morning. The light in the East was just beginning to illuminate the dark. Everyone at home—my mother and father; my youngest brother, Charlie; my little sister, Olga (Steve was still in England, and Harry was at Harvard College)—was still asleep. I paused at the front door, not certain whether to ring the bell for fear of startling them—

no one except strangers ever came to the front door of our house—or to go to the rear as I had always done. Then, hearing a faint stirring at the top of the staircase leading from the front door to the second floor and surmising that the screech of the truck's breaks had awakened one of the sleepers, I rang the doorbell and peered through the curtained window. I saw my mother in a white nightgown, her long gray hair disheveled from sleep flowing down her back, coming down the stairs like a ghost. I held my breath. When she had descended to the landing, she parted the curtains and peered anxiously out the window. She looked at me for an eternal moment, dumbfounded, then screamed, "Billy! . . . *Vaios, einai o Vasilis! To paidi mas eilthai!*" ("Vaios, it's Billy! Our boy has returned!"), and collapsed before she could unlock the door.

A few seconds later my father came racing down the stairs trailed by Charlie and Olga. He opened the door, stepped outside, and wrapped his powerful arms around my shoulders, hugged me with all his strength, and said (in Greek), "Welcome home, my son!" We picked my mother up and walked her carefully down the short hallway to the tiny kitchen table. As my father was ministering to her, I turned my attention to my young brother, who was now sixteen, taller than me and very handsome, and, embracing him warmly, I said, "Hi, pal! I can't believe it's you." Then I turned to my eleven-year-old sister. She was incredibly pretty, her dark brown eyes bright as burning coals, her shining black hair hanging down to the middle of her back, and her breasts beginning to flower. As I gazed at her, she suddenly metamorphosed into the young girl I had picked up in my arms in the rubble of Dresden. I bent down and kissed her on the cheek with tears in my eyes. "Hi! Sweetie, your favorite brother's home," I said with all the courage I could muster. Then I turned to my good and gentle mother, who had recovered from her shock. "*Heraitai, Ma-ma!* Your prodigal son's back." She put her arms around me, her tears flowing, and said softly, "*Ach, Vasili, pedhaki mou,* my lost little boy!"

I was back home. And I was elated by the reunion with my family, which, in the midst of my captivity, I had thought would never happen. But at the center of the circle of the long journey I had taken, there was a black, infernal hole that I could never fill, that I had to acknowledge and confront as a spectral presence even though I had no directives, except the vague but irresistible imperative not to forget it, not to force it into a story. As my mother was holding me to her bosom, I realized with a kind of finality that I had to live always in the time of the now that, like a crater, the firebombing of Dresden had opened up to me.

Coda

The intellectual makes it his task to convert the dynastic role thrust upon him by history or habit. He does not see himself as subordinate even to concepts such as "truth" or "knowledge" insofar as those *descend* (figuratively or literally) from on high or *ascend* from the Origin to the surface.

EDWARD W. SAID, *Beginnings*

I am on a two-week furlough in Newport, from Camp Oglethorpe in Georgia, where I had been in "rehabilitation" for two months, a process that consisted of eating bland food, occasionally exercising, and above all, drinking a lot of beer with a couple of former prisoners of war in the local, often unfriendly and dangerous, segregated bars. My body has recovered from jaundice. I have returned to moderately good health. But my psyche remains volatile. After my furlough I am scheduled by them, for reasons beyond my comprehension, to join an armored tank unit at Fort Knox in Kentucky. I am standing with Kathryn at the top of the cement staircase of the Newport Public Library on Main Street, across the way from the Newport Commons, where in the summers we listened to band concerts and in the winters we skated. I am wearing civilian clothing, no longer able to tolerate the army khakis that now feel like living in a straitjacket.

It is August 15, 1945, and we are watching the people of Newport celebrate the surrender of Japan and the termination of World War II—

V-J Day, in the language of the acronym that, emerging during the war, threatens to banalize the rich complexities of human life. On August 6, 1945, an American B-29 bomber named the *Enola Gay*, had dropped an atomic bomb on the people of Hiroshima. A few days later, on August 9, another B-29 bomber, *Bock's Car*, dropped another atomic bomb on the people of Nagasaki. The devastation these bombings perpetrated compelled the Japanese government to capitulate to the United States. The officials in the government and the media that reported the event told us, in the language of apocalyptic annunciation, that the explosive power of these atomic bombs exceeded that of hundreds of tons of conventional bombs, that they had destroyed the evil empire and brought the war in the Pacific to a triumphant end, that the whole world had been blessed that it was America and not the Nazis or the Japanese that had been able to develop this fearsome weapon, and that, in the hands of the "American people," the atomic bomb assured the benighted world that war was now obsolete.

Down below us two marching bands are playing, one a Souza march, the other, in a bizarre counterpoint, "The Battle Hymn of the Republic," about the righteous wrath of God:

Mine eyes have seen the glory
Of the coming of the Lord.
He is trampling out the vintage
Where the grapes of wrath are stored,
He hath loosed the fateful lightning
Of His terrible swift sword
His truth is marching on.

There is, as far as I can tell, jubilation everywhere. The bells of the churches are ringing. People are milling in the streets, waving American flags, making the V sign with their fingers, singing "God Bless America." Ticker tape is falling profusely from the office buildings on Main Street. Several soldiers and sailors in uniform have been hoisted onto the shoulders of the elated marchers. The long world-encompassing war has come to its end.

America, the promised land. Americans, the chosen people. America, the redeemer nation. She has been led through fire and brimstone to everlasting peace by the terrible swift sword of a protective higher power.

As I stand on the landing of the library steps with Kathryn, watching the people of my hometown rejoice in this ending, I, too, feel relieved that the war is finally over, that humanity everywhere can now begin the task of rebuilding, maybe a better world. Not least, after three years dislocated and mired in an utterly hopeless, nightmarish middle, I am, here at this ending, able to think about the future. Yet I am profoundly troubled. In announcing the great victory that had brought the war to its sudden termination, those "higher-ups" have said nothing about the role that the emergent "Cold War" with the Soviet Union played in President Harry Truman's decision to drop the atomic bomb on Japan, though we all knew that, two days after the atomic bombing of Hiroshima, Stalin had attacked and almost immediately destroyed the Japanese army in Manchuria and was moving in on North Korea. Far more disturbing, they hadn't said anything to us about the seventy thousand innocent human beings—young and old; children, men, women—in Hiroshima and the sixty thousand in Nagasaki whom our atomic bombs had instantly and indiscriminately incinerated and the untold number that would die and live unspeakably horrible deaths by radiation in its aftermath. Try as I might to subdue these unwanted thoughts, they remain curled suffocatingly around my brain, transforming the music and rejoicing below into a raucous cacophony. I feel a profound kinship with the dead and maimed in the smoldering poisoned ashes of Hiroshima and Nagasaki. I have *been there*. I have borne witness to their horror in Dresden.

Kathryn says to me, "Bill, why aren't you celebrating? You're so quiet! The war's over. The world's at peace now. Our country has saved it!"

I don't know what to say to her in response. She is not ignorant; she is an intelligent and generous young woman whose sensitivity has contributed to awakening my dormant sense of possibility. I feel guilty for not joining her. I'm physically here in Newport, which has become the center of the world, but in my mind and heart I'm far away, in the midst of another center. I'm in a sepulchral city of ashes, Dresden/Hiroshima/ Nagasaki. The world of zero. And yet in a perverse way that I can't explain even to myself, I feel in the very abyss of my anguished heart, inextricably, the tentative stirring of a beginning not of a new story but a *now time* that bears within it, always, like a chalice, that infernal time.

I say, in response, "I *am* celebrating, Kitty. I *am!*"